BOOSTING
PRODUCTIVITY
IN
SUB-SAHARAN
AFRICA

BOOSTING
PRODUCTIVITY
IN
SUB-SAHARAN
AFRICA

POLICIES AND INSTITUTIONS TO PROMOTE EFFICIENCY

César Calderón

 **WORLD BANK GROUP**

Contents

Maps

Tables

Acknowledgments

This report was prepared by a team led by César Calderón (Lead Economist), under the guidance of Albert G. Zeufack (Chief Economist of the Africa Region) and Hafez Ghanem (Vice President). Core members of the team included Fernando Aragón, Diego Barrot, Catalina Cantú, Chaoran Chen, Margarida Duarte, Robert Fattal-Jaef, Nicolas Pierre P. Gonne, Aparajita Goyal, Megumi Kubota, Emmanuel K. K. Lartey, Taye Alemu Mengistae, Diego Restuccia, Juan Pablo Rud, Luis Servén, Rishab Sinha, and Måns Soderbom. Kenneth Omondi provided able administrative support to the report team. The report was edited by Mary Anderson.

The following background papers served as important inputs:

- Aragón, Fernando M., and Juan Pablo Rud. 2018. "Weather, Productivity and Factor Misallocation: Evidence from Ugandan Farmers." Unpublished manuscript, Department of Economics, Simon Frasier University.
- Barrot-Araya, Luis Diego, César Calderón, and Luis Serven. 2019. "Growth in Sub-Saharan Africa: A TFP Boost is Needed." Unpublished manuscript, World Bank, Washington, DC.
- Barrot-Araya, Luis Diego, César Calderón, and Luis Serven. 2019. "Sectoral Productivity Shifts in Sub-Saharan Africa." Unpublished manuscript, World Bank, Washington, DC.
- Chen, Chaoran, and Diego Restuccia. 2018. "Agricultural Productivity Growth in Africa." Unpublished manuscript, Department of Economics, University of Toronto.
- Cirera, Xavier, Robert N. Fattal Jaef, and Hibret B. Maemir. 2000. "Taxing the Good? Distortions, Misallocation, and Productivity in Sub-Saharan Africa." *World Bank Economic Review* 34 (1): 75–100.
- Duarte, Margarida, and Diego Restuccia. 2018. "Structural Transformation and Productivity in Sub-Saharan Africa." Unpublished manuscript, Department of Economics, University of Toronto.
- Goyal, Aparajita, Keith Fuglie, and Felipe Dizon. 2018. "Agriculture Productivity and Economic Transformation in Sub-Saharan Africa." Unpublished manuscript, World Bank, Washington, DC.
- Jones, Patricia, Emmanuel Lartey, Taye Mengistae, and Albert Zeufack. 2019. "Market Size, Sunk Costs of Entry, and

Transport Costs: An Empirical Evaluation of the Impact of Demand-Side Factors versus Supply-Side Factors on Manufacturing Productivity." World Bank Group Policy Research Working Paper 8875, Washington, DC.

- Sinha, Rishabh, and Xican Xi. 2018. "Agronomic Endowment, Crop Choice and Agricultural Productivity." Unpublished manuscript, World Bank, Washington, DC.
- Söderbom, Måns. 2018. "Productivity Dispersion and Firm Dynamics in Ethiopia's Manufacturing Sector." Unpublished manuscript, Department of Economics, School of Business, Economics and Law, University of Gothenburg.

We are grateful to the peer reviewers who supported the preparation of this report from the concept stage, through the authors' workshop, to the decision stage: Luc Christiaensen (World Bank), Daniel Lederman (World Bank), and Richard Rogerson (Princeton University). Several World Bank staff provided valuable comments and engaged in productive discussions at various stages of the development of this report. Our thanks also go to the production team, including Mary Fisk, production editor; Jewel McFadden, acquisitions editor; and Orlando Mota, print and electronic conversion coordinator.

About the Author

César Calderón, a Peruvian national, is a Lead Economist in the Office of the Chief Economist of the Africa Region (AFRCE). He joined the World Bank in 2005. Before joining the AFRCE, he worked in the Latin America and the Caribbean Regional Chief Economist Office and the Finance and Private Sector Development (FPD) Chief Economist Office, as well as on the *World Development Report*. He was a core team member of the *Global Financial Development Report 2013: Rethinking the Role of the State in Finance* and the *World Development Report 2014: Risk and Opportunity: Managing Risk for Development*, where he authored the chapter on macroeconomic risk management.

Since 2014, he has been a core team member of the "Africa's Pulse" regional flagship on recent macroeconomic developments in Sub-Saharan Africa. He also has been a task team leader of AFRCE regional research projects, such as *Africa's Macroeconomic Vulnerabilities*. He has worked on issues of open economy macroeconomics, growth, and development—especially the growth impact of infrastructure development and outward-oriented strategies.

He is currently working on issues of trade diversification and growth, digital infrastructure and development, and policy determinants of macroeconomic resilience. He holds a master's degree and a PhD in economics from the University of Rochester, New York.

Abbreviations

AfCFTA	African Continental Free Trade Area
AFRCE	Office of the Chief Economist of the Africa Region (World Bank)
CBA	Commercial Bank of Africa Ltd.
CPIA	Country Policy and Institutional Assessment
CES	constant elasticity of substitution
COVID-19	coronavirus disease 2019
DT	digital technology
EAP5	East Asian "dragons" (Indonesia, the Republic of Korea, Malaysia, Singapore, and Thailand)
EWS	early warning systems
FAO	Food and Agriculture Organization
FCS	fragile and conflict-affected states
GAEZ	Global Agronomic Ecological Zones
GDP	gross domestic product
GIS	geographic information system
GPS	Global Positioning System
GSS	Ghana Statistical Services
HCI	Human Capital Index
ICT	information and communication technology
ICP	International Comparison Program
ILO	International Labour Organization
ISA	Integrated Survey of Agriculture
ISIC	International Standard Industrial Classification
ISP	input subsidy program
ISPC	Simplified Tax for Small Taxpayers
LLMCs	low- and lower-middle-income countries
LSMS-ISA	Living Standards Measurement Studies–Integrated Surveys on Agriculture
MPK	marginal product of capital
NGO	nongovernmental organization
NIPA	national income and product accounts

NIS	National Innovation System
OECD	Organisation for Economic Co-operation and Development
PIM	perpetual inventory method
PPP	purchasing power parity
PWT	Penn World Table
R&D	research and development
RFID	radio frequency identification
SIC	Standard Industrial Classification
SMS	short message service
SSA	Sub-Saharan Africa
TFP	total factor productivity
TFPQ	total factor productivity quantity
TFPR	total factor productivity revenue
UMICs	upper-middle-income countries
UN-NAC	United Nations National Accounts
WBES	World Bank Enterprise Surveys
WDI	World Development Indicators

Boosting Productivity in Sub-Saharan Africa

Introduction

A stylized fact of development economics is the wide disparity in output per worker across the world's countries. On the one hand, there are large disparities in labor productivity *across countries* at any point in time. The richest countries (top decile) were 23 times as productive as the poorest nations (bottom decile) in 1960 (Feenstra, Inklaar, and Timmer 2015). That gap increased to 37 times by 2017. The productivity gap between the richest countries and those in the middle of the distribution has fluctuated by about fourfold between 1960 and 2017.

On the other hand, *a country's own* output per worker also tends to move significantly over time—such that the country's growth successes and failures may be unrelated to the initial level of development. For instance, Botswana, a very poor country at 3.8 percent of United States gross domestic product (GDP) per worker in 1960, rose to 30.8 percent of US GDP per worker by 2017. In contrast, Malawi, at a similar stage of development in 1960 (at about 4.4 percent of the US GDP per worker), dropped to 2.2 percent in 2017.[1]

There has been an intense debate as to whether the observed variation in output per worker across countries is attributable to differences in factor accumulation or to differences in total factor productivity (TFP). The evidence shows that TFP accounts for most of the differences in income per worker across countries (Caselli 2005; Hall and Jones 1999; Hsieh and Klenow 2010; Jones 2016; Klenow and Rodríguez-Clare 1997). This implies that some countries, sectors, and firms produce more than others with the same amount of inputs (labor, human and physical capital, land, and intermediate inputs, among others). In fact, TFP overwhelmingly explains the cross-country differences in income per capita (Caselli 2005; Jones 2016). An important lesson emerges from these aggregate accounting exercises: productivity improvement is essential to sustained economic growth (Kim and Loayza 2019).

Theoretical and empirical efforts to go beyond the country-level analysis and to understand the microeconomic foundations of aggregate behavior have also provided valuable insights on productivity. Two different but complementary explanations may account for the productivity differences between richer and poorer countries: The first emphasizes the slow diffusion and adaptation of technology as well as (production organization and management) best practices to poorer countries (Bloom and Van Reenen 2007; Bloom et al. 2013; Parente and Prescott 2000, 2005). The second focuses on the differences across sectors and firms in the allocation of resources in the production process.

The literature on misallocation of resources, which is the focus of this volume, argues that poorer countries are less effective than wealthier countries in allocating their factors of production to their most efficient uses. Conversely, the efficient allocation of resources across firms and sectors boosts TFP by enabling productive firms to grow, low-productivity firms to exit the market, and new firms to emerge (Foster, Haltiwanger, and Krizan 2001; Hsieh and Klenow 2009; Restuccia and Rogerson 2008, 2013, 2017).

History and Context

Economic growth in the Sub-Saharan Africa region historically has been plagued by a series of shocks: wars, political instability, natural disasters, epidemics, terms-of-trade deterioration, and sudden stops in capital inflows, among others. These shocks have had lingering effects on the factors of production (physical capital and human capital) as well as on TFP because of structural characteristics that exacerbate the impact of those shocks. These characteristics include, among others, the lack of diversification of economic activity, reliance on volatile commodity exports, weak governance, inadequate regulation in labor and output markets, shallow land markets, and underdeveloped financial markets with low access to financial products. Some of these features are the outcome of policies and institutions that distort the allocation of resources from their most efficient use.

The aggregate productivity gap of African countries relative to high-income economies (notably, the United States) reflects substantial productivity differences across

sectors of economic activity and across production units (farms or firms). This is particularly important in agriculture, where (a) sectoral productivity of African countries is extremely low relative to that of high-income countries, and (b) the sector employs most of the population. That so much of the population works in a sector of very low economic activity explains why Sub-Saharan Africa lags the rest of the world's regions in structural transformation (Duarte and Restuccia 2010, 2018).

At the production unit level, the low productivity of African countries can be explained by policies and institutions that foster a systematic redistribution of resources from the more-productive establishments to the less-productive ones. This allocative inefficiency across African production units can be attributed to market imperfections (for example, regarding credit and land), preferential trade policies, size-dependent taxation policies, and informality, among other causes.

Effects of COVID-19

The COVID-19 (Coronavirus) pandemic has significantly hit output and productivity across African countries, sectors, and firms. This asymmetric supply shock has led to a disproportionate fall in demand as production shuts down in some sectors, and the lower demand is transmitted to less-contact-intensive sectors. In other words, the COVID-19 shock has caused a reduction in aggregate demand larger than the original reduction in labor supply. This type of shock has been labeled as a "Keynesian supply shock" (Guerrieri et al. 2020).

Uncertainty increased dramatically at the onset of this dramatic health shock, and this higher uncertainty has caused firms to temporarily suspend their hiring and investment spending. Amid the COVID-19 pandemic, aggregate productivity is expected to fall sharply as the decline in hiring and investing slows the reallocation of resources from low- to high-productivity firms (Baker et al. 2020; Bloom 2014). This productivity impact underlies the theories of uncertainty-driven business cycles, which emphasize how uncertainty shocks reduce investment, hiring, and productivity (Bloom et al. 2018).

The policy response to COVID-19 currently focuses on (a) *emergency relief measures* to protect lives (such as strengthening the health sector; securing the food supply; and enhancing access to water, sanitation, and handwashing stations); and (b) *policies to protect livelihoods* (for example, providing income support to the most vulnerable workers and extending credit to still-viable firms). However, the policy response should also consider measures to protect the future of the Africa region. Such a response requires a comprehensive productivity policy agenda that addresses the human capital crisis, leverages digital technologies for trade and government effectiveness, and fosters intra-African value chains under the umbrella of the African Continental Free Trade Area (AfCFTA).

Policy makers in the region need to engage with development partners to think ahead and design policies that build greater resilience and boost productivity so that African economies can recover faster and thrive in the post–COVID-19 era. A robust productivity policy agenda would not only shorten the region's recovery time but also put it on a path of economic transformation with more, better, and more-inclusive jobs (World Bank 2020a).

Sub-Saharan Africa's Long-Term Performance: Still Far from the Frontier

Overall Economic Growth and Poverty Reduction

From 1996 to 2014, growth of real economic activity in Sub-Saharan Africa sharply accelerated to an annual average rate of 4.8 percent, up from 1.4 percent in 1978–95.[2] Most countries in the region experienced the rising hopes and expectations that came along with robust growth. Six of the world's 10 fastest-growing countries were in Sub-Saharan Africa (*Economist* 2011). After nearly

two decades of uninterrupted growth, the "Afro-pessimism" of the 1980s was being replaced by "Afro-optimism." In 13 of the 19 years from 1996 through 2014, Sub-Saharan Africa grew faster than East Asia. In the aftermath of the Global Financial Crisis and amid a growth slowdown in high-income economies, the region still grew at an average annual rate of 4.8 percent from 2011 to 2014.

However, the region's growth performance is less stellar when accounting for population growth. Real GDP per capita grew at an annual average rate of 1.95 percent from 1996 through 2014. Amid the "Africa Rising" euphoria after 2000—given the persistence of the region's rapid economic growth—the poverty rate in Sub-Saharan Africa decreased (from 54.3 percent in 1990 to 40.1 percent in 2018), albeit more slowly than in East Asia (from 61.6 percent in 1990 to 2.3 percent in 2018) and South Asia (from 47.3 percent in 1990 to 12.4 percent in 2018) (World Bank 2020b). However, the number of poor people in Sub-Saharan Africa increased from 278 million in 1990 to 416.4 million in 2015, as the region's population continued to expand rapidly. Most of the world's poor live in Sub-Saharan Africa, and without drastic policy actions, that number will only continue to grow.[3]

Performance against Benchmarks

The sluggish growth of output per worker in Sub-Saharan Africa widened the region's labor productivity gap relative to two familiar benchmarks: a global efficiency benchmark and an aspirational development benchmark. The former is proxied by the United States,[4] while the latter refers to the "East Asian dragons" (or "EAP5," comprising Indonesia, the Republic of Korea, Malaysia, Singapore, and Thailand).

Global Efficiency Benchmark
According to Penn World Table 9.1 data (updated from Feenstra, Inklaar, and Timmer 2015), the (population-weighted) average output per worker in Sub-Saharan Africa relative to that of the United States declined

from 11.9 percent in 1960 to 7.7 percent in 2017 (figure 1.1).[5] This reveals not only stagnant but also very low labor productivity in Sub-Saharan Africa over the past half century.

The same cannot be said about the (population-weighted) average output per worker in the EAP5 countries, which climbed from 8.5 percent in 1960 to 29.8 percent in 2017 (figure 1.1). Unlike East Asia, Sub-Saharan Africa failed to make headway against the global efficiency benchmark.

Aspirational Development Benchmark

The labor productivity trends show that Sub-Saharan Africa lost its productivity edge over the EAP5 countries over the past six decades. Workers in Sub-Saharan Africa during the 1960s were, on average, about 40–45 percent more productive than those in the EAP5. By the 2010s, workers in the EAP5 were more than three times as productive as

those in Sub-Saharan Africa. The contrasting evolution of labor productivity in Sub-Saharan Africa and the EAP5 indicates not only differences in the pace of (human and physical) capital accumulation but also a growing divergence in TFP between the two regions.

Zooming in on the evolution of output per worker in Sub-Saharan Africa relative to the EAP5 shows that, in 1960, the region as a whole had a head start in terms of labor of productivity relative to Korea (by 20 percent), Indonesia (by 30 percent), and Thailand (more than double), while its labor productivity was almost equal to Singapore's (figure 1.2, panel a). In the 1980s, however, labor productivity contracted in Sub-Saharan Africa while it monotonically increased in all the EAP5 countries—albeit at varying speeds. By 2017, workers in Indonesia and Thailand were more than twice as productive as those in Sub-Saharan Africa, and those in Korea and Singapore were more than 6 and

FIGURE 1.1 **Output per Worker in Sub-Saharan Africa and EAP5 Countries, Relative to the United States, 1960–2017**

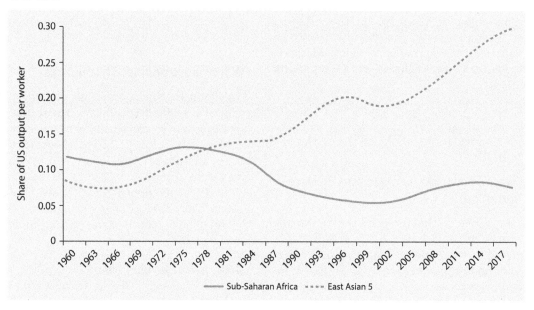

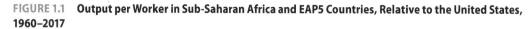

Sources: Penn World Table (PWT) 9.0 and PWT9.1 updates (Feenstra, Inklaar, and Timmer 2015).
Note: "EAP5" (or "East Asian 5") refers to five East Asian economic "dragons": Indonesia, the Republic of Korea, Malaysia, Singapore, and Thailand. The aggregate real output per worker for Sub-Saharan Africa and the EAP5 is a population-weighted average. These calculations use the output-side real GDP per capita at chained purchasing power parity (PPP) rates (in US$, millions, at 2011 prices). The figure presents the Hodrick-Prescott permanent component of the ratio of output per worker of each region relative to the United States (US output per worker = 1.0).

FIGURE 1.2   Output per Worker in Sub-Saharan Africa versus Selected Country Groups, 1960–2016

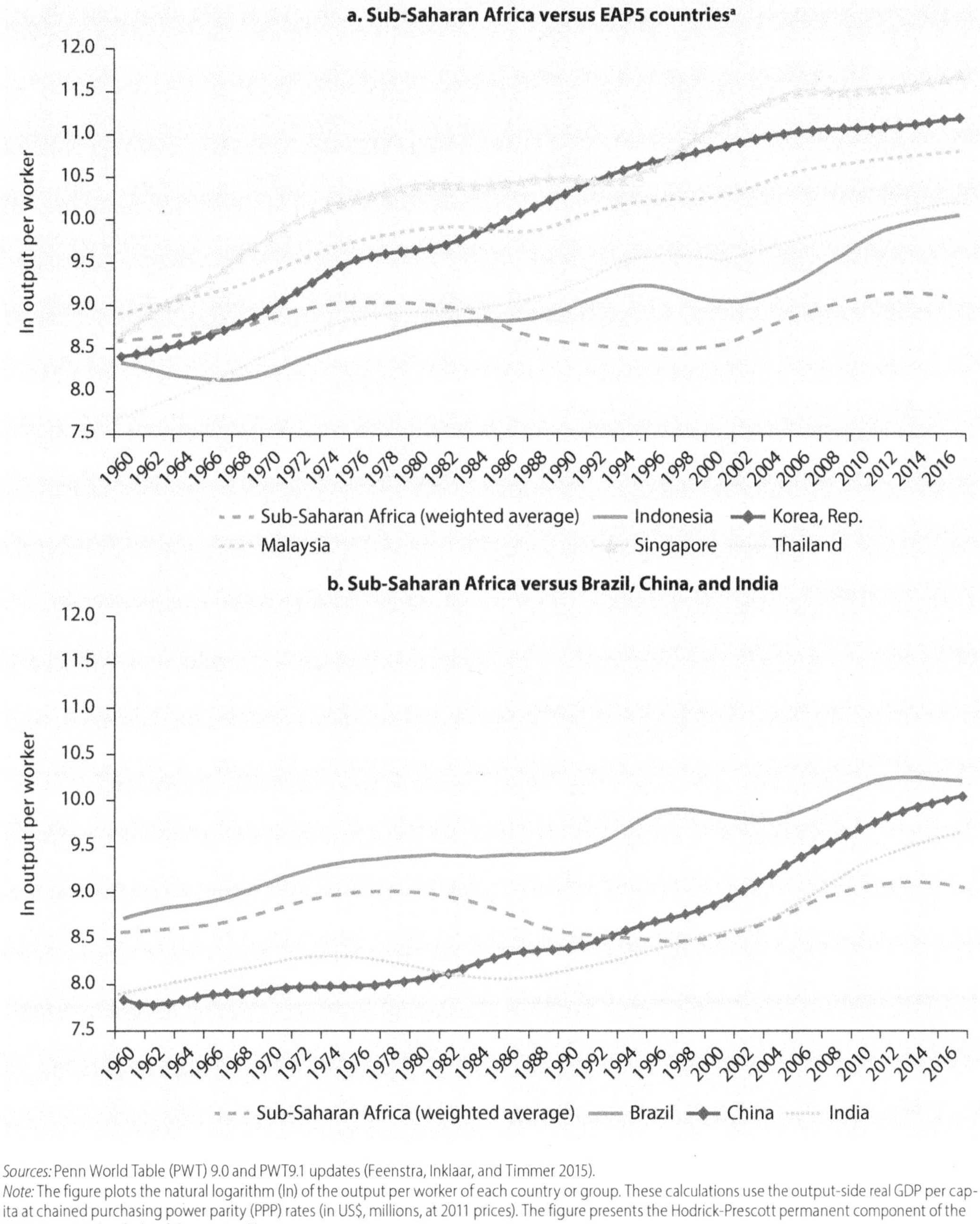

a. Sub-Saharan Africa versus EAP5 countries[a]

Legend: - - - Sub-Saharan Africa (weighted average)   —— Indonesia   ◆ Korea, Rep.
········ Malaysia   Singapore   Thailand

b. Sub-Saharan Africa versus Brazil, China, and India

Legend: - - - Sub-Saharan Africa (weighted average)   —— Brazil   ◆ China   ······ India

Sources: Penn World Table (PWT) 9.0 and PWT9.1 updates (Feenstra, Inklaar, and Timmer 2015).
Note: The figure plots the natural logarithm (ln) of the output per worker of each country or group. These calculations use the output-side real GDP per capita at chained purchasing power parity (PPP) rates (in US$, millions, at 2011 prices). The figure presents the Hodrick-Prescott permanent component of the output per worker (in logs). ln = natural log.
a. "EAP5" refers to five East Asian economic "dragons": Indonesia, the Republic of Korea, Malaysia, Singapore, and Thailand.

10 times as productive, respectively. Overall, there is a clear divergence in labor productivity between Sub-Saharan Africa and its aspirational development benchmark.

Finally, labor productivity in Sub-Saharan Africa also lost ground relative to three large and dynamic emerging market economies: Brazil, China, and India. Labor productivity in Sub-Saharan Africa was double that of China and India in 1960, while it was slightly lower than Brazil's (figure 1.2, panel b). The region's boom-bust cycles in labor productivity led it to gradually diverge from these other countries. By 2017, labor in India was nearly twice as productive, China more than 2.5-fold, and Brazil more than triple that of Sub-Saharan Africa.

Sources of Productivity Growth

Drawing on firm-level census data, this report evaluates the sources of firm productivity growth. Productivity gains within each sector of economic activity are primarily the outcome of increased dynamism within production units. Resource reallocation from less- to more-productive firms and activities also contributes to industry-level productivity growth in any market economy—especially in low-income economies with greater distortions.

Broadly speaking, the sources of productivity growth at the firm level (for countries either pushing the production possibility frontier or catching up to the productivity leaders) are as follows (Cusolito and Maloney 2018):

- *The within component*, which accounts for the productivity growth within firms. It depends on changes in the efficiency and intensity with which inputs are used in production (that is, to upgrade firms) owing to increased firm capabilities (including improved managerial skills, labor skills, innovation, and technology adoption capacity).
- *The between component*, which reflects the role of factor reallocation across firms in aggregate productivity growth. Increases in the "between" component imply that the most-productive firms would command the most resources—thus rendering the largest output and productivity gains. However, multiple distortions may limit the productivity gains arising from this component.
- *The selection component*, which accounts for the gains arising from the entry of high-productivity firms (relative to the

industry average) and the exit of low-productivity firms (relative to the industry average). It captures the aggregate effect of firm churning (or turnover) on productivity growth.

A growing strand of the literature investigates aggregate productivity as the result of firm-level decision-making processes, whereby firms are assumed to have different levels of productivity even within narrowly defined economic activities. (See, for instance, Bartelsman, Haltiwanger, and Scarpetta 2013; Foster, Haltiwanger, and Krizan 2001; and Syverson 2011.) In this context, the seminal work by Restuccia and Rogerson (2008) and Hsieh and Klenow (2009) has argued that the microstructure of production establishments in different economic sectors can help explain the development gap between rich and poor countries. In their framework, the production units exhibit different levels of productivity and hence size. Aggregate TFP is, in turn, influenced by the distribution of productivity across production units, those units' corresponding allocation of resources, and the number of firms per capita.[6]

Role of Resource Misallocation

This report will focus on resource misallocation as a potential explanation of low productivity (levels and growth) in Sub-Saharan Africa.[7] Resource misallocation refers to distortions in the allocation of inputs (such as capital, land, and labor) across production units of varying sizes. In other words, it occurs when different production establishments are taxed at different rates. This focus on misallocation is grounded in the following dimensions:

- First, the increasing role of TFP differences in explaining the labor productivity gap between African countries and both the global efficiency and aspirational development benchmarks.
- Second, the limited availability of firm-level census data that would primarily permit the testing of the static effects of misallocation on aggregate productivity. In the few

countries with longitudinal data from firm-level censuses (for example, Côte d'Ivoire and Ethiopia), there will be an exploration of the static and dynamic implications of misallocation (which includes not only reallocation among incumbents but also reallocation by churning).

- Third, the prevalence of policies and institutions (including social norms) in Sub-Saharan African countries that drive production units away from efficiency benchmarks.

Framework of Resource Allocation–or Misallocation

This strand of the literature on resource misallocation assumes that aggregate output is produced by several producers (N) that have different (individual) levels of productivity (A_i). Firm i's technology is summarized by a production function (f) that is strictly increasing and strictly concave. There is a fixed cost of operation (c) for any producer. Given an aggregate demand of labor (H) and capital (K),

there is a unique allocation of labor and capital across producers that maximizes total output net of fixed operating costs.

Theoretically, inefficiencies in the allocation of labor and capital across heterogeneous producers will affect aggregate output and productivity through three different channels:

- *The technology channel* reflects the level of productivity of each producer. If technological changes increase the productivity of all producers, output will be greater.
- *The selection channel* reflects the choices of producers that would operate in a given industry, given the costs of entry and their levels of productivity.
- *The misallocation channel* reflects the allocation of capital and labor among the operating producers.

These three channels are not independent: any policy or institution that *misallocates* resources across producers will potentially generate additional effects through both the *selection* and *technology* channels (figure 1.3).

FIGURE 1.3   Sources of Resource Misallocation That Reduce Total Factor Productivity

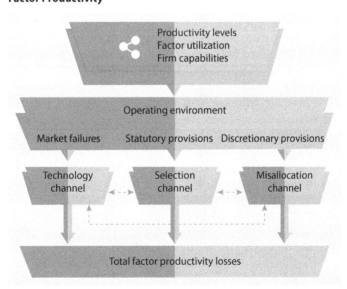

Source: Original figure for this publication.

According to this framework, lower values of A_i reflect either slow adoption or inefficient use of technology. The efficient allocation in this economy maximizes final output and is characterized by two decisions: (a) the number of operating establishments (that is, establishments that can pay the fixed cost, c); and (b) the allocation of capital and labor across the operating establishments. If either of these decisions is distorted, the economy will have lower output and hence lower aggregate TFP—as aggregate factor inputs (K and H) in the industry are constant.

An allocation of inputs that *maximizes* output across production units (say, either firms or farms) takes place when, conditional upon their operation, the marginal (and average) products are equal across all production units. In this equilibrium, no output gains would be obtained by reallocating inputs of production (such as capital, land, and labor) from production units with low marginal products to those with high marginal products. In the efficient allocation, the most productive operating establishments will demand more inputs. In other words, a production unit's productivity and size are positively associated in the efficient allocation. In addition, production units with similar productivity levels command the same amount of inputs and are of identical size.

Deviations from the efficient allocation of resources across firms may have implications for aggregate output and productivity. Input choices that differ from the efficiency model, even if they allocate more factors to the more-productive production units, will generate lower aggregate output. Given the constant aggregate amount of inputs (such as capital, land, and labor), the output loss associated with an inefficient allocation is also an aggregate TFP loss. In this context, misallocation refers to situations where resources are not allocated efficiently across production units, and the cost of misallocation is typically measured in terms of aggregate output or TFP losses.

If the misallocation of resources across these different producers helps explain cross-country differences in aggregate productivity levels, it is then crucial to investigate the sources of misallocation. Resource misallocation across different production units might reflect the following (Restuccia and Rogerson 2017):

- *Statutory provisions,* including some features of the tax code and regulations—for instance, tax code provisions that vary with firm characteristics (say, age or size); tariffs targeting certain groups of goods; employment protection measures; and land regulations, among others
- *Discretionary government (or bank) provisions* that favor or penalize specific firms—for instance, subsidies, tax breaks, or low-interest loans granted to specific firms; preferential market access; and unfair bidding practices for government contracts, among others
- *Market imperfections* such as monopoly power; market frictions (for example, in credit and land markets); and enforcement of property rights.

Dimensions of the Productivity Assessment

The main objective of this report is to characterize the evolution of output and productivity in Sub-Saharan Africa. To accomplish this task, the report documents the region's (labor and multifactor) productivity trends on an international, regional, and country basis. It benchmarks productivity levels and growth in Sub-Saharan Africa in relation to countries in other regions as well as in various African country groups, classified by their degree of natural-resource abundance and condition of fragility.[8] Overall, the analysis of productivity trends is conducted for three different levels of data aggregation: aggregate, sectoral, and establishment.

Aggregate Level

First, the report estimates the level and growth of labor and multifactor productivity in Sub-Saharan Africa (for the region as a whole as well as across countries) and the extent and nature of productivity gaps in relation to international benchmarks at the *aggregate level*. Labor productivity is measured by the ratio of real GDP to the number of persons employed.

The report not only illustrates the region's labor productivity trends but also identifies the sources of the persistent differences in labor productivity between Sub-Saharan Africa and benchmark countries or regions. To that end, the *development accounting* framework is used to decompose the differences in the level of labor productivity into (a) differences in input intensity (such as capital-use intensity and land-use intensity); and (b) differences in production efficiency (Hsieh and Klenow 2010).

In addition, the *growth accounting* framework is used to examine the sources of growth of African economies. In other words, it quantifies the proportion of growth attributed to factor accumulation and TFP growth (Solow 1957). The analysis of the sources of variation of labor productivity using these two frameworks is fully presented in chapter 2.

Sectoral Level

Second, the report depicts labor productivity trends at the *sectoral level* in Sub-Saharan Africa. Current research typically classifies economic activity into three broad sectors: agriculture, industry, and services (see, for instance, Duarte and Restuccia 2010; Herrendorf, Rogerson, and Valentinyi 2014). This classification has been broadly used to analyze the role of structural change—captured by the reallocation of labor from low- to high-productivity sectors—in explaining the differences in labor productivity in low- and middle-income countries (Diao, McMillan, and Rodrik 2017; Gollin, Lagakos, and Waugh 2014; McMillan, Rodrik, and Verduzco-Gallo 2014) and particularly in African countries (McMillan and Harttgen 2014; McMillan, Rodrik, and Sepulveda 2017).

The report uses input-output data, the United Nations National Accounts Database, and International Labour Organization statistics to unbundle the industry and services sectors. Within the industry sector, it distinguishes manufacturing from nonmanufacturing activities (such as construction; mining and quarrying; and electricity, water, and gas). In the services sector, it classifies the different activities as either market or nonmarket services. (Market services include wholesale and retail trade; hotels and restaurants; transportation, storage, and communications; financial intermediation; and real estate. Nonmarket services comprise public administration and defense; education; health and social work; and other community, social, and personal service activities.) Using data on labor productivity and labor shares, this report examines the shifts of resources across sectors over the recent decades.

Establishment Level

Third, the report presents evidence on (labor and multifactor) productivity at the *establishment level*. Using the World Bank's Living Standards Measurement Studies–Integrated Surveys on Agriculture (LSMS–ISA) and manufacturing firm-level censuses of select Sub-Saharan African countries, the report calculates quantity and revenue productivity (TFPQ and TFPR, respectively) at the farm level in agriculture and at the firm level in manufacturing. The coverage of countries in the region as well as time periods depends on the availability of microeconomic data.

The *core analysis* of this report will rest upon the assessment of the implications of aggregate productivity of production decisions across agricultural farms and manufacturing firms in Sub-Saharan Africa. Using farm- and firm-level data, it will assess the performance of production units in terms of their productivity levels across African establishments relative to an efficiency benchmark by computing the extent of resource misallocation. This calculation will provide information on the role of allocative inefficiencies in explaining productivity differences between establishments across Sub-Saharan African countries relative to those of other benchmark countries or regions.

The establishment-level analysis identifies and discusses the different policies and institutions that affect productivity and drive the misallocation of resources across farms and firms in Sub-Saharan Africa. Specifically, it discusses a comprehensive but not exhaustive set of policies and institutions that are categorized by these potential sources of misallocation (Restuccia and Rogerson 2017):

- *Market imperfections.* The analysis discusses credit market imperfections (that is, lack of access to finance due to the lack of collateral); lack of land titling, affecting the allocation of land; and information frictions, affecting producers that are not connected to markets or farmers who have inadequate information on weather forecasts.
- *Statutory provisions.* Also discussed are size-dependent policies—more specifically, tax provisions and regulations that depend on features of the different production units (such as size and age) as well as trade policies that protect specific categories of goods.
- *Discretionary provisions.* In addition, the report captures government provisions that favor or penalize certain types of production units—for instance, subsidies to farmers, low-interest lending to specific firms, and preferential market access for specific groups of producers, among others.

Finally, this report—launched and financed by the World Bank's Office of the Chief Economist of the Africa Region (AFRCE)—is part of the Bank's programmatic agenda on the drivers of productivity worldwide, emphasizing the factors that explain the productivity gap of emerging markets (and, notably, Sub-Saharan African countries) relative to the high-income world. Box 1.1 succinctly describes the goals of some of these research projects.

Data and Measurement Issues

One of the main challenges of empirical work in low- and middle-income countries, notably in Sub-Saharan Africa, is the issue of data quality. The poor quality of the data on macroeconomic, financial, and structural indicators for less-developed countries and for economies with large informal sectors—particularly in Sub-Saharan Africa—has been well documented (Jerven 2010, 2013a, 2013b, 2013c).

Empirical work on productivity in Sub-Saharan Africa is plagued by problems concerning data availability, comparability, and quality. At the national level, these problems are often tied to issues of capacity: The production of high-quality data for national income and product accounts (NIPA), consumption surveys, and firm-level censuses is technically complex. It involves the large-scale mobilization of sizable financial and human resources as well as the setup of robust quality control mechanisms. Additionally, the failure of statistical offices to adhere to methodological and operational standards leads to data comparability and quality issues (Beegle et al. 2016).

At the aggregate level, problems with NIPA quality in Sub-Saharan African countries have been extensively reported (Jerven 2010). Inaccuracies in the output and productivity data reported by national statistical systems have led to (potentially) misleading country productivity rankings. Output and productivity estimates in international currency showed significant variation across countries because of the varying reliability of the data sources or differences in the methods chosen to express the data in international currency.[9]

Output and productivity estimates across African countries can also be volatile, not only because of the low quality of statistical services but also partly because of the large weight of sectors (such as agriculture) that are prone to volatile domestic shocks and vulnerable to fluctuating international commodity prices. This report highlights some of the data production problems facing the region's

BOX 1.1   Building upon the World Bank's Productivity Research Agenda

This report is part of the World Bank Group's programmatic agenda on productivity and part of the regional studies program of the Bank's Office of the Chief Economist of the Africa Region (AFRCE). It complements other research projects conducted or already published in the region as well as the output from the Productivity Project, an initiative of the Vice Presidency for Equitable Growth, Finance and Institutions.

The Productivity Project seeks to bring frontier thinking on the measurement and determinants of productivity, grounded in the developing-country context, to global policy makers. Among its reports are the six described below.

The Innovation Paradox: Developing-Country Capabilities and the Unrealized Promise of Technological Catch-Up (Cirera and Maloney 2017) documents the small investments in innovation undertaken by low- and middle-income country firms and governments even though the returns from these investments are potentially high. Underlying this "innovation paradox," the evidence suggests, is the lack of complementary physical and human capital—in particular, firm managerial capabilities—needed to reap the returns to innovation investments. Countries need to build firms' capabilities and embrace an expanded concept of the National Innovation System (NIS), incorporating a broader range of market and systemic failures.[a]

Productivity Revisited: Shifting Paradigms in Analysis and Policy (Cusolito and Maloney 2018) presents a "second wave" of thinking in productivity analysis and its implications for productivity policies. It tests these hypotheses across select middle-income countries (for instance, Chile, Colombia, and Malaysia). It provides a more accurate calculation of distortions and examines more rigorously their importance as the primary barrier to productivity growth. It recommends a more comprehensive analysis of firm performance that includes efficiency, quality upgrading, and demand expansion. The authors advocate an integrated approach to productivity analysis that accounts for the need to (a) reduce distortions, (b) create human capital capable of identifying opportunities offered to follower countries, and (c) upgrade firm capabilities.

High-Growth Firms: Facts, Fiction, and Policy Options for Emerging Economies (Grover Goswami, Medvedev, and Olafsen 2019) examines whether targeting high-potential firms can enable more economic dynamism. It presents evidence on the occurrence, features, and determinants of high-growth firms

in Brazil, Côte d'Ivoire, Ethiopia, Hungary, India, Indonesia, Mexico, South Africa, Thailand, Tunisia, and Turkey. Its findings reveal that high-growth firms are powerful engines of job and output growth. They also create positive spillovers for other businesses along the value chain.

Harvesting Prosperity: Technology and Productivity Growth in Agriculture (Fuglie et al. 2019) uses recent impact evaluations to examine the constraints to farmers' adoption of technology and dissemination of productivity-enhancing technologies. It also discusses recent developments in agriculture value chains and the emergence of new institutional arrangements to include smallholder farms in these value chains.

Industrializing for Jobs in Africa? (Abreha et al., forthcoming) addresses (a) the lack of industrialization in postindependence Sub-Saharan Africa and some countries' patterns of deindustrialization; (b) the prospects for the region's countries to undergo industrialization through participation in regional or global manufacturing value chains over the next two decades; and (c) industrial policy tools that might foster country participation in the right regional or global manufacturing value chains. The authors' analysis is conducted at three levels of aggregation: country level, country groups defined by resource abundance, and income groups and natural trade groupings.

Inclusive Digital Africa (Begazo-Gomez, Blimpo, and Dutz (forthcoming) addresses why digital technology (DT) is important for Africa's development. It focuses on understanding the current drivers of DT adoption by individuals, households, and enterprises, as well as the linkages between DT adoption and business-driven productivity growth, output, and aggregate jobs expansion as a contribution to poverty reduction and inclusion outcomes in Africa today. More specifically, it addresses the extent to which (a) barriers impede DT adoption in Africa; (b) DT adoption by existing and new enterprises (firms and farms, both formal and informal), as well as by people who are or could be working in these enterprises, can generate productivity gains and aggregate output and jobs expansion; and (c) these gains can have greater impact on poverty reduction and inclusion outcomes.

a. The NIS refers to the institutions, human capital, and interactions between them that facilitate the creation and diffusion of knowledge. They focus on policies that not only foster research and development (R&D) investments but also upgrade firm capabilities. In addition to addressing barriers to knowledge capital accumulation, an NIS should also consider barriers to the accumulation of all types of capital—barriers such as business climate, bankruptcy laws, poor product and factor regulation, and so on (Maloney 2017).

national statistical systems and some of the data usage problems facing researchers.

Outdated Output and Productivity Estimates

The recent slew of national account rebasing exercises (updating the base year of constant price estimates) in Sub-Saharan Africa (for example, in Ghana and Zambia in 2010, and in Kenya, Nigeria, Tanzania, and Uganda in 2013) have called attention to the use of outdated economic structures, lack of adherence to international standards of national accounts measurement, and more broadly, the unreliability of income and product estimates.

For instance, the Ghana Statistical Services (GSS) revised its 2010 GDP to ₵44.8 billion, 60.3 percent higher than its previous estimate of ₵25.6 billion (Jerven 2013a). The upward revision was attributed to the inclusion of new data on unmeasured parts of the economy as the GSS changed the base year from 1993 to 2006.

Nigeria revised its 2013 GDP upward to US$509 billion after changing the base year for calculation from 1990 to 2010. It now includes previously uncounted industries like telecoms, information technology, music, online sales, airlines, and film production. Thanks to this new calculation, Nigeria overtook South Africa as the largest economy in the region and the 26th largest in the world (Blas and Wallis 2014).

The rebasing of output and productivity estimates in Sub-Saharan Africa reveals that important segments of economic activity had gone missing for decades—say, air transportation and information and communication technology (ICT) services—and that the lack of backward estimates thwarts the accurate accounting of economic history in these countries based on official statistics (Jerven 2013b). These revisions also reconfigure the map of income, productivity, and growth in Sub-Saharan Africa. And they raise concerns about the status of income and product statistics in other Sub-Saharan African countries—many of whose national statistical

systems are trapped in a vicious circle where inadequate funding undermines the production of high-quality data, in turn reducing demand for the data, which further reduces resources as well (Jerven 2013c).

Many statistical offices in the region still use outdated methods and data, and they lack the capacity to handle an efficient and transparent revision of their national accounts. Even if more of the region's statistical offices were to apply more recent standards of national accounts (say, base year 2008), they are unequally adapted at the national level. Moreover, there is no agreement on methods to deal with the growth effects of these revisions. The best practice in the buildup of NIPA data should focus not only on international standardization (such as the International Comparison Program [ICP] or the Penn World Tables) but also on fostering local conditions across statistical offices to timely and reliably produce and disseminate surveys.

Bias in Human Capital Assessment: Overstating School Enrollment Data

There is evidence of systematic biases in administrative data systems in the reporting of primary schooling enrollment data. These biases do not necessarily reflect the lack of analytical capacity. In some cases, they are the outcome of incentives to overestimate progress in the sector. Overestimation of school enrollment data results, at least partly, from incentives provided by the governance and funding structures of the Ministries of Education, especially in low-income, highly aid-dependent countries (Sandefur and Glassman 2015).

As national government and line ministries seek to allocate resources between school districts and evaluate teacher performance, the decision process is fed by information from administrative systems based on teacher self-reporting. The administrative data show significant evidence of overreporting of enrollment growth: the average change in enrollment is nearly one-third higher (3.1 percentage points) in administrative data than in survey data across 21 African countries, and this optimistic bias is completely absent in data outside Africa (Sandefur and Glassman 2015).[10] Overall, the resulting systemic misreporting undermines the government's ability to manage public services, especially in remote rural areas.

Unreliable Employment and Wage Labor Estimates

The importance of nonmonetary, subsistence, informal, or unrecorded economic activities in Sub-Saharan Africa may place into question the reliability of the reported data on labor and income. Informality alone makes it difficult to draw the production boundary of Sub-Saharan African economies (Jerven 2010). For instance, recent employment surveys in Tanzania suggest that self-employment is by far the most prevalent type of employment relationship in the informal economy.

Wage labor in Sub-Saharan African countries might also be underestimated for two other reasons (Rizzo, Kilama, and Wuyts 2015): (a) labor force surveys that lump it together with self-employment, and (b) poor understanding of the trends toward subcontracting of informal labor services (instead of direct production of goods). In the case of Tanzania, labor surveys failed to capture the heterogeneity of employment relations found in the informal economy and the heterogeneity of relationships between capital and labor that mediate poor people's participation in the (informal) economy (Rizzo, Kilama, and Wuyts 2015). Remedial measures include abandoning the misplaced aggregation in the classification of labor regimes, which results from conflating into a single catchall category various forms of production and employment that are essentially different.

Inadequate Agricultural Statistics

There are severe weaknesses in the measurement of agricultural outcomes in Sub-Saharan Africa—especially in the poorest countries that depend critically on this sector for the livelihood of large segments of the population. Consequently, their governments cannot assign their limited funding to improvement of statistical quality (FAO 2008; World Bank 2004).

The global strategy spearheaded by the Food and Agriculture Organization (FAO) of the United Nations to improve agricultural and rural statistics, and the corresponding regional action plans, represents efforts to improve agricultural standards and practices. The advent of new (and relatively affordable) technologies and rigorous research is helping foster the adoption or improvement of cost-effective standards in agricultural statistics (Carletto, Jolliffe, and Banerjee 2015). Finally, statistical systems need to promote enhanced integration of agricultural data and other types of data sources (for example, on poverty and nutritional, socioeconomic, and environmental conditions) to better inform sectoral policies.

Limited Availability of Firm-Level Census Data

The scope and breadth of the microeconomic analysis of productivity in this report is limited by the sparse availability of firm-level census data across Sub-Saharan African countries. Fewer than a handful of countries in the region conduct surveys at the establishment level—and even fewer provide longitudinal firm-level census data. This statistical deficit clearly hurts African countries' ability to formulate good policy decisions. To overcome the lack of firm-level census data across the region's countries, researchers have used alternative sources of data such as the World Bank Enterprise Surveys (WBES).

The evidence suggests that mismeasurement in the distribution of firms at the four-digit Standard Industrial Classification (SIC) level across African manufacturing industries—which might overrepresent large firms relative to firm-level census data—leads to biases in the computed extent, using WBES data, of resource misallocation. Inaccuracies in the measurement of value-added shares of industries in narrower industry groups would likely overestimate or underestimate the degree of misallocation because they would reflect both the true share and a sampling error. The WBES-based measure of misallocation would tend to be overestimated if sectors with higher misallocation are overrepresented relative to their shares in the census. Evidence for African countries shows that most industries would have smaller misallocation in the WBES than their dispersion in the census data. Hence, the WBES might underestimate the true misallocation of each sector and therefore underestimate manufacturing productivity dispersion (Cirera, Fattal-Jaef, and Maemir 2018).

Limited Interpretation of Microeconomic Evidence

One of the most widely used measures of firm-level productivity in the literature is total factor productivity revenue (TFPR)—typically defined as the ratio of firms' sales (or revenues) to input costs (appropriately weighted by their production elasticities). It has been argued that TFPR is a measure of profitability (or firm performance) rather than productivity. Hence, differences in TFPR across firms may capture not only differences in physical efficiency but also differences in prices, which reflect product differentiation and markups in addition to costs (De Loecker and Goldberg 2014). The emergence of (output and less often input) price data and new techniques applied to databases with firm-level prices has enabled researchers to compute more accurate measures of physical efficiency. Evidence on the use of these techniques for emerging markets is presented in Cusolito and Maloney (2018) and references therein.

Future work in Africa needs to distinguish productivity shocks (or technical efficiency) from demand shocks in the measures of TFPR among Sub-Saharan African production establishments. This requires the timely availability and recurrent production of high-quality data on output and input prices at the establishment level—a task that does not preclude improving the country coverage

as well as the methodology and periodicity of firm-level censuses. Such new and increased data impose other challenges: (a) wider availability of output price data rather than input price data at the establishment level; (b) reported output prices that are, in most cases, unit values; and (c) the need to undertake surveys at the product level if most manufacturing establishments in a specific sector are multiproduct.

Having greater data availability on output and input prices does not prevent the need to impose more structure to identify the role played by demand shocks in the measured TFPR. Recent research using firm-level census with price data shows that there is still a larger dispersion of TFPR across manufacturing firms in Ethiopia, and this is mirrored by large differences in physical productivity. Prices tend to vary significantly less than productivity levels and do not constitute a major driving factor of TFPR differences (Söderbom 2018).

Plan of the Volume

This volume documents the productivity trends in Sub-Saharan Africa in three different dimensions, assessing productivity at the aggregate level, the sectoral level, and the establishment level. It characterizes the evolution of productivity in the region relative to other countries and regions as well as country groups in Africa classified by their degree of natural-resource abundance and condition of fragility.

The core of this volume rests upon the assessment of the implications for aggregate productivity of production decisions across agricultural farms and manufacturing firms in Sub-Saharan Africa. The next three chapters will present evidence on aggregate productivity from the perspective of production units, using recent household surveys for farmers and firm-level surveys for select African countries as well as frontier estimation techniques. The empirical work presented in this volume can provide further guidance for productivity analysis and the design of a policy agenda for the region.

Chapter 2, "Needed: Boosting the Contribution of Total Factor Productivity," documents the growth performance of Sub-Saharan Africa over the past half century both across countries and across sectors of economic activity. Despite an uptick in labor productivity since 1996, the region has failed to catch up to either high-income countries (notably, the United States) or to groups of middle- to high-income countries such as the EAP5 (Indonesia, Korea, Malaysia, Singapore, and Thailand). The sizable gap in output per worker between Sub-Saharan African countries and those two benchmark groups is primarily attributed to a lower relative stock of physical and human capital (from the 1960s to the 1980s). During 2000–17, inefficiencies in the region's factor production use have played an increasing role in explaining this gap.

At the sectoral level, the analysis in this volume unpacks the various industry and services sectors into a five-sector classification: agriculture, manufacturing, nonmanufacturing, market services, and nonmarket services. Sectoral labor productivity in Sub-Saharan Africa exhibits long swings in the medium term over the past quarter century, and it is lower than in the United States, especially in agriculture. Broadly speaking, the structural transformation of Sub-Saharan Africa tends to lag that of other world regions. Agricultural employment shares have declined more slowly and remain higher than in other regions.

Chapter 3, "Resource Misallocation in Sub-Saharan Africa: Firm-Level Evidence," documents the extent of resource misallocation across agricultural and manufacturing production units in Sub-Saharan Africa. The agriculture sector analysis uses household-level panel data from the World Bank's LSMS-ISA initiative for selected countries in the region as well as geographically gridded data on actual and potential crops, crop choices, and land endowments from the FAO's Global Agronomic Ecological Zones (GAEZ) database. The manufacturing sector analysis uses firm-level manufacturing census data that adequately accounts for small and medium-size firms as well as large formal sector firms. On the other hand, the unavailability of firm-level data for the services sector prevents us from extending the services sector analysis to African countries.

The evidence shows that agriculture and manufacturing in Sub-Saharan Africa are plagued by severe misallocation of resources. The region's low agricultural productivity is not attributed to the quality of its soil or the amount of rainfall. It is overwhelmingly explained by inefficiencies in the allocation of resources. In manufacturing, the misallocation is captured by TFPR dispersion—which is larger than that of other low- and middle-income countries (China and India) and the efficiency benchmark (United States).

Both agricultural and manufacturing production units tend to face higher distortions in Sub-Saharan Africa than in other regions. In turn, these distortions decelerate the growth of the production units, disincentivize their adoption of productivity-enhancing technologies, and reduce the ability of their peers to learn new techniques.

Chapter 4, "Policies and Institutions that Distort Resource Allocation in Sub-Saharan Africa," explains how policies and institutions have distorted the allocation of inputs (capital, land, and labor) across heterogeneous production units. These policies and institutions can be classified into potential sources of misallocation: (a) *market imperfections* (restricted access to finance, lack of land titling or rental markets, and information frictions affecting market connectivity); (b) *statutory provisions* (size-dependent taxes and regulations); and (c) *discretionary provisions* (targeted subsidies and preferential trade policies).

Allocative inefficiencies affect output and productivity levels through three channels: technology, selection (occupational choices), and misallocation. These three channels can be interdependent. For instance, policies or institutions that lead to resource misallocation can potentially generate additional effects through both the selection and technology channels.

The pervasive misallocation of land in Sub-Saharan Africa can be influenced by the lack of land titling and the underdevelopment of land rental markets. This volume shows evidence that rental activity can help reallocate land from less- to more-productive farms. Still, land markets are subject to other frictions, and farms that rent land operate far from the efficiency benchmark. Credit market imperfections introduce distortions to entry and technology adoption decisions. By distorting entrepreneurs' entry decisions, credit market imperfections can lead to poverty traps. Asset grant programs to the poor can help them escape from poverty by identifying potential high-growth entrepreneurs and facilitating their growth.

This chapter also highlights the adoption of digital technologies to reduce some of these market frictions. For instance, mobile money has raised financial inclusion in several African countries. The insertion of digital technologies in finance has granted individuals access to savings instruments and loan products.

Chapter 5, "Agenda for Future Research," discusses further avenues of research that may provide further insights on the productivity dynamics across countries in the region—for instance, distinguishing demand from supply forces—and identify the different channels of policy transmission to enhance productivity.

Notes

1. Percentages calculated by the author from GDP per worker data in Feenstra, Inklaar, and Timmer (2015).
2. Regional economic growth data for Sub-Saharan Africa are calculated by the author.
3. The rising concentration of extreme poverty in Sub-Saharan Africa over the past quarter century can be attributed to two primary factors: (a) economic growth that has been neither as fast as population growth nor inclusive enough to put a big dent in poverty, and (b) the persistently low contribution of TFP to economic growth.
4. The development accounting literature uses the United States as a benchmark given that it is a large, stable, and diverse country that is still at the world's technological frontier (Duarte and Restuccia 2006; Restuccia 2011).
5. These figures roughly implied that the average US worker produced in 28 days what the average worker in Sub-Saharan Africa produced throughout a year in 2017, down from an average of 43 days in 1960.
6. See Hopenhayn (2014) for a unifying theoretical framework and review of the literature on misallocation.
7. The report will not focus on the drivers of within-firm productivity. In other words, productivity improvements due to better managerial practices, greater input quality, product innovation and research and development (R&D) investments, and firm structure decisions, among others, are beyond the scope of this report. For a comprehensive review of these issues, see Cirera and Maloney (2017), Syverson (2011), and the references therein.
8. Resource-rich countries, in this report, are those nations with rents from natural resources (excluding forests) that exceed 10 percent of GDP; that is, the sum of oil rents, natural gas rents, coal rents (hard and soft), and mineral rents should exceed 10 percent of GDP over the past decade. Estimates of natural-resource rents are based on Lange, Wodon, and Carey (2018). On the other hand, fragile and conflict-affected situations are defined as economies having either (a) a harmonized Country Policy and Institutional Assessment (CPIA) rating of 3.2 or less, or (b) the presence of a United Nations and/or regional peacekeeping or peace-building mission during the past three years.
9. In this context, the extent of inaccuracies in the data cannot be easily evaluated because it also reflects the underdevelopment of the region's different countries.
10. Discrepancies between administrative and survey data series in Kenya and Rwanda were concomitant with the shift from bottom-up financing of education (through user fees) to top-down finance (through per pupil central government grants). This highlights the interdependence of public finance systems and the integrity of administrative data systems.

References

Abreha, Kaleb G., Woubet Kassa, Emmanuel K. K. Lartey, Taye A. Mengistae, Solomon Owusu, and Albert G. Zeufack. Forthcoming.

The Prospects of Industrialization in Sub-Saharan Africa: Seizing Opportunities in Global Value Chains. Washington, DC: World Bank.

Baker, Scott R., Nicholas Bloom, Steven J. Davis, and Stephen J. Terry. 2020. "COVID-Induced Economic Uncertainty." Working Paper No. 26983, National Bureau of Economic Research, Cambridge, MA.

Bartelsman, Eric, John Haltiwanger, and Stefano Scarpetta. 2013. "Cross-Country Differences in Productivity: The Role of Allocation and Selection." *American Economic Review* 103 (1): 305–34.

Beegle, Kathleen, Luc Christiaensen, Andrew Dabalen, and Isis Gaddis. 2016. *Poverty in a Rising Africa.* Washington, DC: World Bank.

Begazo-Gomez, Tania, Moussa P. Blimpo, and Mark A. Dutz. Forthcoming. *Digital Africa: Building the Infrastructure Foundations and Facilitating the Adoption of Technologies for Jobs.* Washington, DC: World Bank.

Blas, Javier, and William Wallis. 2014. "Nigeria Almost Doubles GDP in Recalculation." *Financial Times*, April 7.

Bloom, Nicholas. 2014. "Fluctuations in Uncertainty." *Journal of Economic Perspectives* 28 (2): 153–76.

Bloom, Nicholas, Benn Eifert, Aprajit Mahajan, David McKenzie, and John Roberts. 2013. "Does Management Matter? Evidence from India." *Quarterly Journal of Economics* 128 (1): 1–51.

Bloom, Nicholas, Max Floetotto, Nir Jaimovich, Itay Saporta-Eksten, and Stephen J. Terry. 2018. "Really Uncertain Business Cycles." *Econometrica* 86 (3): 1031–65.

Bloom, Nicholas, and John Van Reenen. 2007. "Measuring and Explaining Management Practices across Firms and Countries." *Quarterly Journal of Economics* 122 (4): 1351–1408.

Carletto, Calogero, Dean Jolliffe, and Raka Banerjee. 2015. "From Tragedy to Renaissance: Improving Agricultural Data for Better Policies." *Journal of Development Studies* 51 (2): 133–48.

Caselli, Francesco. 2005. "Accounting for Cross-Country Income Differences." In *Handbook of Economic Growth*, Vol. 1, Part A, edited by Philippe Aghion and Steven Durlauf, 679–741. Amsterdam: Elsevier.

Cirera, Xavier, Roberto Fattal-Jaef, and Hibret Maemir. 2018. "Taxing the Good? Distortions, Misallocation, and Productivity in Sub-Saharan Africa." *World Bank Economic Review* 34 (1): 75–100.

Cirera, Xavier, and William F. Maloney. 2017. *The Innovation Paradox: Developing-Country Capabilities and the Unrealized Promise of Technological Catch-Up.* Washington, DC: World Bank.

Cusolito, Ana Paula, and William F. Maloney. 2018. *Productivity Revisited: Shifting Paradigms in Analysis and Policy.* Washington, DC: World Bank.

De Loecker, Jan, and Pinelopi Koujianou Goldberg. 2014. "Firm Performance in a Global Market." *Annual Review of Economics* 6 (1): 201–27.

Diao, Xinshen, Margaret McMillan, and Dani Rodrik. 2017. "The Recent Growth Boom in Developing Economies: A Structural Change Perspective." Working Paper 23132, National Bureau of Economic Research, Cambridge, MA.

Duarte, Margarida, and Diego Restuccia. 2006. "The Productivity of Nations." *Federal Reserve Bank of Richmond Economic Quarterly* 92 (3): 195–223.

Duarte, Margarida, and Diego Restuccia. 2010. "The Role of the Structural Transformation in Aggregate Productivity." *Quarterly Journal of Economics* 125 (1): 129–73.

Duarte, Margarida, and Diego Restuccia. 2018. "Structural Transformation and Productivity in Sub-Saharan Africa." Unpublished manuscript, University of Toronto.

Economist. 2011. "Africa Rising." December 3.

FAO (Food and Agriculture Organization of the United Nations). 2008. "Agricultural Bulletin Board on Data Collection, Dissemination and Quality of Statistics (ABCDQ) project" developed by the FAO Statistics Division. http://faostat.fao.org/abcdq/.

Feenstra, Robert C., Robert Inklaar, and Marcel P. Timmer. 2015. "The Next Generation of the Penn World Table." *American Economic Review* 105 (10): 3150–82.

Foster, Lucia, John C. Haltiwanger, and C. J. Krizan. 2001. "Aggregate Productivity Growth: Lessons from Microeconomic Evidence." In *New Developments in Productivity Analysis*, edited by Charles R. Hulten, Edwin R. Dean, and Michael J. Harper, 303–72. Chicago: University of Chicago Press.

Fuglie, Keith, Madhur Goyal, Aparajita Gautam, and William F. Maloney. 2019. *Harvesting Prosperity: Technology and Productivity Growth in Agriculture.* Washington, DC: World Bank.

Gollin, Douglas, David Lagakos, and Michael E. Waugh. 2014. "Agricultural Productivity Differences across Countries." *American Economic Review* 104 (5): 165–70.

Grover Goswami, Arti, Denis Medvedev, and Ellen Olafsen. 2019. *High-Growth Firms: Facts, Fiction, and Policy Options for Emerging Economies.* Washington, DC: World Bank.

Guerrieri, Veronica, Guido Lorenzoni, Ludwig Straub, and Iván Werning. 2020. "Macroeconomic Implications of COVID-19: Can Negative Supply Shocks Cause Demand Shortages?" Working Paper No. 26918, National Bureau of Economic Research, Cambridge, MA.

Hall, Robert E., and Charles I. Jones. 1999. "Why Do Some Countries Produce So Much More Output per Worker than Others?" *Quarterly Journal of Economics* 114 (1): 83–116.

Herrendorf, Berthold, Richard Rogerson, and Ákos Valentinyi. 2014. "Growth and Structural Transformation." In *Handbook of Economic Growth* Vol. 2, edited by Philippe Aghion and Steven Durlauf, 855–941. Amsterdam: Elsevier.

Hopenhayn, Hugo A. 2014. "Firms, Misallocation, and Aggregate Productivity: A Review." *Annual Review of Economics* 6 (1): 735–70.

Hsieh, Chang-Tai, and Peter J. Klenow. 2009. "Misallocation and Manufacturing TFP in China and India." *Quarterly Journal of Economics* 124 (4): 1403–48.

Hsieh, Chang-Tai, and Peter J. Klenow. 2010. "Development Accounting." *American Economic Journal: Macroeconomics* 2 (1): 207–23.

Jerven, Morten. 2010. "African Growth Recurring: An Economic History Perspective on Africa Growth Episodes, 1690–2010." *Economic History of Developing Regions* 25 (2): 127–54.

Jerven, Morten. 2013a. "Comparability of GDP Estimates in Sub-Saharan Africa: The Effect of Revisions in Sources and Methods Since Structural Adjustment." *Review of Income and Wealth* 59 (S1): S16–S36.

Jerven, Morten. 2013b. *Poor Numbers: How We Are Misled by African Development Statistics and What to Do about It.* Ithaca, NY: Cornell University Press.

Jerven, Morten. 2013c. "Why We Need to Invest in African Development Statistics: From a Diagnosis of Africa's Statistical Tragedy towards a Statistical Renaissance." *African Arguments* (online platform of the Royal African Society), September 26.

Jones, Charles I. 2016. "The Facts of Economic Growth." In *Handbook of Macroeconomics, Vol. 2A,* edited by John B. Taylor, and Harald Uhlig, 3–69. Amsterdam: Elsevier.

Kim, Young Eun, and Norman V. Loayza. 2019. "Productivity Growth: Patterns and Determinants across the World." Policy Research Working Paper 8852, World Bank, Washington, DC.

Klenow, Peter J., and Andrés Rodríguez-Clare. 1997. "The Neoclassical Revival in Growth Economics: Has It Gone Too Far?" In NBER Macroeconomics Annual 1997, edited by Ben S. Bernanke and Julio J. Rotemberg, 73–103. Cambridge, MA: MIT Press.

Lange, Glenn-Marie, Quentin Wodon, and Kevin Carey, eds. 2018. *The Changing Wealth of Nations 2018: Building a Sustainable Future.* Washington, DC: World Bank.

Maloney, William F. 2017. "Revisiting the National Innovation System in Developing Countries." Policy Research Working Paper 8219, World Bank, Washington, DC.

McMillan, Margaret, and Kenneth Harttgen. 2014. "What Is Driving the 'African Growth Miracle'?" Working Paper 20077, National Bureau of Economic Research, Cambridge, MA.

McMillan, Margaret, Dani Rodrik, and Claudia Sepulveda. 2017. "Structural Change, Fundamentals and Growth: A Framework and Case Studies." Working Paper 23378, National Bureau of Economic Research, Cambridge, MA.

McMillan, Margaret, Dani Rodrik, and Íñigo Verduzco-Gallo. 2014. "Globalization, Structural Change, and Productivity Growth, with an Update on Africa." *World Development* 63: 11–32.

Parente, Stephen L., and Edward C. Prescott. 2000. *Barriers to Riches.* Cambridge, MA: MIT Press.

Parente, Stephen L., and Edward C. Prescott. 2005. "A Unified Theory of the Evolution of International Income Levels." In *Handbook of Economic Growth, Vol. 1, Part B,* edited by Philippe Aghion and Steven Durlauf, 1371–1416. Amsterdam: Elsevier.

Restuccia, Diego. 2011. "Recent Developments in Economic Growth." *Federal Reserve Bank of Richmond Economic Quarterly* 97 (3): 329–57.

Restuccia, Diego, and Richard Rogerson. 2008. "Policy Distortions and Aggregate Productivity with Heterogeneous Establishments." *Review of Economic Dynamics* 11 (4): 707–20.

Restuccia, Diego, and Richard Rogerson. 2013. "Misallocation and Productivity." *Review of Economic Dynamics* 16 (1): 1–10.

Restuccia, Diego, and Richard Rogerson. 2017. "The Causes and Costs of Misallocation." *Journal of Economic Perspectives* 31 (3): 151–74.

Rizzo, Matteo, Blandina Kilama, and Marc Wuyts. 2015. "The Invisibility of Wage Employment in Statistics on the Informal Economy in Africa: Causes and Consequences." *Journal of Development Studies* 51 (2): 149–61.

Sandefur, Justin, and Amanda Glassman. 2015. "The Political Economy of Bad Data: Evidence from African Survey and Administrative Statistics." *Journal of Development Studies* 51 (2): 116–32.

Söderbom, Måns. 2018. "Productivity Dispersion and Firm Dynamics in Ethiopia's Manufacturing Sector." Unpublished manuscript, University of Gothenburg, Sweden.

Solow, Robert M. 1957. "Technical Change and the Aggregate Production Function." *Review of Economics and Statistics* 39 (3): 312–20.

Syverson, Chad. 2011. "What Determines Productivity?" *Journal of Economic Literature* 49 (2): 326–65.

World Bank. 2004. "The Marrakech Action Plan for Statistics. Better Data for Better Results: An Action Plan for Improving Development Statistics." Paper presented at the Second International Roundtable on Managing for Development Results, Marrakech, Morocco, February 4–5.

World Bank. 2020a. *Africa's Pulse: Assessing the Impact of COVID-19 and Policy Responses in Sub-Saharan Africa,* vol. 21 (April). Washington, DC: World Bank.

World Bank. 2020b. *Poverty and Shared Prosperity 2020: Reversals of Fortune.* Washington, DC: World Bank.

Needed: Boosting the Contribution of Total Factor Productivity | 2

The Divergent Paths of Malaysia and Senegal

In 1960, the productivity stories of Malaysia and Senegal were roughly similar. Despite their geographical distance—one in East Asia, the other in West Africa—the two countries were quite close in terms of labor productivity and its corresponding deep fundamentals: factor endowments and total factor productivity (TFP).

For instance, the 1960 output per worker in Malaysia and Senegal was US$7,261 and US$7,899, respectively (in 2011 dollars at current purchasing power parity [PPP] prices).[1] That is, labor productivity in Malaysia was about 92 percent that of Senegal. The capital per worker and capital-output ratios in Malaysia were also close to those in Senegal.[2] Physical capital per worker in Malaysia and Senegal in 1960 was US$22,874 and US$23,175, respectively (in 2011 dollars at current PPP prices), while their corresponding capital-output ratios were 3.15 and 2.94. In addition, Malaysia's human capital index was 29 percent higher than Senegal's in 1960.[3] Finally, workers in the East Asian country were about 70 percent as productive as those in the West African country. Arguably, these two countries had similar initial conditions in terms of labor productivity and similar factor endowments (figure 2.1).

By 2017, labor productivity in Malaysia had already navigated a different path from that of Senegal. Output per worker in Malaysia was 6.6 times larger than in Senegal (US$49,630 and US$7,532, respectively, in 2011 dollars at current PPP prices). Although the capital-output ratios of Malaysia and Senegal have remained almost invariant over the past six decades, the amount of physical capital per worker in the East Asian country is now more than six times that of the West African country—specifically, 6.4 times as large in 2017. Human capital continues to be higher in Malaysia than in Senegal, although the gap has increased, from about 29 percent in 1960 to 92 percent in 2017. In addition, Malaysian workers became more productive than Senegalese workers—by 2017, 3.5 times as productive (figure 2.1).

In sum, the greater gap in labor productivity between Malaysia and Senegal over the past six decades could be attributed not only to greater differences in factor endowments but also to differences in TFP. In other words, Senegal lost ground to Malaysia not only because of lower investment (in physical

FIGURE 2.1   **Outputs, Inputs, and Productivity Gaps between Malaysia and Senegal, 1960 and 2017**

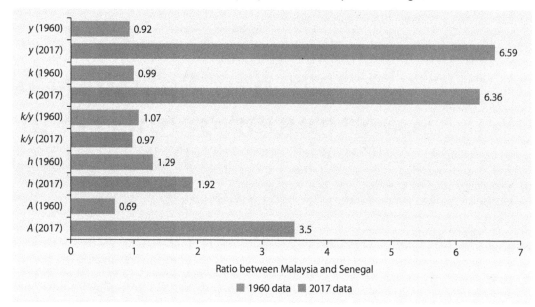

Source: Penn World Table (PWT) 9.0 and PWT9.1 updates (Feenstra, Inklaar, and Timmer 2015).
Note: The bars display ratios of Malaysian to Senegalese indicators in their corresponding years. y = labor productivity; k = capital stock per worker; k/y = capital-output ratio; h = PWT human capital index; A = relative total factor productivity (TFP). The year of measurement is shown in parentheses.

and human capital) but also because of lower efficiency in combining the different factors of production.

Development Accounting

The divergent (labor and multifactor) productivity paths of Malaysia and Senegal is only one example of Sub-Saharan Africa's failure to converge economically with the five East Asian "dragons" (referred to here as the "EAP5," comprising Indonesia, the Republic of Korea, Malaysia, Singapore, and Thailand) and the United States, as further discussed in chapter 1. In fact, labor productivity in all the region's countries declined sharply relative to the EAP5 between 1960 and 2017—with half of the Sub-Saharan African countries having 2017 labor productivity levels that were less than or equal to only a quarter of their corresponding levels in 1960. From these facts, a question emerges: What explains Sub-Saharan Africa's dismal performance on labor productivity compared with the rest of the low- and middle-income world?[4]

This report proposes several explanations: First, physical capital is scarce (as manifested by low capital per worker), and economic activities in Sub-Saharan Africa are less capital-intensive than in other regions where growth took off (say, among the EAP5 countries). The gap in physical capital per worker persists despite increased public and private investment spending in the region.

Second, the region exhibits relatively poorer levels of human capital and declining educational quality as a result of insufficient investment and poor learning outcomes. In fact, 23 of the 25 countries with the lowest Human Capital Index (HCI) are in Sub-Saharan Africa (World Bank 2019).

Finally, the region's poor economic performance is attributed not only to scarce (and low-quality) resources but also to inefficiencies in the operation of production technologies. These inefficiencies reflect the prevalence of policies and institutions among the region's countries that impede the more-productive establishments from demanding more factors of production, thus limiting the growth of their respective firms or farms. For instance, nonmarket mechanisms of land allocation, differential access to bank credit, tax evasion, and informality may help explain why different factors of production in the economy are not necessarily reallocated from the least- to the most-productive units. In other words, scarce resources, compounded by inefficient allocation across the different productive units, translate into low aggregate labor productivity.

Sub-Saharan Africa needs policies to boost productivity across all sectors of economic activity, especially in those sectors where most poor people make their living. The region needs policies that improve productivity in the agriculture sector, foster rural development, and create jobs for the youth bulge that is joining the labor force.

Impacts of Low Resource Endowments and Production Inefficiency

Relative Labor Productivity

The aggregate growth performance of the region masks the very different growth experiences across Sub-Saharan African countries—where surges, expansions, recessions, and collapses have taken place throughout the economic history of the African subcontinent. From 1980 to 2017, about two-thirds of the region's countries (30 of 44) experienced a decline in the relative gross domestic product (GDP) per worker (figure 2.2). Relative labor productivity in 2017 was less than half that of 1980 for nine countries in the region: the Central African Republic, the Comoros, the Democratic Republic of Congo, Guinea, Liberia, Niger, Nigeria, Togo, and Zimbabwe. In contrast, two countries (Botswana and Equatorial Guinea) saw their GDP per worker more than double during the 1980–2017 period.

Labor Productivity

There is great dispersion of labor productivity across countries in Sub-Saharan African countries relative to the United States, which is the global frontier benchmark (map 2.1). The region houses the largest number of countries with the lowest labor productivity relative to this benchmark. In about 80 percent of the region's countries (37 out of 44), the output per worker is less than one-fifth that of the United States. Within this group, the relative GDP per worker of five countries was below 2.5 percent of the US benchmark in 2017 (Burundi, the Central African Republic, Liberia, Malawi, and Niger). In contrast, the output per worker in eight countries exceeded 20 percent of the US benchmark—and within this group, it exceeded 40 percent of the benchmark in three countries (Gabon, Mauritius, and the Seychelles).[5]

Capital-Labor Ratio

The substantial gap in output per worker between Sub-Saharan Africa and the United States is attributable to the region's scarce availability of inputs of production (physical and human capital) as well as its less efficient combination of these inputs. Many countries in the region (31 out of 45) had 2017 capital-labor ratios below US$50,000 at 2011 prices (map 2.2). The stock of capital per worker in this undercapitalized group of countries in 2017 ranged from US$2,500 to US$41,400—with a median capital-labor ratio of US$12,093—and 12 of them had capital-labor ratios below US$10,000.

Only 21 countries outside the region had capital-labor ratios below US$50,000, but the median ratio for this group (about US$33,319) was significantly higher than in Sub-Saharan Africa. At the other end of the spectrum, only 3 countries in the region had 2017 capital-labor ratios exceeding US$200,000 (Equatorial Guinea, Gabon, and the Seychelles), while that was the case for 52 countries outside Sub-Saharan Africa.

Human Capital Index

The issue of resource scarcity is not limited to physical capital in Sub-Saharan Africa. Human capital is also scarce and of low quality, as measured by the World Bank's 2017 Human Capital Index (HCI).[6] The HCI assigns values between 0 and 1 that reflect worker productivity relative to a benchmark of complete education and full health (World

FIGURE 2.2   Relative Labor Productivity of Sub-Saharan African Countries, 1980 versus 2017

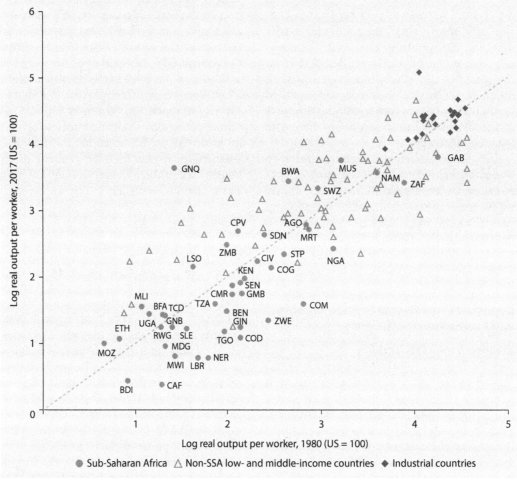

● Sub-Saharan Africa   △ Non-SSA low- and middle-income countries   ◆ Industrial countries

Source: Penn World Table (PWT) 9.0 and PWT9.1 updates (Feenstra, Inklaar, and Timmer 2015).
Note: The figure depicts the output per worker of all countries relative to that of the United States (US = 100). The ratio is then expressed in logs. "Industrial" countries refers to high-income Organisation for Economic Co-operation and Development (OECD) economies. Selected countries and economies are labeled using International Organization for Standardization (ISO) alpha-3 codes.
GNB = Guinea Bissau; BFA = Burkina Faso; TCD = Chad; MRT = Mauritania; STP = São Tomé and Principe.

Bank 2019). On this measure, 24 out of 40 countries with HCI data in Sub-Saharan Africa registered low HCI scores (below 0.4) in 2017, varying within a narrow band from 0.361 to 0.396 (map 2.3). The median HCI score for this group of 24 countries (0.37) implies that the future productivity of a child born in 2017 is 63 percent below what the child could have achieved with complete education and full health.

Only three countries outside the region (Iraq, Pakistan, and the Republic of Yemen)

had HCI scores below 0.4, varying from 0.369 to 0.398. Among the Sub-Saharan African countries with HCI scores above 0.4 (16 out of 40 countries), the median was 0.42, varying from 0.476 to 0.678.

Efficiency of Production

The low relative output per worker of several African countries can be attributed not only to low stocks of capital per worker but also to poor human capital. However, the region's large and persistent gap in output

MAP 2.1   Labor Productivity, by Country, Relative to the United States, 2017

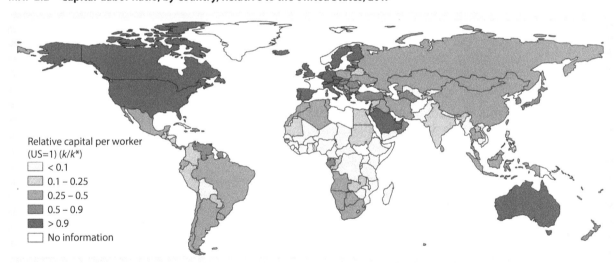

Source: Penn World Table (PWT) 9.0 and PWT9.1 updates (Feenstra, Inklaar, and Timmer 2015).
Note: Relative labor productivity of a given country, y/y^*, is the ratio of the output per worker in that country to output per worker in the United States (US = 1.0).

MAP 2.2   Capital-Labor Ratio, by Country, Relative to the United States, 2017

Source: Penn World Table (PWT) 9.0 and PWT9.1 updates (Feenstra, Inklaar, and Timmer 2015).
Note: The relative capital-labor ratio of a given country, k/k^*, is the stock of physical capital per worker (US = 1.0).

per worker relative to comparator country groups (say, the EAP5 countries or the United States) is not only a story of scarce (physical and human) capital but also of low efficiency in the combination of the scarce factors of production.

On this score, the TFP of the global efficiency benchmark (the United States) is at

MAP 2.3   Human Capital Index, by Country, 2017

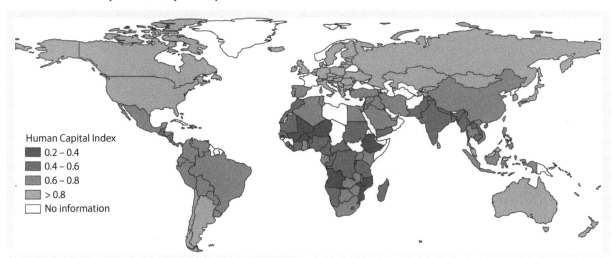

Human Capital Index
- 0.2 – 0.4
- 0.4 – 0.6
- 0.6 – 0.8
- > 0.8
- No information

Sources: Penn World Table (PWT) 9.0 and PWT9.1 updates (Feenstra, Inklaar, and Timmer 2015).
Note: The figure plots the values of the World Bank's 2017 Human Capital Index (HCI) for all countries. The HCI measures three components: probability of survival, expected learning-adjusted years of school, and health. The HCI values (from 0 to 1.0) reflect prospective worker productivity relative to a benchmark (1.0) of complete education and full health.

least five times that of 31 countries (out of 37) in Sub-Saharan Africa (map 2.4). Specifically, US TFP is 5 times that of Botswana, Côte d'Ivoire, and Kenya; 10 times that of Ghana and Zambia; and more than 20 times that of Nigeria and Tanzania.[7]

Drivers of Labor Productivity Gaps between Sub-Saharan Africa and the United States

Development Accounting Analysis
Labor productivity in Sub-Saharan Africa, relative to the global efficiency benchmark (the United States), exhibits long swings (from 5 percent to 15 percent) between 1960 and 2017 (figure 2.3, panel a). This relative productivity declines from an average of 12 percent in the 1970s to a trough of 6 percent in the 1990s, and then it recovers to 8 percent from 2010 to 2017.

The development accounting analysis shows that, from the 1960s to the mid-1980s, more than half of the differences in

output per worker between Sub-Saharan Africa and the United States were driven by differences in the relative endowment of (physical and human) capital. Since the 1990s, differences in TFP became the main driver explaining the output-per-worker gaps (figure 2.3, panel b).[8]

Overall, two findings emerge from this analysis of the widening gap in aggregate labor productivity between the United States and Sub-Saharan Africa:

- Differences in output per worker were mainly driven by undercapitalization in Sub-Saharan Africa from the 1960s to the mid-1980s. The region's lower relative accumulation of (physical and human) capital became the main culprit of the labor productivity gap.
- Gaps in factor accumulation between Sub-Saharan Africa and the United States still play a role in explaining differences in relative output per worker. However, the gap in the region's efficiency in combining its factors of

MAP 2.4   Efficiency of Production, by Country, Relative to the United States, 2017

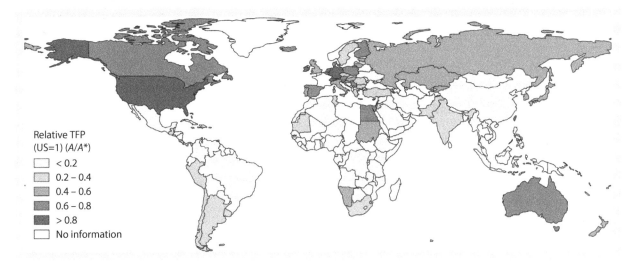

Source: Penn World Table (PWT) 9.0 and PWT9.1 updates (Feenstra, Inklaar, and Timmer 2015).
Note: The relative total factor productivity (TFP) of each country, A/A*, was computed using data on output per worker, capital-output ratios, human capital, and the share of labor in output relative to the US (= 1.0).

production—as captured by the share due to TFP—has become increasingly relevant to explanations of productivity gaps from 2000 to 2014. The decrease in TFP in Sub-Saharan Africa relative to the United States could be attributed, among other things, to resource misallocation.

There is a shift in the narrative of what explains the persistent gap in labor productivity between Sub-Saharan Africa and the United States. It has shifted from an *undercapitalization story* (reflected by the substantially lower relative capital-output ratios from the 1960s to the mid-1980s) to a *production inefficiency story* (captured by the region's lower relative TFP). In turn, Sub-Saharan Africa's lower TFP levels could be attributed, among other things, to resource misallocation. In sum, the region's scarce physical and human capital, compounded by the misallocation of these resources, translates into an even lower level of (labor and total factor) productivity.

Drivers of the Labor Productivity Gap

The extent and persistence of the labor productivity gap between Sub-Saharan Africa and the United States differ markedly across countries in the region. However, country evidence supports the aggregate story of changes in the main drivers of these persistent gaps in output per worker.

First, output-per-worker differences between Sub-Saharan African countries and the United States from 1980 to 1989 were primarily driven by differences in the stocks of physical and human capital.[9] Lower capital-output ratios and human capital relative to the United States explain more than half of the labor productivity gap during that period in 22 out of 37 Sub-Saharan African countries. The median share of labor productivity differences attributed to factors of production was about 67 percent.

Second, disparities in labor productivity between Sub-Saharan African countries and the United States were larger in 2010–17 than in 1980–89. Furthermore, factor accumulation and TFP played increasing roles in

FIGURE 2.3   Sources of the Labor Productivity Gap between Sub-Saharan Africa and the United States, 1960–2017

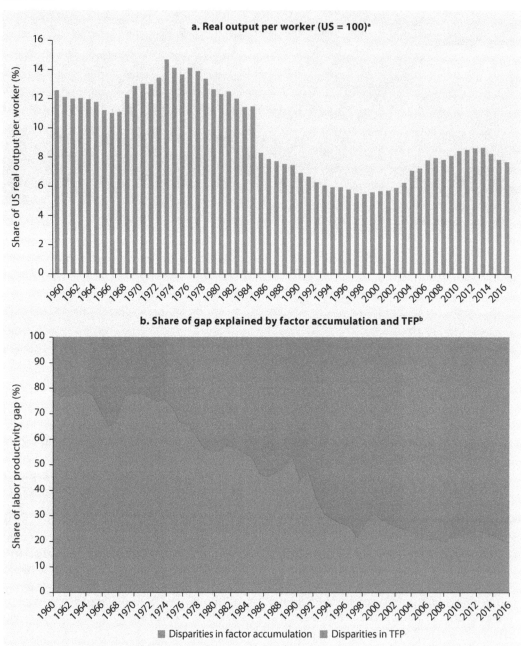

Source: Penn World Table (PWT) 9.0 and PWT9.1 updates (Feenstra, Inklaar, and Timmer 2015).
Note: TFP = total factor productivity.
a. Panel a shows the employment-weighted average of relative real output per worker among countries in Sub-Saharan Africa, as a percentage of that in the United States (US = 100).
b. Panel b shows the proportion of the differences in output per worker that are attributed to either factor accumulation or TFP differences.

driving these differences. Out of 37 countries in the region, the *undercapitalization narrative* (that is, factor accumulation explaining more than 50 percent of the labor productivity differences) holds for 3 countries (with a median share due to factor accumulation of 59 percent). On the other hand, the *inefficiency narrative* (that is, TFP differences explaining more than 50 percent of the labor productivity differences) holds for the remaining 34 countries in the region. For these 34 countries, about 75 percent of the output-per-worker differences are attributed to differences in the efficiency with which workers combine the factors of production.

Third, TFP differences have played a larger role in explaining the gap in relative output per worker across Sub-Saharan African countries over time. The share attributed to TFP has increased for all 37 countries in the region between 1980–89 and 2010–17 (figure 2.4). The median share due to TFP increased from 44 percent in 1980–89 to 76 percent in 2010–17. This finding implies that the narrative of "inefficient use of current technologies"—attributed partly to resource misallocation—is getting more mileage when explaining output-per-worker differences in Sub-Saharan Africa.

Dismal Growth Performance: The Negligible Contribution of TFP Growth

Sub-Saharan Africa has failed to catch up with both the aspirational development and global efficiency benchmarks—the EAP5 and the United States, respectively—over the past six decades. From 1960 to 2017, Sub-Saharan Africa registered the lowest annual average growth per worker of any region in the world (figure 2.5): its average annual rate of growth per worker over the 57-year period was 1 percent—smaller than that of either industrial (high-income) countries (2.1 percent) or the EAP5 countries (3.5 percent).[10]

Main Source of Productivity Growth: Factor Accumulation

Overall Trends

Growth per worker in Sub-Saharan Africa has been overwhelmingly driven by physical capital accumulation from 1960 to 2017. Almost three-quarters of the region's labor productivity growth from 1960 to 2017 is explained by growth of physical capital per worker. The contribution of TFP, on the other hand, is negligible. The narrative on the economic performance of Sub-Saharan Africa is one of growth at the extensive margin rather than at the intensive margin—a typical feature of low- and lower-middle-income economies. Growth per worker and the role played by factor accumulation (relative to TFP growth) in the region is comparable to that of Latin America and the Caribbean.

Labor productivity growth in the EAP5 countries was more than triple that of Sub-Saharan Africa (average annual growth rates of 3.5 percent and 1.0 percent, respectively) over the 1960–2017 period. The contribution of TFP growth has also been far more significant: more than 20 percent of the growth per worker in the EAP5 countries was driven by greater efficiency in combining the factors of production. Growth per worker in India (3.3 percent per year) is comparable to that of the EAP5, and the contribution of TFP growth is significantly higher (about 50 percent).

Intraregional Trends

Resource-rich versus non-resource-rich countries. Within Sub-Saharan Africa from 1960 to 2017, non-resource-rich countries outperformed resource-rich countries in terms of growth per worker (with annual average rates of 1.2 percent and 0.7 percent per year, respectively). The engines that supported the growth records of these country groups were also different. Capital accumulation was the main engine of growth for both resource-rich

FIGURE 2.4 **Share of Labor Productivity Differences due to TFP in Sub-Saharan African Countries, 1980–89 versus 2010–17**

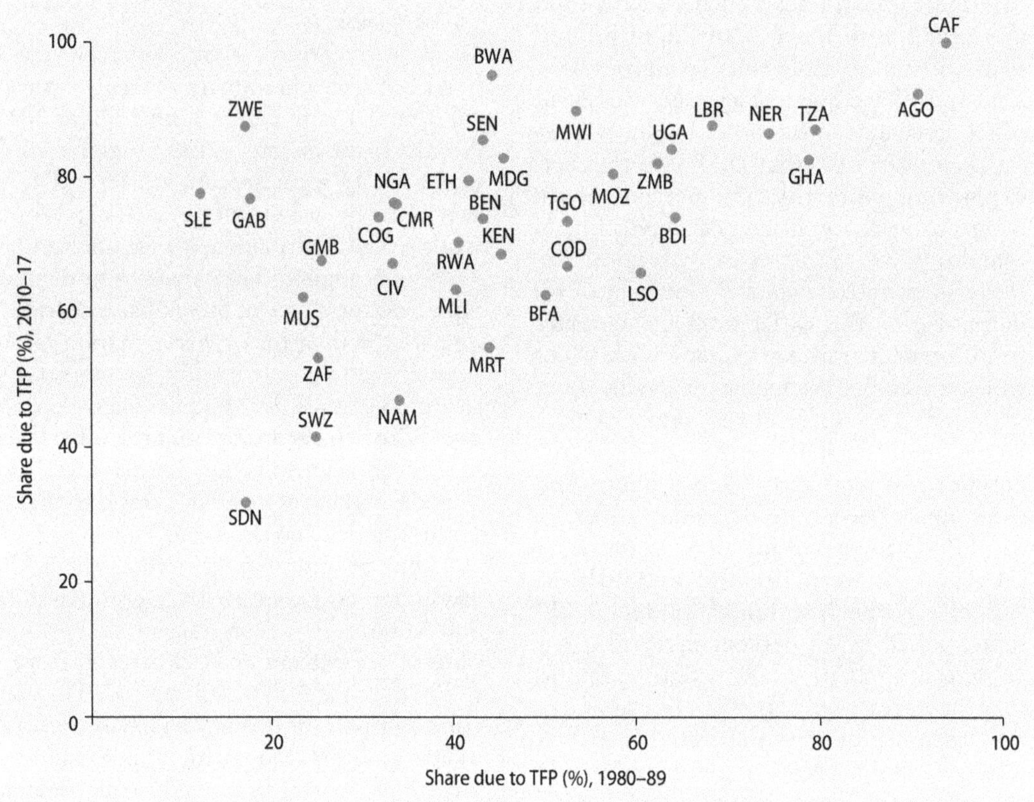

Source: Penn World Table (PWT) 9.0 and PWT9.1 updates (Feenstra, Inklaar, and Timmer 2015).
Note: TFP = total factor productivity. Selected countries and economies are labeled using International Organization for Standardization (ISO) alpha-3 codes.

and non-resource-rich countries; but in resource-rich countries, declines in TFP dragged down the growth in overall labor output (figure 2.5). This suggests that, in this group of countries, either (a) part of the capital expenditure may not have translated into a greater amount of physical capital, or (b) the combination of factors of production may have been largely inefficient. Growth per worker in the non-resource-rich countries, on the other hand, was primarily explained by factor accumulation, but TFP growth had a positive and economically important contribution (about 20 percent).

Swings in productivity growth over time. Growth per worker in Sub-Saharan Africa exhibited long swings from 1960 to 2017: The expansion of real GDP on a per worker basis during 1960–77, bolstered by favorable oil prices, was followed by a 1978–95 contraction characterized by adverse external shocks and macroeconomic instability. From 1996 onward, growth per worker recovered and continued to expand amid a favorable external environment (commodity price boom and ample capital inflows), improved macroeconomic frameworks, and adequate (policy and liquidity) buffers. These buffers, built during the years of expansion, allowed some African countries to formulate policies to withstand the unprecedented 2008–09 external shock of the Global Financial Crisis.

Changes in sources of growth. These swings in labor productivity growth were accompanied by changes in the relative importance of the different sources

FIGURE 2.5   Traditional Solow Decomposition of Labor Productivity Growth, Selected Regions and Country Groups, 1960–2017

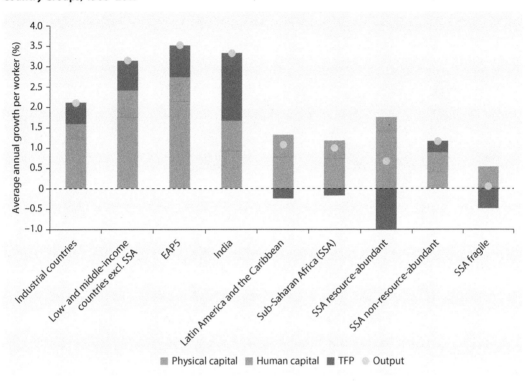

Source: Penn World Table (PWT) 9.0 and PWT9.1 updates (Feenstra, Inklaar, and Timmer 2015).
Note: Group averages are employment-weighted averages. "Industrial" countries refers to high-income Organisation for Economic Co-operation and Development (OECD) countries. "Fragile" refers to fragile and conflict-affected states, as defined by the World Bank. "EAP5" refers to five East Asian economic "dragons": Indonesia, the Republic of Korea, Malaysia, Singapore, and Thailand. SSA = Sub-Saharan Africa; TFP = total factor productivity. For the detailed definitions and methodology, see appendix A.

of growth. Despite the swings in economic performance over time, the fortunes of growth in Sub-Saharan Africa are still tightly connected to factor accumulation (figure 2.6). For instance, the region's acceleration of growth per worker in 1996–2017 (2.3 percent per year, up from 0.7 percent per year in 1978–95) is mostly accounted for by the accumulation of physical and human capital (about 65 percent). The relative contribution of TFP growth (about 35 percent in 1996–2017) is comparable to that of other low- and middle-income countries (about 30 percent). However, these findings should be taken with caution because the contribution of TFP growth might be overstated by the omission of factors such as the accumulation of natural capital (box 2.1).

Within Sub-Saharan Africa, the rebound of labor productivity growth between 1996 and 2017 was experienced by resource-abundant, non-resource-abundant, and fragile countries alike. This recovery came along with an acceleration of TFP growth. For instance, average annual growth per worker of non-resource-rich countries jumped from −0.5 percent in 1978–95 to 2.4 percent in 1996–2017 (with TFP growth increasing from -0.7 percent to 0.8 percent, respectively). In fact, TFP contributed positively to growth per worker in all regional country groups: its relative contribution amounted to 33 percent of growth per worker in non-resource-abundant countries, 40 percent in resource-abundant countries, and 43 percent in fragile countries.[11]

FIGURE 2.6 **Traditional Solow Decomposition of Labor Productivity Growth in Sub-Saharan Africa, by Country Group and Period, 1961–2017**

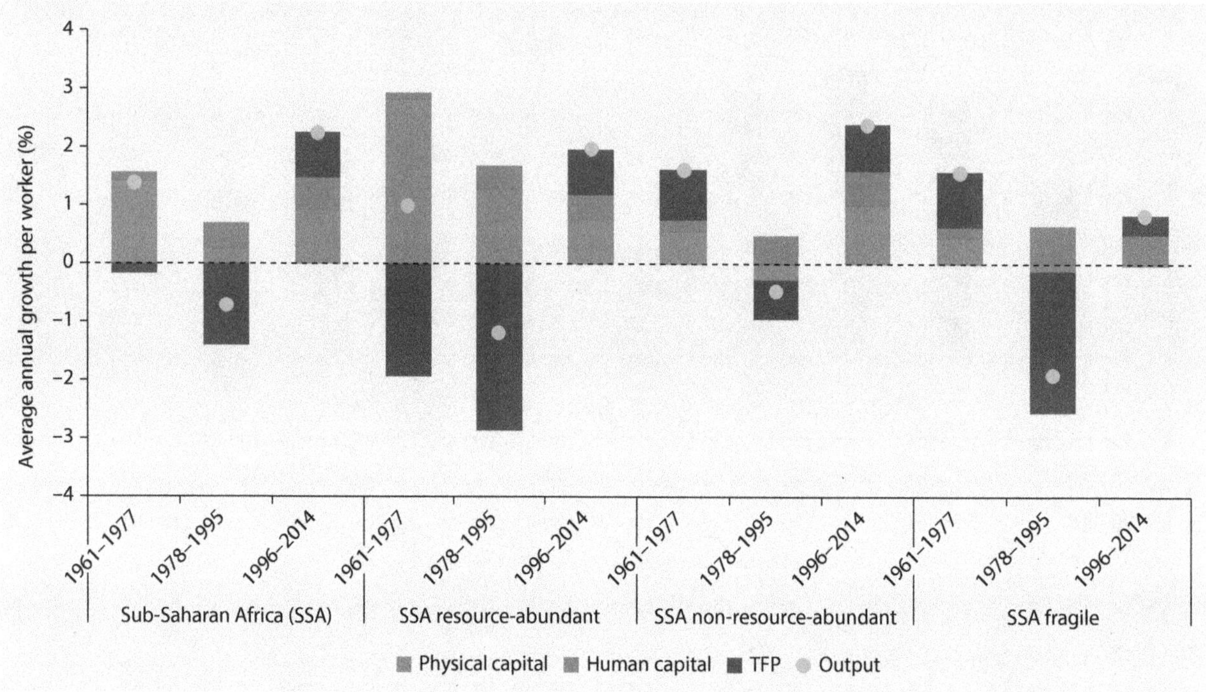

Source: Penn World Table (PWT) 9.0 and PWT9.1 updates (Feenstra, Inklaar, and Timmer 2015).
Note: Group averages are employment-weighted averages. "Fragile" refers to fragile and conflict-affected states, as defined by the World Bank. TFP = total factor productivity. For the detailed definitions and methodology, see appendix A.

Role of Public Capital in Sub-Saharan Africa's Economic Growth

Public investment can be an important catalyst of economic growth by delivering important public services as well as connecting citizens, farms, and firms to economic opportunities. After the Global Financial Crisis, public investment played (and still plays) a role in supporting long-term growth by deploying (own and borrowed) resources to finance infrastructure projects—especially among Sub-Saharan African countries (IMF 2015). From 1960 to 2017, the stock of public capital grew faster than the stock of private capital only in Sub-Saharan Africa (by 1.9 percent and 1.4 percent per year, respectively), although public and private capital both grew more slowly than in industrial countries and in other low- and middle-income countries.

Public capital has been an important driver of economic growth in Sub-Saharan Africa from 1960 to 2017: about half of the region's growth per worker is attributed to the accumulation of public capital (figure 2.7). The slump of TFP growth in this period might be partly associated with inefficiencies in public spending.[12] This pattern of growth and capital accumulation is even more pronounced among the region's resource-abundant countries, where physical capital accumulation (and especially the dynamics of public investment) explains growth per worker over the past six decades. However, the extent of inefficient public investment spending is translated into greater misallocation of resources and a negative contribution of TFP growth.[13]

Higher public investment may not automatically translate into commensurate increases in the capital stock or in higher growth benefits, because of a low-quality

BOX 2.1   The Contribution of Natural Capital to Growth per Worker

The contribution of total factor productivity (TFP) to growth per worker across Sub-Saharan Africa, especially among the resource-abundant countries, tends to decline when the production technology accounts for the use of natural capital as an additional factor of production. Natural capital—the stock of all extractable resources such as geology, soils, air, water, and living organisms—accounted for more than half of the region's growth per worker from 1996 to 2017.

The increased share of growth due to TFP in the region might be attributed to the contribu-tion of natural capital in sectors such as energy (as in Chad, the Republic of Congo, Gabon, and Nigeria) and extractives (as in Botswana, the Democratic Republic of Congo, and Zambia). Accounting for the accumulation of natural capital reduces the contribution of TFP to growth per worker by almost 1 percentage point per year. This decline is even larger (more than 150 basis points per year) for Sub-Saharan African countries that are abundant in minerals and metals (figure B2.1.1).

FIGURE B2.1.1   Decomposition of Labor Productivity Growth, Including Natural Capital, in Sub-Saharan Africa, 1996–2017

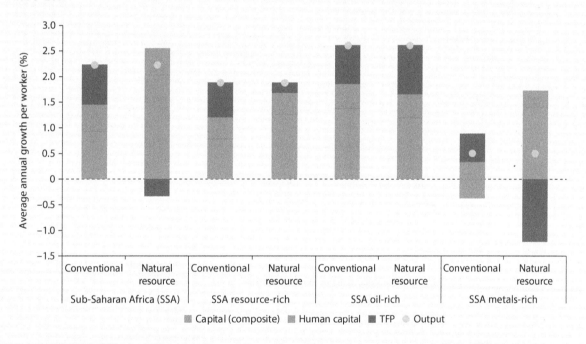

Source: Penn World Table (PWT) 9.0 and PWT9.1 updates (Feenstra, Inklaar, and Timmer 2015).
Note: Natural capital refers to the stock of all extractable resources such as geology, soils, air, water, and living organisms. The "natural resource" decomposition treats natural capital as a factor of production; the "conventional" decomposition does not. Group averages are population-weighted averages. The methodology to compute the output elasticity of physical capital and natural capital as well as the specification of technology and the computation of total factor productivity (TFP) growth is described in appendix B, "Country Productivity Analysis in Sub-Saharan Africa." SSA = Sub-Saharan Africa.

pipeline of investment projects or inefficiencies and waste in the selection and implementation of these projects. This disconnect is particularly acute when governance is weak—as it is in Sub-Saharan African countries (Keefer and Knack 2007). Closing efficiency gaps in public investments could significantly increase the public investment multiplier. For instance, closing the gap between the top and bottom quartiles of

FIGURE 2.7 Decomposition of Labor Productivity Growth, including Role of Public Capital, in Selected Regions and Country Groups, 1961–2014

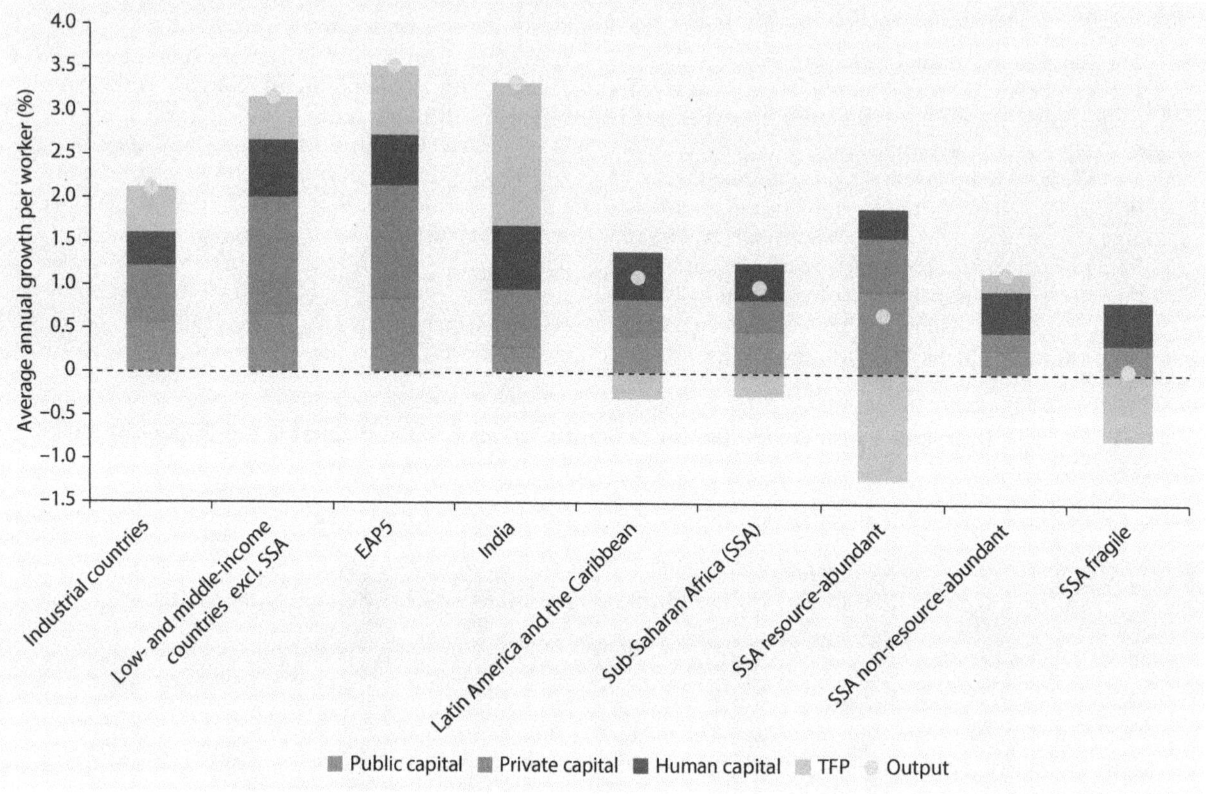

Sources: Penn World Table (PWT) 9.0 data from Feenstra, Inklaar, and Timmer 2015; PWT 9.1 updates by World Bank.
Note: Group averages are population-weighted averages. "Industrial" countries refers to high-income countries such as Organisation for Economic Co-operation and Development (OECD) member countries. "Fragile" refers to fragile and conflict-affected states, as defined by the World Bank. "EAP5" refers to five East Asian economic "dragons": Indonesia, the Republic of Korea, Malaysia, Singapore, and Thailand. SSA = Sub-Saharan Africa; TFP = total factor productivity. For the detailed definitions and methodology, see appendix A.

public investment efficiency could double the impact of such investment on growth (IMF 2015).

Lagging Structural Transformation

One of the main features of sectoral structure and long-term growth in Sub-Saharan Africa is the region's substantial lag in structural transformation for two reasons: A large share of people still work and make a living from agriculture across countries in the region. And the region's employment share in agriculture has been declining more slowly than has historically been the case in other world regions (figure 2.8).

Sectoral Employment

In 1990, the region's share of agricultural employment was about 40 percent—higher than in either high-income economies or the low- and middle-income countries of other regions (figure 2.8). By 2016, this share had declined to only 31 percent, which is still substantially greater than in high-income economies (2 percent) and other low- and middle-income countries (18 percent) (Barrot, Calderón, and Servén 2018b).

Although the average share of agricultural employment in the region still exceeded 30 percent in 2016, countries varied greatly in the proportion of people engaged in agricultural activities. It remains above 60 percent

FIGURE 2.8 Sectoral Employment Shares, Sub-Saharan Africa versus Low- and Middle-Income Countries in Other Regions, 1990–2016

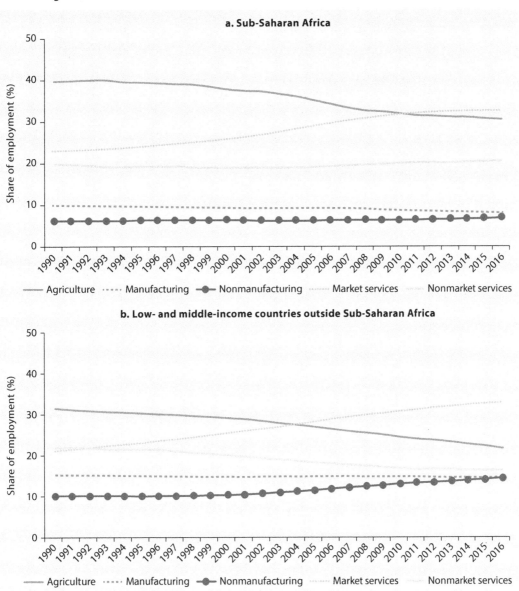

Source: Barrot, Calderón, and Servén 2018b.
Note: Regional sectoral labor shares are GDP-weighted averages of country sectoral labor shares. For detailed definitions and methodology, see appendix A.

in 13 (out of 28) countries: Burundi, Cameroon, the Central African Republic, Eswatini, Madagascar, Malawi, Mali, Mauritania, Mozambique, Niger, Nigeria, Rwanda, and Uganda. This finding reflects the fact that countries with higher shares of agricultural

employment tend to exhibit low levels of agricultural productivity (Duarte and Restuccia 2010, 2018; Herrendorf, Rogerson, and Valentinyi 2014).

The region's share of manufacturing employment remains low, declining from 10.3

percent in 1990 to 8.4 percent in 2016. Within the region, 10 countries have a manufacturing employment share below 5 percent: Angola, Botswana, Burundi, Gabon, Mali, Mozambique, Rwanda, Sierra Leone, Uganda, and Zambia. On the other hand, Sub-Saharan Africa is experiencing a rapid shift of workers from agriculture to market services.

The aggregate employment share in market services increased from 23 percent in 1990 to 33 percent in 2016 (figure 2.8, panel a). This trend holds for countries across the region regardless of income level and the extent of resource abundance, albeit at different speeds. Only three countries have an employment share in market services below 10 percent

FIGURE 2.9 Sectoral Labor Productivity Relative to Agriculture: Sub-Saharan Africa and Low- and Middle-Income Countries in Other Regions, 1990–2016

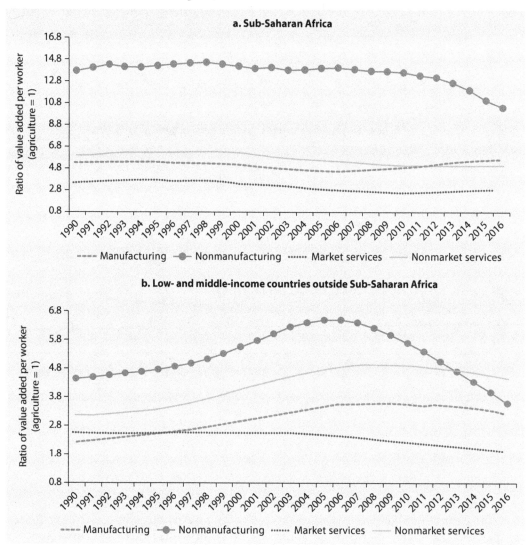

Source: Barrot, Calderón, and Servén 2018b.
Note: Regional sectoral labor productivity figures are GDP-weighted averages of country sectoral labor productivity relative to agriculture (=1.0). For detailed definitions and methodology, see appendix A.

(Burundi, the Central African Republic, and Malawi), whereas the share exceeds 40 percent in another three countries (the Gambia, Mauritius, and South Africa).

Sectoral Labor Productivity

Sectoral labor productivity exhibits large swings over time in most Sub-Saharan African countries. However, it has improved in most of the region's countries since the mid-1990s (Duarte and Restuccia 2018). Labor productivity experienced sharp upswings in agriculture (averaging 4.5 percent per year) and manufacturing (averaging 3 percent per year) from 1990 to 2016. Productivity growth in market and nonmarket services was less dynamic (with annual average growth rates of 1.6 percent and 1.1 percent, respectively).

In spite of its faster growth, labor productivity is lower in agriculture than in the region's nonagricultural activities—namely, manufacturing, nonmanufacturing, and market and nonmarket services. By 2016, the ratio of value added per worker relative to that of agriculture was 2.9 in market services, 5.7 in manufacturing, and 10.4 in nonmanufacturing activities (figure 2.9).

The region's sectoral productivity gaps relative to agriculture have remained slightly invariant or have declined at a sluggish pace over the past quarter century. However, among the non-resource-rich countries, these gaps have been declining steadily. In contrast, among resource-rich countries, they have declined at a slower pace in all sectors but manufacturing.

Overall, sectoral labor productivity growth in Sub-Saharan Africa is consistent with the process of structural change and aggregate performance. However, there is substantial heterogeneity across countries and over time. A standard structural transformation model shows that low growth in agricultural productivity translates into weak structural change—although faster productivity growth since 1995 has almost doubled the pace of reallocation out of agriculture. The presence of medium-term cycles in trended productivity across countries and over time may reflect either frictions in labor allocation or issues in measurement and specification (Duarte and Restuccia 2018).

Notes

1. Productivity data and ratios for Malaysia and Senegal are the author's calculations using Penn World Table (PWT) data.
2. The capital-output ratio is the amount of capital needed to produce each extra unit of output. As such, it is an indicator of how efficiently new investment contributes to economic growth.
3. The human capital index is calculated from the average years of schooling and an assumed rate of return to education, on the basis of Mincer equation estimates, around the world. For a detailed explanation on how the data are compiled and used to construct the index, see "Human Capital in PWT 9.0" (https://www.rug.nl/ggdc/docs/human_capital_in_pwt_90.pdf).
4. Throughout the "Development Accounting" section, the sample of Sub-Saharan African countries varies by the type of productivity, ratio, or index being measured because of the countries' varying data availability. For example, a TFP calculation requires complete information on output, inputs, and shares of labor in output, which several countries did not have, resulting in a relatively low total sample (37 countries) for that measurement.
5. Relative to the aspirational development benchmark (represented by the EAP5 countries), the output per worker in 35 (out of 45) countries in Sub-Saharan Africa is less than half the EAP5 average—and less than one-fifth the EAP5 average among 24 of those countries.
6. The HCI has three components: probability of survival, expected learning-adjusted years of school, and health. It reflects the human capital of the next generation given the risks of inadequate education and health in the country where they live (World Bank 2019).
7. Outside Sub-Saharan Africa, only 11 countries had such low relative TFP—although US TFP is, on average, no more than eight times that of this group.
8. Appendix B of this report, "Country Productivity Analysis of Sub-Saharan Africa," presents a visual analysis of the development accounting exercises for all countries in the region, with data available on output,

employment, physical capital, human capital, and the labor share of output.

9. Here we depict the development accounting exercise for Sub-Saharan African countries in 1980–89 rather than 1960–69 because the 1980–89 period (a) increased the regional coverage from 21 countries to 37 countries, and (b) includes some of the largest countries in the region (for example, Angola and Sudan).

10. This section is based largely on Barrot, Calderón, and Servén (2018a).

11. "Fragile" refers to fragile and conflict-affected states (FCS), defined on the basis of financial and security status by the World Bank's Fragile, Conflict and Violence group. For more information, see the Bank's online topical overview: https://www.worldbank.org/en/topic/fragility conflictviolence/overview.

12. The calibration of the elasticity of output to public and private capital as well as the methodology to compute TFP growth are discussed in appendix A, "Output per Worker, Factor Accumulation, and Total Productivity."

13. Note that the relative contribution of public capital accumulation and TFP to growth per worker is similar among industrial countries and the EAP5 countries (about 25 percent and 24 percent, respectively).

References

Barrot, Luis-Diego, César Calderón, and Luis Servén. 2018a. "Growth in Sub-Saharan Africa: A TFP Boost Is Needed." Unpublished manuscript, World Bank, Washington, DC.

Barrot, Luis-Diego, César Calderón, and Luis Servén. 2018b. "Sectoral Productivity Shifts in Sub-Saharan Africa." Unpublished manuscript, World Bank, Washington, DC.

Duarte, Margarida, and Diego Restuccia. 2010. "The Role of the Structural Transformation in Aggregate Productivity." *Quarterly Journal of Economics* 125 (1): 129–73.

Duarte, Margarida, and Diego Restuccia. 2018. "Structural Transformation and Productivity in Sub-Saharan Africa." Unpublished manuscript, University of Toronto.

Feenstra, Robert C., Robert Inklaar, and Marcel P. Timmer. 2015. "The Next Generation of the Penn World Table." *American Economic Review* 105 (10): 3150–82.

Herrendorf, Berthold, Richard Rogerson, and Ákos Valentinyi. 2014. "Growth and Structural Transformation." In *Handbook of Economic Growth* Vol. 2, edited by Philippe Aghion and Steven Durlauf, 855–941. Amsterdam: Elsevier.

IMF (International Monetary Fund). 2015. "Making Public Investment More Efficient." Staff report, IMF, Washington, DC.

Keefer, Philip, and Stephen Knack. 2007. "Boondoggles, Rent-Seeking, and Political Checks and Balances: Public Investment under Unaccountable Governments." *Review of Economics and Statistics* 89 (3): 566–72.

World Bank. 2019. *World Development Report 2019: The Changing Nature of Work*. Washington, DC: World Bank.

Resource Misallocation in Sub-Saharan Africa: Firm-Level Evidence | 3

Introduction

Why are African countries considerably less productive than high-income economies? What accounts for these differences in (labor and total factor) productivity? And why is firm performance in Sub-Saharan Africa lower and more volatile than that of their counterparts in either the "aspirational development" or the "global efficiency" benchmark countries?[1] This report argues that distortions in decision-making processes at the firm level have implications for a country's aggregate output and productivity and might also help explain aggregate productivity differences across countries. It suggests that low-income countries are not as effective in allocating inputs of production to their most efficient use.

The effectiveness of resource allocation is indicated in relation to an efficiency benchmark in a model economy where firms maximize final output. It is characterized by (a) decisions about setting the number of establishments to be operating in the industry, and (b) the allocation of capital and labor across those operating establishments. Distortions in each of these two stages of decision making will reduce aggregate output

and productivity. This argument lies at the heart of the literature on resource misallocation and takes center stage in the report's analysis of low productivity in Sub-Saharan Africa. (Box 3.1 summarizes the theoretical underpinnings of the relationship between the number of operating firms and their distribution, misallocation, and aggregate productivity.)

Empirical research on resource misallocation as a source of low aggregate productivity in Sub-Saharan Africa is growing, but it is still incipient. The lack of available firm-level census data (across countries and over time) in the region is still a binding constraint. The existing evidence for the region focuses on both direct and indirect approaches to quantifying the extent of resource misallocation across Sub-Saharan African countries and its influence on aggregate total factor productivity (TFP). While some papers measure the total net effects of distortions on aggregate productivity (the indirect approach), others assess specific sources of distortions.

This report finds evidence of severe misallocation in agriculture and manufacturing across Sub-Saharan African countries. Low agricultural productivity is primarily explained by inefficiencies in the allocation

BOX 3.1   Resource Misallocation: Theoretical Underpinnings

Resource misallocation refers to distortions in the allocation of inputs (capital, land, and labor, among others) across production units of different sizes. This misallocation typically occurs when the different production establishments are taxed at different rates. This strand of the literature assumes that aggregate output is produced by several producers (N) with different levels of productivity (A_i). Firm i's technology is summarized by a production function (f) that is strictly increasing and strictly concave. There is a fixed cost of operation (c) for any producer. Given an aggregate demand of labor (H) and capital (K), there is a unique allocation of labor and capital across producers that maximizes total output net of fixed operating costs.

According to this framework, lower values of A_i reflect either slow adoption or inefficient use of technology. The efficient allocation in this economy maximizes final output and is characterized by two decisions: (a) the number of operating establishments (that is, establishments that can pay the fixed cost, c); and (b) the allocation of capital (K) and labor (H) across the operating establishments. If either of these decisions is distorted, the economy will have lower output and hence lower aggregate total factor productivity (TFP)—because the aggregate factor inputs (K and H) in the industry are constant.

The allocation of inputs that *maximizes* output across production units (say, either firms or farms) takes place when, conditional upon their operation, the marginal (and average) products are equal across all production units. In this equilibrium, no output gains would be acquired by reallocating inputs of production (say, capital, land, and labor) from production units with low marginal products to those with high marginal products. In the efficient allocation, the most productive operating establishments will demand a greater amount of inputs. In other words, a production unit's productivity and size are positively associated in the efficient allocation. In addition, production units with similar levels of productivity command the same amount of inputs and are of identical size.

Deviations from the efficient allocation of resources across firms may have implications on aggregate output and productivity. Input choices that are different from the efficiency model, even if they allocate more factors to the more-productive

production units, will generate lower aggregate output. Given the constant aggregate amount of inputs (say, capital, land, and labor), the output loss associated with an inefficient allocation is also an aggregate TFP loss. In this context, misallocation refers to situations were resources are not allocated efficiently across production units, and the cost of misallocation is typically measured in terms of aggregate output or TFP losses.

Theoretically, inefficiencies in the allocation of labor and capital across heterogeneous producers will affect aggregate output and productivity through three different channels:

- *The technology channel*—the higher the productivity for all firms, the greater the output
- *The selection channel*—based on the choice of operating producers
- *The misallocation channel*—based on the allocation of capital and labor among operating producers.

These three channels are not independent: any policy or institution that distorts the allocation of resources across producers will potentially generate additional effects through both the selection and technology channels.

If the misallocation of resources across these different producers helps explain cross-country differences in aggregate productivity levels, it is then crucial to investigate the sources of misallocation. Resource misallocation across different production units might reflect the following (Restuccia and Rogerson 2017):

- *Statutory provisions,* including some features of the tax code and regulations—for instance, provisions of the tax code that vary with firm characteristics (say, age or size); tariffs targeting certain groups of goods; employment protection measures; and land regulations, among others
- *Discretionary government (or bank) provisions* that favor or penalize specific firms—for instance, subsidies, tax breaks, or low-interest loans granted to specific firms; preferential market access; and unfair bidding practices for government contracts, among others
- *Market imperfections*—for instance, monopoly power; market frictions (such as in credit and land markets); and enforcement of property rights.

(Box continues next page)

BOX 3.1 **Resource Misallocation: Theoretical Underpinnings** *(continued)*

The resource misallocation literature examines (a) the extent of factor misallocation in the economy, (b) its impact on TFP differences across countries and over time, and (c) the underlying factors driving misallocation. Two main approaches have been followed to tackle these questions—the direct approach and the indirect approach (Restuccia and Rogerson 2013, 2017).[a]

The direct approach seeks to ascertain the underlying sources of misallocation and evaluates their consequences through a structural model. Assessing the degree of misallocation requires computation of a counterfactual. However, the direct approach also requires quantitative measures of the source of misallocation. If the main drivers of misallocation come from discretionary rather than statutory provisions, there will be severe measurement problems. Furthermore, the complexity of measuring drivers such as regulation (especially its differences across industries) may make it complicated to build, calibrate, and simulate a structural model.

The indirect approach quantifies the extent of resource misallocation and does not dig deeply into the underlying factors that generate the distortions driving the inefficient allocation of resources. It measures the total net effect of these distortions without fully identifying their main sources. The efficient allocation of resources equalizes their marginal products across all operating production units. A direct examination of the dispersion of marginal products provides a measure of the degree of misallocation. This approach does not require a full structural model; however, it needs the specification of the technology of production. Still, the indirect approach faces an important challenge: efficient allocations may not require that marginal products be equalized across production units *at every point in time*—especially if input choices precede the realization of the individual productivity shock or are in the presence of adjustment costs.

In sum, resource misallocation is closely related to a specific model economy and to a benchmark allocation relative to that economy. In this model economy, inputs are homogeneous, and the only source of heterogeneity among productive units is the productivity of their operating establishments. The output-maximizing allocation of factors in the model economy is the commonly used benchmark.

It is not optimal to allocate the entire endowment of inputs to any individual production unit—even if it is the most productive one—because the increase in output for a given increase in inputs declines as the size of the establishment increases. Resource misallocation can arise both across production units with different levels of productivity and across units with similar productivity. An important interpretation of misallocation is that production units effectively face different prices or wedges to their inputs or output. That is, production units face idiosyncratic distortions (Restuccia and Rogerson 2008). These wedges or distortions support the observed allocation, which differs from the efficient allocation, as an equilibrium outcome.

Sources: Restuccia 2011; Restuccia and Rogerson 2008, 2013, 2017.
a. The direct and indirect approaches have been commonly applied to census data on manufacturing firms. See Restuccia and Rogerson (2008), Hsieh and Klenow (2009), and the empirical literature that arose from those seminal papers.

of resources across farmers rather than agronomic endowments. The most productive farms cannot command more factors of production, and their growth is impeded. Resource misallocation also has dynamic implications for agricultural productivity by disincentivizing the adoption of new technologies and reducing the farmers' ability to learn new techniques.

In manufacturing, the large dispersion of revenue productivity (TFPR) is an indication of severe misallocation across manufacturing firms in select Sub-Saharan African countries.[2] This dispersion is greater than in other low- to middle-income countries (China and India) as well as that of the global efficiency benchmark (the United States). Furthermore, the positive correlation between TFPR and quantity (or physical) productivity (TFPQ)[3] across Sub-Saharan African manufacturing firms indicates that the region's more-productive firms tend to face higher distortions—especially output distortions. These higher distortions decelerate the growth of firms over their life cycles and discourage the adoption of new technologies.

Resource Misallocation in Agriculture

This report has so far corroborated some of the stylized facts found in the literature:

- There are large and persistent differences in real output per worker across countries (Hsieh and Klenow 2010; Jones 2016; Restuccia 2011).
- Poorer countries tend to allocate most of their labor to agriculture (Duarte and Restuccia 2010, 2018; Herrendorf, Rogerson, and Valentinyi 2014).
- The productivity of agriculture (relative to nonagriculture sectors) in poorer countries tends to be lower than in richer countries (Adamopoulos and Restuccia 2014; Gollin, Lagakos, and Waugh 2014; Restuccia, Yang, and Zhu 2008).

These three stylized facts stress the important role played by agriculture in understanding the large disparities in real output per worker across countries.[4]

Differences in Agricultural Productivity: About Efficiency, not Geography

Are the differences in agricultural productivity between Sub-Saharan Africa and the aspirational and global efficiency benchmarks explained by land quality and geography? Or are these differences in productivity (say, differences in yields) attributable to inefficient use of agricultural inputs?

Agricultural output and productivity can depend on the region's geographical features—exogenous factors such as rainfall, temperature, and soil quality.[5] In many Sub-Saharan African countries, rural farmers who operate at subsistence levels and lack the appropriate infrastructure make up a larger share of the population than in other world regions. Under these conditions,

farmers may produce crops that may not be suitable to the geographical features of the land they operate (Adamopoulos and Restuccia 2014; Gollin and Rogerson 2014).

However, low agricultural productivity in low-income countries—and, notably, in Sub-Saharan Africa—is primarily attributable to inefficiencies in the use of resources rather than poor agronomic conditions (such as low-quality land and unfavorable weather). Worldwide evidence shows that approximately 80 percent of agricultural productivity differences between poor and rich countries can be attributed to production inefficiencies. In other words, agricultural productivity in low-income countries is not low because they have lower potential yields. It is low because the actual yields lie far from their potential ones (Adamopoulos and Restuccia 2018).

Counterfactual Exercise, with Crop Selection Constant

What would be the gains in agricultural output in Sub-Saharan African countries if actual yields were raised to their potential ones? A spatial productivity growth accounting in agriculture was conducted for five large countries in the region: the Democratic Republic of Congo, Ethiopia, Kenya, Nigeria, and Tanzania.[6] The benefits of closing the actual-potential yield gap is conducted under three scenarios of input use and water supply but holding constant the farmers' crop choices (table 3.1). The different scenarios considered are (a) low input use under rainfed cultivation, (b) high input use under rainfed cultivation, and (c) high input use under irrigated cultivation (Sinha and Xi 2018).

Under the least productive scenario (low input use under rainfed cultivation), actual yields are higher than potential ones for the Democratic Republic of Congo and Nigeria. On aggregate, this implies that both countries have moved beyond the least productive scenario. In contrast, Ethiopia, Kenya, and Tanzania still can reap productivity gains from closing the actual-potential gap, even using the least sophisticated

TABLE 3.1 Gap between Actual and Potential Agricultural Yields, Selected Sub-Saharan African Countries, 2000

Country	Change in yield (%)		
	Low input use[a] Rainfed	High input use[a] Rainfed	High input use[a] Irrigated
Congo, Dem. Rep.	−36	88	102
Ethiopia	32	367	450
Kenya	40	314	380
Nigeria	−16	174	230
Tanzania	47	347	442

Source: Sinha and Xi 2018.
Note: The Global Agronomic Ecological Zones (GAEZ) database provided data on crop-specific yields, crop choices, and land endowments as well as potential crop yields (at the grid level) under different scenarios of water supply and input use (at the farm level). The scenarios hold the farmers' crop choices constant. The GAEZ data are complemented with the Food and Agriculture Organization's (FAO) harmonized crop calendars and country-level crop prices.
a. Input use is classified into (a) *low* (labor-intensive and subsistence agricultural practices); (b) *intermediate* (market participation, use of better seed varieties, hand tools, livestock, and preliminary methods of mechanization); and (c) *high* (modern practices, production for market purposes only, completely mechanized, no shortfalls in use of fertilizers and chemicals).

method of cultivation. For instance, agricultural yields in Tanzania can increase by about half under this scenario.

Aggregate yield gains become larger as agricultural production scenarios become more sophisticated. However, there is a great deal of heterogeneity in productivity gains across countries. Under the intermediate scenario (high input use and rainfed cultivation), agricultural yields nearly double for the Democratic Republic of Congo—yet these gains are much smaller than in the other countries, especially Ethiopia, Kenya, and Tanzania. The contribution of irrigation to farmers' productivity, on the other hand, is limited once they use inputs at their highest level. If farmers were to raise their input use from low to high (holding constant the nature of the water supply), their potential productivity gains would increase between 7 and 11 times for Ethiopia, Kenya, and Tanzania. If, on the other hand, the cultivation method shifts from rainfed to irrigation (while maintaining high input use), the potential gains are significantly lower. For instance, the marginal yield gains of using irrigation fluctuate from a paltry 14 percentage points (the Democratic Republic of Congo) to 95 percentage points (Tanzania). Overall, changes in input use appear to play a greater role than the nature of water supply when explaining agricultural

productivity improvements in Sub-Saharan African countries (Sinha and Xi 2018).

Counterfactual Exercise, with Crop Selection Optimized

What role does crop selection play in explaining the changes in aggregate agricultural yields? Table 3.2, column [1], reports the yield gains when farmers' optimal crop choice is cultivated under actual levels of input use and water supply (in short, under actual yields).[7] Optimal crop selection raises farmers' productivity, although these gains vary widely across countries. The smallest productivity gains are attained in the Democratic Republic of Congo and Tanzania, while yields nearly double among Nigerian farmers. The largest gains are achieved by farmers in Ethiopia and Kenya (about 5.3 and 6.5 times their actual output, respectively).

Moving from the actual-yield benchmark, the role of crop selection is evaluated under three scenarios: (a) low input use under rainfed cultivation (table 3.2, column [2]); (b) high input use under rainfed cultivation (column [3]); and (c) high input use under irrigation (column [4]). Under the least productive scenario, optimal crop choice expands agricultural output by 25 percent in the Democratic Republic of Congo and 44 percent in Nigeria. Agricultural output grows

TABLE 3.2 **Optimal Crop Choice and Aggregate Yield Gains, Selected Sub-Saharan African Countries, 2000**

Country	Percent change in yield			
	Actual input use Actual water supply [1]	Low input use[a] Rainfed [2]	High input use[a] Rainfed [3]	High input use[a] Irrigated [4]
Congo, Dem. Rep.	116	25	217	238
Ethiopia	532	125	628	948
Kenya	645	275	943	1,110
Nigeria	197	44	421	450
Tanzania	108	217	838	1,330

Source: Sinha and Xi 2018.
Note: "Optimal" crop choice refers to the selection of the possible crops cultivated on a farm that maximizes output. The Global Agronomic Ecological Zones (GAEZ) database provided data on crop-specific yields, crop choices, and land endowments as well as on potential crop yields (at grid level) under different scenarios of water supply and use of intermediate inputs (at the farm level). The GAEZ data are complemented with the Food and Agriculture Organization's (FAO) harmonized crop calendars and country-level crop prices.
a. Input use is classified into (a) low (labor-intensive and subsistence agricultural practices); (b) intermediate (market participation, use of better seed varieties, hand tools, livestock, and preliminary methods of mechanization); and (c) high (modern practices, production for market purposes only, completely mechanized, no shortfalls in use of fertilizers and chemicals).

1.25 times in Ethiopia and more than doubles in Kenya and Tanzania.

Yet the productivity gains grow exponentially under high input use—even if we keep the nature of the water supply invariant. The meager gains registered in the Democratic Republic of Congo and Nigeria under the least productive scenario expand by eight to nine times if input use is enhanced (column [3]), while they are considerably higher for the other countries—especially Kenya, which potentially would achieve a nearly tenfold increase in actual output.

Under the most productive scenario (column [4]), the marginal returns from irrigation (while keeping input use constant) remain modest compared with the returns from increasing input use (while keeping constant the nature of the water supply). The marginal gains from irrigation (measured as a percentage change in yields) are particularly small for the Democratic Republic of Congo and Nigeria (20 and 30 percentage points, respectively). In Tanzania, however, the marginal returns from the use of irrigation techniques are larger: yields are more than 12 times as large as those obtained with actual production (table 3.2).

Aggregate Consequences of Inefficient Resource Allocation across Farms

Measuring the misallocation of resources across farms requires the definition of a conceptual efficiency benchmark. Two-sector general equilibrium models with heterogeneous production units argue that the efficient allocation of factors is achieved when the marginal product of land and labor are equal across farmers (Adamopoulos and Restuccia 2014; Aragón and Rud 2018). The optimal decision rules of farmers suggest the following testable implications on factor allocative efficiency: First, the more productive farmers should be able to demand more intermediate inputs (say, labor, capital, and land). Second, agricultural yields should be uncorrelated with farmers' productivity.[8]

Farm-level evidence for Ethiopia, Malawi, and Uganda shows the following (Aragón and Rud 2018; Chen, Restuccia, and Santaeulàlia-Llopis 2017; Restuccia and Santaeulàlia-Llopis 2017):

• The more productive farmers tend to have greater use of intermediate inputs; however, the relationship between input use and productivity is flatter than the one suggested by the allocative efficiency criteria.

- The more productive farmers tend to exhibit greater agricultural yields. In other words, yields and farmers' productivity fail to be uncorrelated.

In sum, the relationships between input use and farmers' productivity and between yields and farmers' productivity do not conform with the predicted implications of the efficient allocation of resources. This implies that there is substantial evidence of factor

misallocation across farmers. Figure 3.1 illustrates the misallocation of resources across Ugandan farmers (Aragón and Rud 2018).

The lack of correlation between the actual allocation of land across farmers and the corresponding level of farmers' productivity (figure 3.1, panel a) is consistent with land allocation mechanisms that are governed by inheritance norms and redistribution, whereas market mechanisms (or rent and sale) are severely more restricted. Farmers'

FIGURE 3.1   Farmers' Productivity, by Input Use and Yields, in Uganda

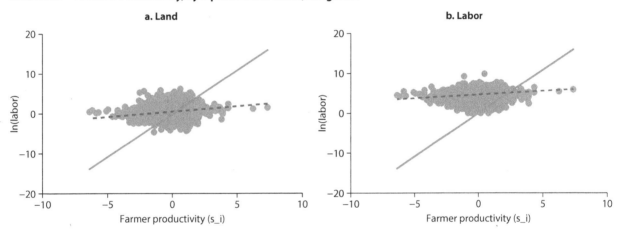

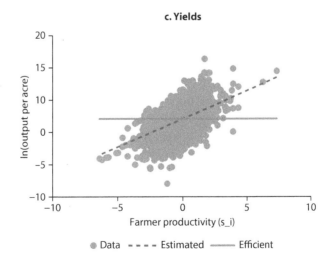

● Data   ---- Estimated   —— Efficient

Source: Aragón and Rud 2018.
Note: The data on farmers' productivity, yields, and input use are taken from the Uganda Panel National Survey (UNPS), a household-level panel dataset collected as part of the World Bank's Living Standards Measurement Studies–Integrated Surveys on Agriculture (LSMS-ISA) project. This survey, with representative information at the urban/rural and regional levels, has four available rounds (2009–10, 2010–11, 2011–12, and 2013–14). It collects agricultural information for cropping seasons taking place in either the first or second semester each year. Given that the period of analysis is the cropping season, the time dimension of the panel consists of eight periods at best. ln = natural logarithm. s_i = time-invariant total factor productivity of farmer *i*.

insecure property rights and land market restrictions limit their ability to raise capital for agricultural production (Besley and Ghatak 2010; de Soto 2000). Eliminating resource misallocation in agriculture may yield significant aggregate output and productivity gains in Sub-Saharan Africa—for example, an increase of about 200 percent in Ethiopia (Chen, Restuccia, and Santaeulàlia-Llopis 2017) and 260 percent in Malawi (Restuccia and Santaeulàlia-Llopis 2017).

Resource Misallocation in Manufacturing

The inefficient allocation of inputs across manufacturing firms plays an important role in understanding underdevelopment: resource misallocation can explain up to 60 percent of aggregate TFP differences between poor and rich countries (Bartelsman, Haltiwanger, and Scarpetta 2013; Hsieh and Klenow 2009; Restuccia and Rogerson 2008). Firm-level evidence from select Sub-Saharan African countries shows substantial misallocation of capital—as reflected in a greater dispersion in marginal products of capital (as well as domestic interest rates).[9] In this context, smaller firms tend to display the largest degree of misallocation, which might be tied to their higher cost of capital relative to medium and large firms.[10] More broadly, there is severe misallocation of resources across manufacturing firms as resources are shifted from the more-productive firms to the less-productive ones. This implies the coexistence of few productive firms with many low-productivity ones.

The efficient allocation of resources (say, capital and labor) is achieved when the marginal products of the factors of production are equal across manufacturing firms. In the presence of multiple intermediate inputs, efficiency is attained when TFPR is equal across firms. Hence, dispersion in TFPR signals resource misallocation, which in turn can be attributed to distortions in output and capital. Evidence from firm-level manufacturing census data of Côte d'Ivoire (2003–12), Ethiopia (2011), Ghana (2003), and Kenya

(2010) shows that there is pervasive misallocation of resources across Sub-Saharan African manufacturing firms (Cirera, Fattal-Jaef, and Maemir 2018).

A look at the distribution of quantity and revenue productivity (TFPQ and TFPR, respectively) shows that there is also substantial variation in firm-level productivity in all four of these Sub-Saharan African countries. The productivity dispersion across manufacturing firms in Sub-Saharan Africa is larger than in more productive benchmarks—say, China, India, and the United States (Hsieh and Klenow 2009).

The magnitude of this productivity dispersion is particularly striking in Kenya, where less-productive firms coexist with a few very productive ones. Kenyan firms in the top decile of TFPQ are 290 percent more productive than firms in the bottom decile. The gap between the most and the least productive firms is about 87 percent in Ghana, 39 percent in Ethiopia, and 26 percent in Côte d'Ivoire (table 3.3) (Cirera, Fattal-Jaef, and Maemir 2018).

The dispersion of TFPR across manufacturing firms in the selected Sub-Saharan African countries is significantly higher than that of manufacturing firms in China, India, and the United States. For instance, the gap between the most and the least productive firms (as measured by the ratio of top to bottom TFPR deciles) is equal to 51 in Kenya, 17 in Ghana, 13 in Ethiopia, and 7 in Côte d'Ivoire. These gaps are substantially larger than those in China (4.9), India (5.0), and the United States (3.3). A plausible explanation for the excessive dispersion of TFPR across manufacturing firms is that policies and institutions in Sub-Saharan Africa may prevent the most-productive firms from expanding and replacing the least-productive ones. The potential productivity gains from better allocation of resources across manufacturing establishments would be substantial. An equalization of TFPR across firms in each industry would raise manufacturing productivity by 31.4 percent in Côte d'Ivoire, 66.6 percent in Ethiopia, 75.5 percent in Ghana, and 162.6 percent in Kenya.[11]

TABLE 3.3 **Dispersion of Revenue and Quantity Productivity across Manufacturing Firms, Selected Sub-Saharan African Countries**

Metric	Cote d'Ivoire[a]		Kenya[b]		Ghana[c]		Ethiopia[d]	
	TFPR 2003–12	TFPQ 2003–12	TFPR 2010	TFPQ 2010	TFPR 2003	TFPQ 2003	TFPR 2011	TFPQ 2011
Standard deviation	0.65	1.24	1.52	2.41	0.95	1.75	0.78	1.30
Ratio of percentiles								
75-25	0.88	1.74	1.99	3.34	1.43	2.61	1.26	1.94
90-10	1.99	3.25	3.94	5.67	2.89	4.47	2.56	3.67
Cov(TFPQ, TFPR)	0.70		0.85		0.69		0.74	
Reg. Coeff.	0.42		0.52		0.44		0.53	
NObs	4,146	4,146	757	757	1151	1151	4,012	4,012

Source: Cirera, Fattal-Jaef, and Maemir 2018.
Note: Output and input data were obtained from firm-level manufacturing censuses of Côte d'Ivoire (2003–12), Ethiopia (2011), Ghana (2003), and Kenya (2010). The censuses (specified in notes a.–d. below) are nationally representative, adequately including both small and large firms in the formal sector. Revenue and quantity productivity (TFPR and TFPQ, respectively) are expressed in logs and are demeaned by industry-specific averages. Industries are weighted by their value-added shares. NObs = number of observations; Cov = covariance; Reg. Coeff. = Regression coefficient; TFPQ = Quantity total factor productivity; TFPR = Revenue total factor productivity.
a. The Côte d'Ivoire data are from the Registrar of Companies for the Modern Enterprise sector, collected by the National Statistics Institute. The Côte d'Ivoire statistics are calculated by taking the average for the years 2003–12.
b. The Kenyan data come from the 2010 Census of Industrial Production (CIP), conducted by the Kenyan National Bureau of Statistics (KNBS).
c. The Ghanaian data come from the 2003 National Industrial Census (NIC) dataset, conducted by the Ghana Statistical Service (GSS). It is similar in structure to the Ethiopian survey, covers the universe of establishments employing more than 10 workers, and takes a representative sample of firms employing fewer than 10 workers.
d. The datasets used for Ethiopia are the Large and Medium Scale Manufacturing Industries Survey (LMSMI) and the Small-Scale Manufacturing Industries Survey (SSMI), both of which are conducted by the Ethiopian Central Statistical Agency (CSA).

Within-industry dispersion of TFPR across manufacturing firms in Sub-Saharan Africa is also quite substantial (table 3.3). The distortions associated with the observed dispersion in TFPR would be costlier if they were positively associated with the firms' TFPQ—as noted by Restuccia and Rogerson (2008) and Bartelsman, Haltiwanger, and Scarpetta (2013). In other words, distortions would have a more deleterious impact on aggregate productivity if they were to "tax" the most-productive firms relative to the least-productive ones.

Firm-level evidence shows that there is a strong positive relationship between TFPQ and TFPR for select countries in the region (figure 3.2). This finding confirms that the region's most productive manufacturing firms face the largest distortions to resource allocation. The presence of these "correlated distortions" is consistent with evidence found for manufacturing firms in other low- and middle-income countries. For instance, the estimated elasticity of log(TFPR) on log(TFPQ) is 0.42 for Côte d'Ivoire, 0.53 for Ethiopia, 0.44 for Ghana, and 0.52 for Kenya (Cirera, Fattal-Jaef, and Maemir 2018). How do these elasticities compare with the global efficiency benchmark? The computed elasticity of TFPR with respect to TFPQ for the US manufacturing sector is 0.09 (Hsieh and Klenow 2014). Hence, TFPR rises more steeply among Sub-Saharan African manufacturing firms than among their counterparts in the United States.

The larger elasticity of the Sub-Saharan African manufacturing sector suggests that the more-productive firms cannot use more resources and use them more efficiently—thus worsening aggregate productivity (Restuccia and Rogerson 2008). That the region's more-productive firms face higher distortions may also decelerate the growth of firms over their life cycles by discouraging them from investment in productivity-enhancing technologies (Bento and Restuccia 2017; Hsieh and Klenow 2014).

FIGURE 3.2 **Quantity versus Revenue Productivity across Selected Sub-Saharan African Countries**

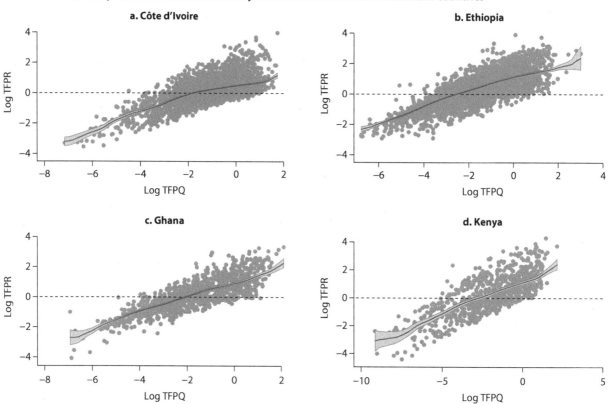

Source: Cirera, Fattal-Jaef, and Maemir 2018.
Note: Revenue total factor productivity (TFPR) and quantity total factor productivity (TFPQ) denote the revenue and physical productivity measures. They are computed for each establishment in industry using firm-level census data from Côte d'Ivoire, Ethiopia, Ghana, and Kenya. TFPR and TFPQ are expressed in logs and scaled by the industry-specific average.

Notes

1. As further discussed in chapter 1, the "aspirational development" benchmark is represented by the five "East Asian dragons" (or "EAP5," comprising Indonesia, the Republic of Korea, Malaysia, Singapore, and Thailand). The "global efficiency" benchmark is proxied by the United States.

2. Total factor productivity revenue (TFPR) is typically defined as the ratio of firms' sales (or revenues) to input costs (appropriately weighted by their production elasticities).

3. Total factor productivity quantity (TFPQ), also called physical productivity, is defined as the ratio of a firm's physical output to physical inputs, appropriately weighted according to their production elasticities.

4. The productivity gap between the world's richest and poorest nations is even larger in the agriculture sector. For instance, agricultural labor productivity in the richest countries was approximately 78 times that of the poorest ones. Additionally, 86 percent of workers in the poorest nations were employed in agriculture—as opposed to 4 percent in the richest nations (Restuccia, Yang, and Zhu 2008).

5. Certain regions might be more suitable for cultivation of particular crops based on geography but may yield dismal output if used to cultivate other crops that require significantly different geographical attributes.

6. These five countries jointly account for just under half of the region's population, and agriculture is an important activity in terms of both employment and value added.

7. This simulation restricts the optimal crop selection to those choices that are actually observed at the farm level. Consequently, the narrow set of crop choices is smaller than the entire set of crop choices including changing

yields constructed using the GAEZ crop calendar information (Sinha and Xi 2018).

8. An additional implication suggests that adverse local productivity shocks should decrease the use of intermediate inputs (Aragón and Rud 2018).

9. In the presence of well-functioning domestic capital markets, efficient allocation is characterized by each firm's marginal product of capital (MPK) being equal to the market interest rate. If firms instead borrow at different interest rates, capital is likely to be misallocated and the MPK will differ across firms. Differential access to informal finance or political connections are among the factors that may explain the variance in interest rates for firms (Kalemli-Ozcan and Sørensen 2016).

10. Smaller firms tend to have more binding constraints than larger firms. Smaller firms are less likely to access credit at more favorable contract terms than larger firms can, given their profits and collateral (Bigsten et al. 2004; Paganini 2016).

11. These productivity gains from reversing misallocation are still small relative to the development gaps in the region; however, they are reasonable lower bounds to the overall cost associated with the extent of misallocation in a country. These calculations do not consider propagation through intersectoral linkages, and they only account for static gains from reallocation.

References

Adamopoulos, Tasso, and Diego Restuccia. 2014. "The Size Distribution of Farms and International Productivity Differences." *American Economic Review* 104 (6): 1667–97.

Adamopoulos, Tasso, and Diego Restuccia. 2018. "Geography and Agricultural Productivity: Cross-Country Evidence from Micro Plot-Level Data." Working Paper 24532, National Bureau of Economic Research, Cambridge, MA.

Aragón, Fernando M., and Juan Pablo Rud. 2018. "Weather, Productivity, and Factor Misallocation: Evidence from Ugandan Farmers." Background paper, World Bank, Washington, DC.

Bartelsman, Eric, John Haltiwanger, and Stefano Scarpetta. 2013. "Cross-Country Differences in Productivity: The Role of Allocation and Selection." *American Economic Review* 103 (1): 305–34.

Bento, Pedro, and Diego Restuccia. 2017. "Misallocation, Establishment Size, and Productivity." *American Economic Journal: Macroeconomics* 9 (3): 267–303.

Besley, Timothy, and Maitreesh Ghatak. 2010. "Property Rights and Economic Development." In *Handbook of Development Economics, Vol. 5*, edited by Dani Rodrik and Mark Rosenzweig, 4525–95. Oxford: North-Holland.

Bigsten, Arne, Paul Collier, Stefan Dercon, Marcel Fafchamps, Bernard Gauthier, Jan Willem Gunning, Abena Oduro, et al. 2004. "Do African Manufacturing Firms Learn from Exporting?" *Journal of Development Studies* 40 (3): 115–41.

Chen, Chaoran, Diego Restuccia, and Raúl Santaeulàlia-Llopis. 2017. "The Effects of Land Markets on Resource Allocation and Agricultural Productivity." Working Paper 24034, National Bureau of Economic Research, Cambridge, MA.

Cirera, Xavier, Roberto Fattal-Jaef, and Hibret Maemir. 2018. "Taxing the Good? Distortions, Misallocation, and Productivity in Sub-Saharan Africa." *World Bank Economic Review* 34 (1): 75–100.

de Soto, Hernando. 2000. *The Mystery of Capital: Why Capitalism Triumphs in the West and Fails Everywhere Else.* New York: Basic Books.

Duarte, Margarida, and Diego Restuccia. 2010. "The Role of the Structural Transformation in Aggregate Productivity." *Quarterly Journal of Economics* 125 (1): 129–73.

Duarte, Margarida, and Diego Restuccia. 2018. "Structural Transformation and Productivity in Sub-Saharan Africa." Background paper, World Bank, Washington, DC.

Gollin, Douglas, David Lagakos, and Michael E. Waugh. 2014. "The Agricultural Productivity Gap." *Quarterly Journal of Economics* 129 (2): 939–93.

Gollin, Douglas, and Richard Rogerson. 2014. "Productivity, Transport Costs and Subsistence Agriculture." *Journal of Development Economics* 107: 38–48.

Herrendorf, Berthold, Richard Rogerson, and Ákos Valentinyi. 2014. "Growth and Structural Transformation." In *Handbook of Economic Growth, Vol. 2*, edited by Philippe Aghion and Steven Durlauf, 855–941. Amsterdam: Elsevier.

Hsieh, Chang-Tai, and Peter J. Klenow. 2009. "Misallocation and Manufacturing TFP in China and India." *Quarterly Journal of Economics* 124 (4): 1403–48.

Hsieh, Chang-Tai, and Peter J. Klenow. 2010. "Development Accounting." *American Economic Journal: Macroeconomics* 2 (1): 207–23.

Hsieh, Chang-Tai, and Peter J. Klenow. 2014. "The Life Cycle of Plants in India and Mexico." *Quarterly Journal of Economics* 129 (3): 1035–84.

Jones, Charles I. 2016. "The Facts of Economic Growth." In *Handbook of Macroeconomics, Vol. 2A*, edited by John B. Taylor, and Harald Uhlig, 3–69. Amsterdam: Elsevier.

Kalemli-Ozcan, Sebnem, and Bent E. Sørensen. 2016. "Misallocation, Property Rights, and Access to Finance: Evidence from within and across Africa." In *African Successes, Volume III: Modernization and Development*, edited by Sebastian Edwards, Simon Johnson, and David N. Weil, 183–211. Chicago: University of Chicago Press for the National Bureau of Economic Research.

Paganini, Monica. 2016. "An Efficiency Analysis of Firms: Evidence from Sub-Saharan Africa." Doctoral dissertation, University of Kent, Canterbury, UK.

Restuccia, Diego. 2011. "Recent Developments in Economic Growth." *Federal Reserve Bank of Richmond Economic Quarterly* 97 (3): 329–57.

Restuccia, Diego, and Richard Rogerson. 2008. "Policy Distortions and Aggregate Productivity with Heterogeneous Establishments." *Review of Economic Dynamics* 11 (4): 707–20.

Restuccia, Diego, and Richard Rogerson. 2013. "Misallocation and Productivity." *Review of Economic Dynamics* 16 (1): 1–10.

Restuccia, Diego, and Richard Rogerson. 2017. "The Causes and Costs of Misallocation." *Journal of Economic Perspectives* 31 (3): 151–74.

Restuccia, Diego, and Raül Santaeulàlia-Llopis. 2017. "Land Misallocation and Productivity." Working Paper 23128, National Bureau of Economic Research, Cambridge, MA.

Restuccia, Diego, Dennis Tao Yang, and Xiaodong Zhu. 2008. "Agriculture and Aggregate Productivity: A Quantitative Cross-Country Analysis." *Journal of Monetary Economics* 55 (2): 234–50.

Sinha, Rishabh, and Xican Xi. 2018. "Agronomic Endowment, Crop Choice and Agricultural Productivity." Background paper, World Bank, Washington, DC.

Policies and Institutions that Distort Resource Allocation in Sub-Saharan Africa | 4

Introduction

Institutions and economic policies may introduce distortions in the decision-making processes of production units (farms and firms) in Sub-Saharan Africa. In turn, these distortions in resource allocation across the different production units may affect not only the quantities they produce but also the economy's aggregate level of output and productivity. The aggregate productivity losses associated with these distortionary policies and institutions, therefore, are transmitted through three distinct and interdependent channels (Restuccia and Rogerson 2017):

- *The technology channel,* which affects the productivity of various production units
- *The selection channel,* which affects the number of operating production units[1]
- *The misallocation channel,* which drives the allocation of capital and labor among operating production units away from an efficiency benchmark.

These three channels are not independent: any policy or institution that *misallocates* resources can potentially generate additional effects through both the *selection* and *technology* channels.

This chapter (a) examines various policies and institutions that affect the productivity of farms and firms; (b) evaluates their (static) impact on resource misallocation; and (c) assesses, to the extent possible, their dynamic effects through distorted occupational choices or inefficient technological decisions. Specifically, this chapter discusses a comprehensive, but by no means exhaustive, set of potentially distortionary policies and institutions (summarized in table 4.1) that are classified by three potential sources of misallocation (Restuccia and Rogerson 2017):

- *Market imperfections.* The analysis discusses (a) credit market imperfections (that is, restricted access to finance due to the lack of collateral); (b) lack of land titling, affecting the allocation of land; and (c) information frictions, affecting producers that are not connected to markets or farmers who have inadequate information on weather forecasts.
- *Statutory provisions.* Also discussed are size-dependent policies—more specifically, tax provisions and regulations that depend on features of the different production units (say, size and age) as well as trade policies that protect specific categories of goods.

TABLE 4.1 Policy-Related Sources of Potential Resource Misallocation Affecting Farm and Firm Productivity

Source	Policies
Market imperfections	• Financial frictions (collateral) • Nonmarket land allocation (land titling, rentals) • Information asymmetries (price dispersion, EWS)
Statutory provisions	• Size-dependent policies (tax provisions) • Age-and size-dependent regulations • Targeted trade policies
Discretionary provisions	• Input subsidy programs for farmers • Preferential lending to specific firms • Preferential market access to certain producers

Source: Restuccia and Rogerson 2017.
Note: EWS = early warning systems.

• *Discretionary provisions.* In addition, the report captures government provisions that favor or penalize certain types of production units—for example, subsidies to farmers, low-interest loans to specific firms, and preferential market access for specific groups of producers, among others.

In focusing on the potential sources of misallocation across agriculture and manufacturing production units in Sub-Saharan Africa, the chapter uses farm- and firm-level information to quantitatively assess the impact of policies and institutions on aggregate productivity. Most of the empirical evidence presented in this chapter uses the *direct approach* to resource misallocation (as further discussed in chapter 3, box 3.1). First, it directly measures the specific policies, institutional factors, and market imperfections that are likely sources of misallocation. Second, it calibrates and simulates a model of heterogeneous production units to evaluate the extent to which these factors can generate effects on aggregate total factor productivity (TFP) through misallocation.[2]

Chapter 3 presented farm- and firm-level evidence of pervasive resource misallocation in agriculture and manufacturing among Sub-Saharan African countries—and these allocative inefficiencies are even greater than in other low- and middle-income countries. Agriculture still plays an important role in the region's economic performance. This primary activity is not only less productive than other sectors (including manufacturing) but also employs a larger share of the region's population. This chapter explores the potential institutional and policy-related sources of misallocation in agriculture and manufacturing, including land market imperfections, agricultural subsidies, size-dependent taxation and informality, preferential trade policies, differential access to infrastructure, and financial market imperfections. These sources have likely led to allocative inefficiencies, primarily through suboptimal selection of operating production units, distorted occupational choices, and disincentives to investment in technological upgrading.

Land Market Imperfections

The underdevelopment of land market institutions is one of the potential sources of resource misallocation in agriculture across Sub-Saharan African countries. The analysis of available household data, integrated with farm-level agricultural production data across the region, has yielded strong evidence of capital and land misallocation in the agriculture sectors (see chapter 3 and the references therein). In turn, it has been argued that institutions governing land allocation mechanisms are connected to the severe misallocation of agricultural resources across farms in Sub-Saharan Africa and impede farm-size growth among the most-productive farmers (Restuccia and Santaeulàlia-Llopis 2017).

Distortions in farm size can hamper agricultural productivity and discourage the uptake of modern technologies. Farm size in low-income countries can be distorted by a wide variety of institutions and farm-level policies. For instance, many countries (including Bangladesh, Ethiopia, and the Philippines) have imposed ceilings on land holdings, partitioning any farms that exceed those ceilings. Others (Indonesia and Zimbabwe) have established both maximum and minimum size constraints. Several countries have also levied progressive land taxes (Namibia and Zimbabwe) or steep progressive income taxes (Ethiopia) on farmers (Restuccia 2016).

In addition, institutional mechanisms for allocating land are tightly linked to inheritance norms and redistribution. They tend to restrict access to land in underdeveloped rental and sale markets. Insecure property rights or inefficient land allocation mechanisms may lead not only to resource misallocation but also to (a) distorted incentives for technological adoption (Aragón and Rud 2018; Chen, Restuccia, and Santaeulàlia-Llopis 2017); and (b) distorted occupational choices by individuals between farming and nonfarming activities—because individuals opting to work in nonagriculture sectors may have to forfeit their untitled land (Chen 2017).

Aggregate Consequences of Inefficient Resource Allocation across Farms

There is a strong relationship between the depth of land markets and the degree of output loss attributed to misallocation. In other words, resource misallocation across countries in the region is greater among farmers without rental markets than those with developed rental markets—as shown in Ethiopia, Malawi, and Uganda (box 4.1). This disparity is captured by the greater dispersion in

---

BOX 4.1   Land Institutions in Selected Sub-Saharan African Countries

Malawi: Dominance of Customary Land Tenure

Most of the land tenure in Malawi is customary, with user rights assigned locally by village chiefs.[a] The country's Customary Land Act (No. 19 of 2016) grants the village head (or superior chiefs administering several villages) the power to allow or ban land transactions and to resolve disputes across villages associated with land limits (Kishindo 2011; Morris 2016). Although the Malawi Land Bill (also passed in 2016) looks to reduce these powers, it has not yet been enacted.

Most household farms in Malawi (83.4 percent) do not operate any marketed land (rented-in or purchased). Of the 16.6 percent of household farms that do operate part of their land from the market, 3 percent rent-in land informally (borrowed for free or moved into without permission); 9.5 percent rent-in land formally (through leaseholds, short-term rentals, or farming as a tenant); 1.8 percent purchase land without a title; and 1.3 percent purchase land with a title (Restuccia and Santaeulàlia-Llopis 2017).

Ethiopia: State Ownership of Land

From 1974 until the early 1990s, the Ethiopian government expropriated and uniformly redistributed the country's rural land and legally prohibited land transactions. Although land ownership still resides with the state and many of the restrictions to land transactions remain in place, some reforms were implemented in the 2000s to grant land certificates to farmers and to allow rentals of the use rights (up to a certain limit). Because land sales are prohibited in Ethiopia, land rentals are the only channel for reallocating farms' operational scale, and hence they constitute a measure of the depth of land markets.

However, the extent of land rentals began to differ substantially across subregions as these reforms were decentralized to local governments (Deininger, Ayalew Ali, and Alemu 2008). For instance, the percentage of rented land varies from 0 percent to more than 73 percent among the 69 zones (with available data) across the country. Among 234 woredas (districts), the percentage of rented land varies from 0 percent to 91 percent. These large differences in

(Box continues next page)

BOX 4.1   Land Institutions in Selected Sub-Saharan African Countries *(continued)*

land rentals across zones and districts reflect substantial heterogeneity among local land market institutions.

Despite the comprehensive land certification reform intended to provide tenure security to farmers, land markets remain highly underdeveloped. Among Ethiopian household farms, 67.6 percent neither rent-in nor rent-out any land; 24.3 percent formally or informally rent-in some land for production; 10.6 percent rent-out land; and 2.5 percent either rent-in or rent-out some land. For a more extensive institutional background on the allocation and use of land in Ethiopia, see Chen, Restuccia, and Santaeulàlia-Llopis (2017).

Uganda: Multiple Land Systems

Uganda provides four types of land tenure: freehold, leasehold, Mailo (a form of freehold), and customary land. The first three systems offer some degree of formal and secure property rights, while customary systems are less secure and lack formal land registries (Coldham 2000; Place and Otsuka 2002).

The Mailo territory (8,000 square miles) was allocated to chiefs and notables after an agreement between the British government and the Kingdom of Buganda (Central region) in 1900. Although Mailo landowners hold their land in perpetuity and have similar rights to freeholders, tenants have security of occupancy as in common-law arrangements (sometimes backed by a certificate) and can only be removed if the land is unattended for at least three years (Coldham 2000).

In regions where noncustomary tenure systems are more prevalent, 47 percent of land holdings have been marketed (purchased or rented). In regions where customary land tenure is more common, 27 percent of land holdings have been marketed. These tenure systems are spatially concentrated as follows: (a) more than 90 percent of land holdings are under customary land tenure in the Northern and Eastern regions, and (b) noncustomary systems are mostly found in the Western and Central regions.

Finally, differences in land tenure appear to matter for economic activity in Uganda: customary land is associated with lower agricultural investment (Place and Otsuka 2002).

Sources: Aragón and Rud 2018; Chen, Restuccia, and Santaeulàlia-Llopis 2017; Restuccia and Santaeulàlia-Llopis 2017.

a. "Customary" land tenure (as opposed to "statutory" tenure) refers to ownership by indigenous communities, administered in accordance with their customs. Common ownership is one form of customary land ownership.

---

total factor productivity revenue (TFPR) and in the marginal product of land for farmers who cannot rent land (table 4.2).[3] For instance, evidence from Ethiopian farmers confirms the following (Chen, Restuccia, and Santaeulàlia-Llopis 2017):

- The dispersion of TFPR is greater for farmers without rental markets (1.10) than for farmers with rental markets (0.96).
- The standard deviation of the marginal product of land is also significantly lower for farmers who rent-in or rent-out land (0.86) than for those who cannot do so (1.05).

In sum, firms with any portion of market land tend to display less resource misallocation.

The output gains from eliminating distortions in land allocation would be larger among farms operating on nonmarketed lands. Evidence at the household farm level in Ethiopia shows that the efficiency gains from reallocation for farmers who do not participate in rentals are larger than those of farmers who rent land (table 4.2). The same finding is obtained for farms in Malawi: the output level of farms without marketed land (about 84 percent of the sample) would be 4.2-fold, compared with the 3.6-fold output gains for the entire sample of farmers in Malawi (Restuccia and Santaeulàlia-Llopis 2017).[4]

The degree of association between farm size and farm TFP is higher among farms operating with marketed land than among those operating without marketed land: these correlations amount to 0.30 and 0.14, respectively, among Malawi farmers (Restuccia and Santaeulàlia-Llopis 2017).

TABLE 4.2 **Impact of Land Rental on Resource Misallocation among Farmers in Ethiopia, 2013/14**

Metric	Full sample	No rentals	Rentals
Efficiency gain (nationwide)	3.07	3.18	2.61
Std Dev (log TFPR)	1.06	1.10	0.96
Std Dev (log MP land)	0.99	1.05	0.86
Observations (no.)	2,887	1,951	936
Sample (%)	100.0	67.6	32.4

Source: Chen, Restuccia, and Santaeulàlia-Llopis 2017, using data from the Ethiopia Integrated Survey of Agriculture (ISA) 2013/14.
Note: A baseline nationwide reallocation is conducted to compute efficiency gains separately for each group of farmers: those with no rental land and those with any percentage of rented-in or rented-out land. MP land = the marginal product of land; Std Dev = standard deviation; TFPR = revenue productivity.

However, the weakness of these correlations suggests that land markets are still limited, even for farmers with access to marketed land; that is, these farmers are still far from operating at their efficient scale.

Despite the alleviating role played by land rentals, the degree of misallocation is still severe, even among farms that rent land. Land rentals help reassign land from less-productive to more-productive farms. However, these farms are still operating far from the sectorally efficient allocation. This finding suggests that land markets in Sub-Saharan Africa remain subject to various frictions. Weak legal institutions may also hinder rental activity.

Distributional Implications of Resource Reallocation

Resource reallocation among farmers to achieve efficient operational scales may have distributional implications. Empirical evidence shows the actual versus the efficient distribution of factors, output, and income across farmers by productivity quintile in Malawi (table 4.3).

The actual land distribution across farm TFP is flat: most farms are operating on less than 2 acres of land. The estimated efficient land distribution, on the other hand, suggests that the most productive farm (top quintile) should operate on almost 6 acres on average (representing 97 percent of total land). These findings point to a substantial redistribution of land to achieve higher

levels of aggregate productivity (Restuccia and Santaeulàlia-Llopis 2017).

The actual distribution of income (and productivity) is widely dispersed despite the relative equalization of inputs (say, capital and land) across farmers in Malawi. For example, the ratio of the top to bottom quintile of agricultural output (a proxy of farm income) is a factor of 34-fold (4.78 for the top quintile and 0.14 for the bottom quintile) although the corresponding ratios of top to bottom quintiles for capital and land use are within a factor of 1-fold to 2-fold. In other words, equal access to land across households does not necessarily translate into income equalization because these farmers differ substantially in their productivity.

Assessing the distributional income effects of the reallocation of inputs across farmers requires the computation of a counterfactual income level that (a) considers the actual distribution of factors as endowments, and (b) allows the efficient allocation to be achieved through perfectly competitive rental markets. Such a simulation yields the following findings for household farms in Malawi:

• First, the least productive farmers reap the largest benefits from the higher factor returns, and overall inequality declines. The income ratio between farmers in the top and bottom quintiles would decline from a factor of 34-fold (actual allocation) to about 3.4-fold (efficient allocation)—that is, a decline of income inequality among these farmers by a factor of 10-fold.

TABLE 4.3   Effects of Actual and Efficient Distribution of Land, Capital, MPL, and MPK among Farms in Malawi

| Variable | Productivity partition | | | | | |
	1st	2nd	3rd	4th	5th	var(ln x)
Farm productivity *(s)*	0.75	2.10	3.72	6.39	21.50	1.435
Land (l):						
Actual	1.19	0.87	1.01	1.03	1.99	0.749
Efficient	0.00	0.01	0.04	0.14	5.91	6.782
Capital (k)						
Actual	55.93	25.35	21.81	24.70	26.71	1.820
Efficient	0.04	0.32	1.10	3.60	149.52	6.782
MP Land (yield)						
Actual	4.21	11.00	17.82	29.10	82.04	1.485
Efficient	76.30	76.30	76.30	76.30	76.30	0.000
MP Capital						
Actual	0.73	2.19	3.94	7.25	24.54	2.154
Efficient	6.03	6.03	6.03	6.03	6.03	0.000
Output (y) - level						
Actual	0.14	0.39	0.69	1.20	4.78	1.824
Efficient	0.00	0.05	0.18	0.60	25.06	6.782
% of total						
Actual	2.01	5.46	9.57	16.67	66.26	..
Efficient	0.02	0.20	0.71	2.33	96.71	..
Agricultural income - level:						
Actual	0.14	0.39	0.69	1.20	4.78	1.824
Efficient	4.28	2.22	2.17	2.56	14.65	1.228
Income gain	23.70	3.88	2.27	1.58	1.99	..
% of total:						
Actual	2.01	5.46	9.57	16.67	66.26	..
Efficient	16.55	8.58	8.41	9.88	56.56	..

Source: Restuccia and Santaeulàlia-Llopis 2017.
Note: Household quintiles are shown in order of farm productivity (1st quintile the lowest, 5th quintile the highest). Land, capital, and output are in per hours terms. "MP land" (MPL) is the marginal product of land and "MP capital" (MPK) the marginal product of capital computed for each bin. "Actual" income is equal to actual agricultural output, whereas "efficient" income is computed assuming that (a) actual allocations are the endowments, and (b) the efficient allocation is achieved via perfectly competitive rental markets. "Income gain" is the ratio of efficient to actual income. .. = not calculated.

- Second, the ratio of efficient to actual income increases for all household farms. However, this increase is largest for the poorest households (a 24-fold increase for the bottom quintile of farmers as opposed to only a 2-fold increase for the top quintile).

This counterfactual suggests that having well-functioning rental markets for capital and land to achieve the efficient allocation of operational scales can lead to substantial increases in agricultural productivity as well as sharp reductions in inequality levels and poverty.

Better Technology, Better Practices

In an efficient allocation, access to marketed land implies that farmers can command more inputs and produce more output. Farmers operating on marketed land are also more likely to have greater access to other markets (say, credit markets) and are likely to be substantially more educated than farmers without marketed land. In addition, the women of these farms are more empowered in terms of labor force participation and market wages, and a larger proportion of these farmers invest in intermediate inputs and technology adoptions (Restuccia 2016; Restuccia and Santaeulàlia-Llopis 2017). For instance, a farm with average productivity in Ethiopia is 18.3 percent more likely to use fertilizer and 20.6 percent more likely to use livestock if it operates on marketed land (Chen, Restuccia, and Santaeulàlia-Llopis 2017). Although fertilizers can boost agricultural productivity almost independently of the size of the cultivated plot, this is not the case for large animals, tractors, and other sizable capital, which, unless rented on a daily or hourly basis, are more likely to pay off only on large operational scales (Chen 2020).

Removing distortions in land allocation generates not only static productivity gains but also dynamic ones. Policies that deepen rental markets in Sub-Saharan Africa will positively influence farmers' decisions on technology upgrading to boost productivity. Spillovers and learning-by-doing effects operate among farmers: the more farmers who learn in the village and the more their improved techniques spill over to neighbors who may not have learned, the more farm productivity will improve. Conversely, misallocation can reduce the returns from learning among the more-talented farmers (Chen and Restuccia 2018).

Simulations for the Ethiopian agriculture sector shows that removing land distortions would raise agricultural productivity (by 264 percent), reduce the share of agricultural employment (from 60 percent to 21 percent), and increase the percentage of farmers who are learning new techniques (from 18.7 percent to 35.1 percent). The agricultural productivity gains can be decomposed into (a) 41.9 percentage points from static gains associated with removing static misallocation among farmers, (b) 103.6 percentage points from eliminating distortions in occupational choices, and (c) 2 percentage points associated with the learning component of the static productivity gain (Chen and Restuccia 2018).

From a dynamic perspective, removing distortions in land allocation will increase the percentage of farmers who learn and hence will shift the technology frontier faster. Labor productivity growth in agriculture then will depend not only on the general equilibrium effects associated with selection and structural transformation but also on the growth of the technological frontier.

Faster productivity growth in agriculture will also accelerate the structural transformation of the Ethiopian economy—by reducing the country's agricultural employment share by 0.16 percentage points per year (Chen and Restuccia 2018). On a regional level, Sub-Saharan Africa's rapid population growth (3 percent per year) tends to slow down the structural transformation process: larger population implies a greater demand for agricultural goods, and as a result, more people work in agriculture, and the sector's TFP decreases because of standard selection effects (Lagakos and Waugh 2013).

Population growth also affects both agricultural productivity and learning in this way: if distortions to resource allocation were eliminated and population growth were reduced to an annual rate of 1 percent, agricultural productivity would grow faster (by 2.75 percent per year), which is more than 1.5 percentage points under the high-population-growth scenario (Chen and Restuccia 2018). The agricultural employment share would also decline faster (by 0.35 percentage points per year)—and this decline is twice as fast as the scenario with high population growth. Faster agricultural productivity growth, resulting from slower population growth, generates agricultural productivity that is 40 percent higher than that of an economy with rapid population growth. Slower population growth could also offset the gains in agricultural productivity by lowering the price of agricultural goods and reducing the percentage of farmers who learn.

Resource misallocation in agriculture has led to an excessive amount of inputs used to produce a certain minimum level of value added per capita in agriculture across Sub-Saharan African countries. This chapter so far suggests that improving the quality of institutions supporting the functioning of land markets can help reduce misallocation (Aragón and Rud 2018; Chen, Restuccia, and Santaeulàlia 2017; Restuccia 2016).

Finally, insecure property rights or inefficient mechanisms to allocate land may lead not only to resource misallocation but also to (a) distorted incentives of technology adoption (Chen, Restuccia, and Santaeulàlia-Llopis 2017); and (b) distorted occupational choices by individuals between farming and nonagricultural activities because individuals opting to work in the nonagriculture sectors may have to forfeit their untitled land (Chen 2017).[5]

How Allocative Inefficiencies Exacerbate the Impact of Climatic Shocks

Climate shocks have detrimental effects on agricultural productivity—impacts that are exacerbated in an environment with allocative distortions, thus raising the costs associated with climate adaptation.[6] Extreme temperature induces a negative shock to productivity: an increase of 1 degree Celsius in the average temperature above the optimal threshold reduces agricultural productivity by 9 percentage points among farmers in Uganda. These harmful effects take place in all regions of the country regardless of the system of land rights.

Resource misallocation is particularly worrisome in light of the current climate change predictions (Aragón, Oteiza, and Rud 2018; Carleton and Hsiang 2016; Chen, Chen, and Xu 2016; Zhang, Zhang, and Chen 2017). In response to high-temperature events, farmers may tend to increase (instead of decreasing) their land use without reducing labor use, especially in the regions with less-developed land markets (say, the Eastern and Northern regions of Uganda) (table 4.4).

TABLE 4.4 Impact of Weather Shocks on Input Use and Output on Farmers in Uganda, 2009–14

Dependent variable	Land ln(T) (1)	Labor ln(L) (2)	Land ln(T) (3)	Labor ln(L) (4)	Output ln(Y) (5)
HDD	0.038**	−0.001	0.047***	0.017	−0.075″
	(0.015)	(0.014)	(0.016)	(0.015)	(0.033)
HDD x	...	...	−0.070*	−0.139***	−0.077
Western/Central	...	...	(0.039)	(0.035)	(0.065)
N	13.113	13.113	13.113	13.113	13.113
R2	0.021	0.025	0.022	0.027	0.050

Source: Aragón and Rud 2018.
Note: ... = variable was not included in the regression specification. Standard errors are clustered at household level (in parentheses). All regressions include household fixed effects; fixed effects by growing season (year) and by cropping season (first and second semester); degree days (DD); harmful degree days (HDD); and natural logarithm ln(precipitation). DD and HDD are two measures of cumulative exposure to heat during the growing seasons. DD measures cumulative exposure to temperatures between a lower bound (usually 8 degrees Celsius) and an upper threshold, while HDD captures exposure to extreme temperature (above the threshold). Columns (3) and (4) include interactions of HDD with an indicator of being in the Western/Central region. N = number of observations. R2 = R-squared, the proportion of variance for a dependent variable explained by an independent variable or variables.
Significance level: * = 1 percent, ** = 5 percent, *** = 10 percent.

The greater use of inputs, especially land, in response to negative supply shocks is interpreted as a risk management strategy of farmers in the context of imperfect markets. That is, absent insurance or access to credit, subsistence farmers may need to increase input use to offset the loss of agricultural output and avoid an undesirable reduction in consumption (Aragón, Oteiza, and Rud 2018; Aragón and Rud 2018). In other words, negative climate shocks can exacerbate allocative inefficiency in environments with imperfect input markets. Reallocating resources from agriculture to other productive uses may attenuate the negative productivity effects of climate change, but imperfect markets might hinder this reallocation.

Climate mitigation and adaptation policies may help reduce the frequency of extreme temperature events and hence their potential impact on agricultural productivity. The introduction of digital technologies to implement early warning systems (EWS) and provide timely information on flood alerts, drought warnings, wildfires, and pest outbreaks can also help farmers manage climate shocks.[7] Additionally, property rights appear to matter for adaptive behavior by farmers exposed to weather shocks. Policies that foster property rights and increase the competitiveness in the allocation of land markets may allow farmers to better cope with climatic shocks.

Agricultural Subsidies

Targeted input subsidy programs (ISPs) are one of the main tools for many African governments to boost fertilizer use. ISPs have yielded short-term benefits for national production and food security. However, their impacts have been weakened by poor crop response to fertilizer implementation features that weaken the programs' contribution to broader fertilizer use.[8] Low crop response to fertilizer has also impeded the growth of commercial demand for fertilizer in Africa, and the ISPs have further crowded out the development of commercial distribution channels (Goyal and Nash 2017).

History and Effects of ISPs

Sub-Saharan Africa phased out most ISPs throughout the 1990s except in Malawi and Zambia, where modest ISPs have been implemented sporadically during the 2010s. Fertilizer subsidy programs were largely ineffective in contributing to agricultural productivity growth, food security, or poverty reduction in the 1980s and 1990s. Instead, they placed a major fiscal burden on African governments (Kherallah et al. 2002; Morris et al. 2007; World Bank 2008).

Fertilizer subsidy programs in the region also led to corruption and state paternalism, often hindering the development of commercial input distribution systems and contributing to local supply gluts that put political pressure on governments to implement costly grain purchases and price-support policies for farmers. For these reasons, international lenders and bilateral donors tended to discourage African governments from relying on ISPs during this period of aid conditionality.

The landscape, however, changed quickly and profoundly since 2005. After African governments committed to increase their agriculture expenditures under the 2003 Maputo declaration,[9] at least 10 countries introduced or reintroduced fertilizer subsidy programs, at a collective cost of roughly US$1 billion annually (figure 4.1).[10] Large-scale input subsidy programs often became the centerpiece of governments' agricultural development programs. Skepticism based on the past performance of these programs was swept aside by arguments that a new vintage of "smart" subsidy programs (further discussed in the next section) could take account of past lessons to maximize the benefits and minimize the problems of prior programs.

What has been the experience of Sub-Saharan African countries with ISPs? Large-scale ISPs have tended to raise beneficiary households' crop yields and production levels, at least in the year that they receive the subsidy. However, the production effects of ISPs are smaller than expected because of low crop-yield responses to fertilizer by most

FIGURE 4.1 **Government Spending on Agricultural Input Subsidies, by Type, in Sub-Saharan African Countries with the 10 Largest ISPs, 2014**

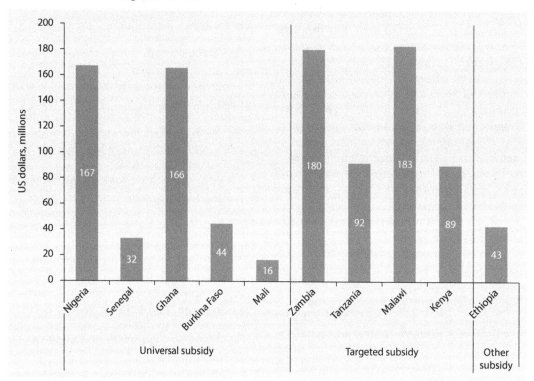

Source: Goyal and Nash 2017.

Note: A "universal" input subsidy program (ISP) is universal in the sense that (in theory) any farmer can access it. The quantity available to a given farmer is determined roughly based on farm size. "Targeted" programs provide subsidies to selected households based on some observable criteria. The "other subsidy" category pertains to Ethiopia, whose government officially states that it does not have an ISP, yet fertilizer is typically made available to farmers at prices roughly 20–25 percent lower than the commercial distributors' price to other countries of the region.

smallholder-managed fields and the tendency of ISPs to partially crowd out commercial fertilizer demand. Subsidies have also had relatively small, transitory effects on the incomes of recipient households.

The lack of persistent yield response and the crowding-out effect are directly linked to the natural effects of ISPs on incomes and poverty (Goyal 2018). Furthermore, fertilizer subsidy programs have only a modest, if not negligible, impact on food prices (for example, maize in Malawi) (Ricker-Gilbert et al. 2013). In other cases, the production effects of subsidy programs are not large enough to have a significant impact on local food markets or rural wage rates.

Moreover, fertilizer subsidy programs fail to kick-start dynamic growth processes. In Mozambique, their impact on production and income appear to decay the year after the farmers receive the subsidies (Carter, Laajaj, and Yang 2014). In Malawi, their impact on fertilizer use or crop production was limited even one year after farmers graduated from the subsidy program following three years of participation (Ricker-Gilbert and Jayne 2012). The lack of effectiveness might be partly attributed to the influence of political and election-related motives on the geographic distribution of subsidies.

Potential Benefits from Reform

A more systematic strategy for raising smallholder crop productivity—focusing on sustainably raising the efficiency and quantity of fertilizer used—will more effectively achieve the region's agricultural, food security, and poverty reduction goals. Such a comprehensive strategy may include ISPs if they can be implemented according to "smart subsidy" criteria. Other important elements of such a strategy include (a) greater public investment in coordinated systems of agricultural research and development (R&D); (b) water management and extension that emphasize bidirectional learning between farmers of varying resource constraints; and (c) input from agroecologists, researchers, and agrodealers (Goyal 2018).

Overall, reforming the design and implementation of ISPs while rebalancing government spending in favor of high-return core public goods and policies could deliver high returns for Sub-Saharan African agriculture systems. Effective science and extension programs are also necessary to interactively work with farmers to identify best practices for maintaining and increasing crop productivity amid changes in economic and biophysical environments.

Taxation and Informality

Taxation constitutes an important source of misallocation, because it interferes with the equalization of marginal products across firms. Tax systems may induce sizable productivity losses. The productivity cost of tax-induced distortions is particularly high in emerging and low- to middle-income economies, where resource misallocation is more pervasive and firm-level productivity more sensitive to distortions (Bento and Restuccia 2017). This implies that tax systems are an even more sizable source of productivity losses in low-income countries than in high-income countries. Tax disparities between productive capital and real estate alone account for as much as a 5–7 percent loss in industrial TFP in emerging and low-income economies (IMF 2017).

Production inefficiencies induced by taxes are amplified if the tax wedges in marginal products across firms are positively associated with their productivity. These production inefficiencies take place if, as a result of taxation, the size of the most (least) productive firms is smaller (larger) than the one indicated by the efficient allocation. This "taxing the good" misallocation is starker in Sub-Saharan African countries relative to countries in other regions. Firm-level data suggest estimated distortion elasticities of productivity of 0.53 for Ethiopia, 0.44 for Ghana, and 0.52 for Kenya (Cirera, Fattal-Jaef, and Maemir 2018).

These "correlated distortions" alter the allocation of inputs and reduce the incentives to invest in innovation (Gabler and Poschke 2013; Ranasinghe 2014). This dynamic inefficiency is likely to both further depress aggregate productivity and widen the efficiency gap between high-income and low- to middle-income economies.

Most distortions caused by tax systems in low- and middle-income countries arise from size-dependent policies and informality. These distortions do not emerge from built-in differentiated effective taxation across assets or sources of financing but rather reflect either de jure statutory provisions (related to the scale of operations) or de facto differentiated treatment (resulting from incomplete enforcement). In the context of low-income countries, size-dependent policies and informality issues are therefore the most salient mechanisms through which taxation causes misallocation and hinders productivity. These distortions hamper the expansion of efficient firms and contribute to the survival of inefficient ones, resulting in lower aggregate productivity.

Size-Dependent Tax Policies

Size-dependent policies interfere with factor demand by (implicitly or explicitly) subsidizing or taxing firms based on their scale of production, thus distorting the size distribution of firms. These policies feature pervasively in tax codes of high-income and low- to middle-income economies alike.

Size-dependent provisions also generate implicit marginal taxes that vary with the scale of operations. For instance, if size-dependent regulations are being phased in as firms expand while licensing, they act effectively as quotas. They create disincentives for firms to grow and take full advantage of scale economies, inducing small-business traps.

The resulting negative impact on production is sizable: estimates from calibrated models suggest that interventions reducing the average size of production units by 20 percent lead to an output contraction of 8 percent (Guner, Ventura, and Xu 2008). Furthermore, although market failures sometimes warrant size-dependent interventions in the short or medium run, the dynamic inefficiency resulting from inertia amplifies the long-run reduction in aggregate production because of the negative impact of such well-intended policies on firm growth (Buera, Moll, and Shin 2013).

Preferential tax regimes for small taxpayers can create disincentives to firm growth. Evidence shows that, to minimize their tax liabilities, firms tend to bunch below the regulatory thresholds created by these regimes (Asatryan and Peichl 2017; Brockmeyer and Hernandez 2016). For example, small taxpayers in Mozambique were offered a simplified tax on gross turnover, called the Simplified Tax for Small Taxpayers (ISPC). Since 2009, this tax replaced the corporate income tax, the personal income tax, and the value added tax. A flat tax rate of 3 percent was imposed on taxpayers with annual business volumes below Mt 2.5 million, while those with business volumes below 36 times the minimum wage were exempt from the tax. A significant bunching of small firms emerged below the eligibility threshold in Mozambique after the ISPC was introduced, as shown in figure 4.2 (Swistak, Liu, and Varsano 2017).

Removing size-dependent tax enforcement in low- and middle-income countries would increase TFP, with productivity gains amounting to 0.8 percent (Bachas, Fattal-Jaef, and Jensen 2018). Making tax systems size-neutral would significantly attenuate inefficiencies in the allocation of resources. Size-dependent policies that generate small-business traps must be eliminated because they implicitly subsidize the least-productive firms and tax the most-productive ones. If governments are to provide tax incentives to spur growth, they should target productivity-enhancing investments to minimize the adverse allocative impact of distorting marginal products. If aimed at relieving the proportionally high fixed costs faced by start-ups, policies should aim at facilitating entry rather than subsidizing small firms.

In Ghana, switching from a size-dependent tax to a uniform rate would substantially raise per capita income. Gollin (2006) calibrates the span-of-control model of Lucas (1978) with self-employment technology and dynamics that match the manufacturing sector's firm-size distribution in Ghana. Ghana's tax policy environment, which includes a three-tiered tax scheme, is compared with a revenue-neutral counterfactual in which the rate of taxation is uniform across firm size. The simulation generates substantial labor reallocation from own-account to wage employment and estimated efficiency gains that amount to an increase of 6.5 percent in per capita income. However, it does not greatly reduce the prevalence of small firms.

FIGURE 4.2 Distribution of ISPC Taxpayers in Mozambique: 2010 versus 2015

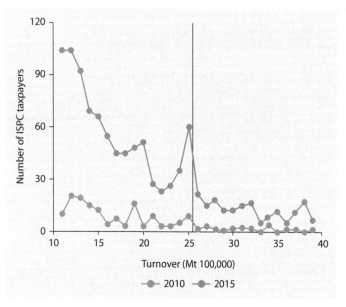

Turnover (Mt 100,000)

—●— 2010 —●— 2015

Source: IMF 2017, using data from Swistak, Liu, and Varsano 2017.
Note: The horizontal axis designates the turnover bins (as multiples of Mt 100,000) by which the business taxpayers are classified. The vertical rule designates the business eligibility threshold for the Simplified Tax for Small Taxpayers (ISPC), to the right of which taxpayers are ineligible. A small number of ISPC taxpayers appear above the threshold, possibly because the registration requirement is applied to turnover in the previous year instead.

Tax-induced distortions can have significant dynamic implications on resource misallocation through the impact that the corresponding allocative inefficiencies have on the firms' incentives to invest in productivity-enhancing technologies. As a result, these firms will exhibit slower life-cycle productivity growth and hence slower employment growth. Empirical evidence shows that productivity growth over a firm's life cycle is flatter among Sub-Saharan African countries relative to more-efficient benchmarks. For example, revenue productivity (TFPR) increases steadily with the age of the establishments in Ethiopia but at a slow pace. This suggests that older firms face bigger distortions. In contrast to the Ethiopian example, older firms in Ghana and Kenya tend to exhibit smaller TFPR as firms age. In sum, tax-induced distortions tend to decelerate firm growth over the cycle and discourage the adoption of productivity-enhancing technologies (Cirera, Fattal-Jaef, and Maemir 2018).

Overall, leveling the playing field regardless of firm size would also generate large productivity gains. Independently of government revenue considerations, better-functioning tax administration would generate productivity gains by putting an end to the distortive implicit subsidies enjoyed by informal, typically low-productivity firms. Moreover, reducing compliance costs would play a part in spurring growth by reallocating resources toward productive activities.

Informality-Related Issues

Informality is widespread in low- and middle-income economies, especially in Sub-Saharan Africa. Informal firms account for up to half of aggregate output in low-income countries, and they typically circumvent taxation. Tax avoidance or evasion and other nonremitted contributions constitute the main benefit from informality (Fajnzylber 2007). Tax compliance increases with development, as the gradual construction of functioning legal and regulatory frameworks makes it more attractive for firms to operate in the formal economy.

Informal, noncompliant firms are significantly less productive than formal, tax-compliant ones. At the country level, there is a significant negative correlation between country TFP and the extent of informality. Firm-level evidence suggests that noncompliant manufacturing firms in low- and middle-income economies have lower productivity than their compliant counterparts; for example, businesses that only report 30 percent of their sales have, on average, a 4 percent lower TFP than those reporting a greater proportion of their sales (IMF 2017).

Informality is a source of misallocation and hinders productivity. The relative cost advantage enjoyed by noncompliant firms affects business dynamism by distorting creative destruction and growth. In this context, informality enables the survival of unprofitable businesses—thus increasing their participation in aggregate output at the expense of more profitable and compliant firms. Differences in the size distribution of all firms relative to formal firms signal the misallocation that arises from such inefficient growth dynamics. The pervasiveness of this resource misallocation is illustrated in the size distribution of manufacturing firms in Cameroon, Rwanda, and Zambia (figure 4.3) (Cirera, Fattal-Jaef, and Maemir 2018).

The size and scope of the informal sector plays an important role in explaining productivity differences within sectors and across countries. General equilibrium model simulations suggest that countries with high entry and operation costs in the formal sector as well as weak debt enforcement tend to have greater allocative inefficiencies and a larger share of output produced by low-productivity informal firms. These frictions tend to generate large informal sectors and exacerbate the misallocation of capital, thus explaining a decline in TFP of up to 25 percent (D'Erasmo and Moscoso Boedo 2012). In other words, the model yields a strong negative association between income per capita and the size of the informal sector.

Finally, incomplete tax enforcement can reduce the capital intensity of informal

FIGURE 4.3 Size Distribution of Formal Firms versus All Firms and US Benchmark, Selected Sub-Saharan African Countries

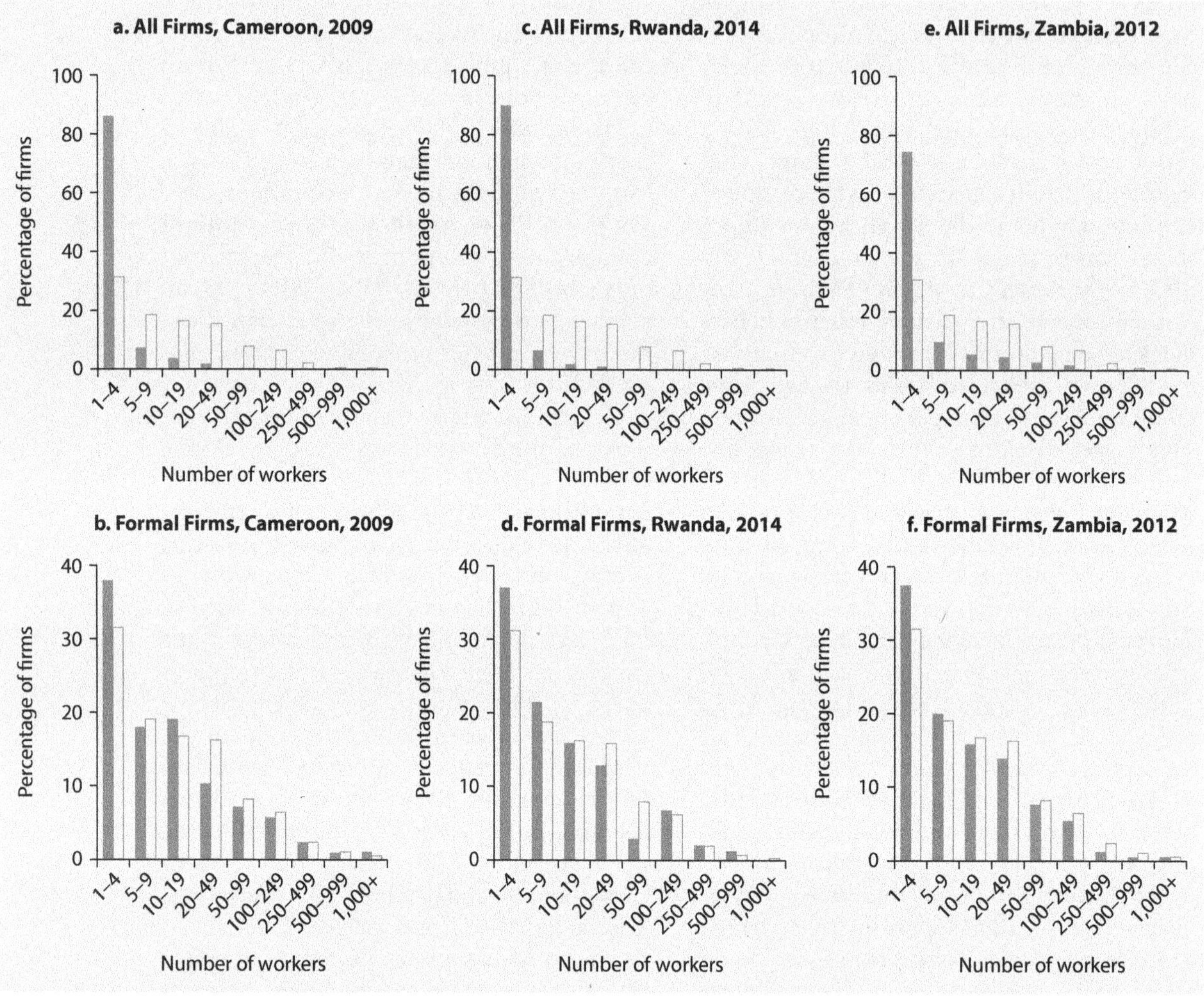

Source: Cirera et al. 2018.
Note: The figure shows the distribution of manufacturing firm size (as measured by the number of workers) in selected Sub-Saharan countries. Outlined bars represent the size distribution in United States, which proxies a global efficiency benchmark.

firms, induce excess entry of less-productive businesses, and lead to the reallocation of inputs toward less-productive firms (Leal Ordóñez 2014).

The coexistence of a sizable informal sector with a formal one poses serious challenges to the design of policies to foster entrepreneurship. Policies that impose barriers on the formal sector tend to lower aggregate productivity through distortions in occupational choice. Different types of frictions (financial, institutional, and others) and their interplay may lead to suboptimal occupational choices.

An individual's choice between formal entrepreneurship, informal entrepreneurship, and nonentrepreneurial work can be influenced by both personal features (skill level and initial wealth) and institutional factors (such as entry costs, taxation enforcement, or financial frictions). The institutional environment of African economies is characterized by high registration costs, imperfect credit markets, and low-enforcement tax collection. Entrepreneurs pay a registration fee to become formal. Afterward, these entrepreneurs pay taxes and have better access to credit. In contrast, informal entrepreneurs evade tax payments and are more likely to face borrowing constraints.

Taxation and registration costs reduce the entry of low-productivity entrepreneurs into the formal sector and induce a larger number of unproductive firms to enter the informal sector. In Cameroon, barriers to entry drive the choice of whether entrepreneurs join the formal sector (Nguimkeu 2015). A counterfactual exercise shows that cutting registration costs by half will double the share of formal enterprises through the formalization of informal firms and new entrants to the industry (figure 4.4, panel a). It also increases aggregate income by 15 percent, and the government's total net tax revenues more than double (figure 4.4, panel b). In sum, the counterfactual exercises for Cameroon show that

an efficient skill allocation and significant income gains can be obtained by reducing registration costs and selecting the optimal tax rate while fostering entrepreneurial skills and enterprise creation through business training and improved access to credit.

Trade Policy

Trade policies can affect firm performance through (a) mechanisms that induce changes *within* firms and hence affect firm-level components of profitability, and (b) mechanisms that induce the reallocation of economic activity *across* firms in an industry. The first channel's impact is summarized in box 4.2. In the case of the second channel, trade may not affect *firm-level* profitability, but the trade-induced factor reallocation from the

FIGURE 4.4 **Simulated Impact of Business Registration Reform on Occupational Choice and Income in Cameroon**

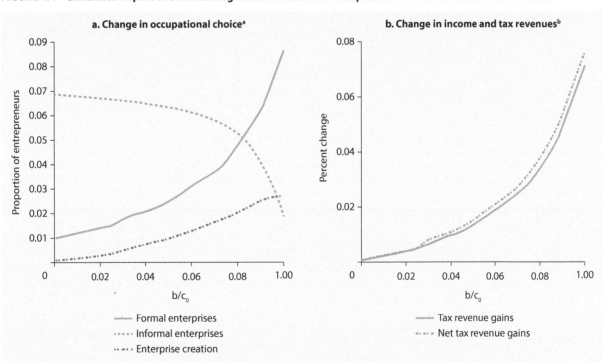

Source: Nguimkeu 2015.
Note: The simulated reform is to cut business registration costs. On the x-axes, b represents the reduction of the entry cost implied by the reform, and c_0 is the fixed entry cost for the entrepreneur to join the formal sector. 0.05 = 5%.
a. Panel a denotes the fraction of formal enterprises, informal enterprises, and new enterprise creation simulated by the corresponding change in entry cost (b/c_0).
b. Panel b indicates the simulated variation in aggregate income gains (computed as the total income gain from all sectors) and the tax revenue gains (computed as the total tax revenues net from forgone registration fees due to reform).

BOX 4.2 Trade Liberalization and Within-Firm Changes

Firms participate in world markets as producers or sellers of goods and as buyers of intermediate inputs used in the production of these goods. Trade policies, therefore, can potentially affect all phases of the firm's production and expenditure decisions:

- Transformation of physical inputs to output
- Upgrade (or downgrade) in the quality of the producers' outputs and inputs
- Remuneration of workers of different skills
- A firm's locational choices.

The channels through which trade reforms affect firms will depend on the specific nature of the trade policy changes and, particularly, on whether these policy changes affect output relative to input markets.

In response to trade shocks, firms are expected to raise their productivity as they undertake actions to become more efficient—say, by adopting better management practices or appointing better managers (Bloom et al. 2013; Schmidt 1997). Productivity improvements are usually linked to investment in new technologies, research and development (R&D), and entry in export markets. Productivity-enhancing actions are associated with inputs; that is, investment will affect not only productivity but also the capital stock (De Loecker 2013).

Input Market Costs

Exposure to international trade can affect the firm's performance through changes in the trade cost of inputs. Lower trade costs lead to the import of new intermediate inputs and an increase in production beyond what the increase in expenditures would predict. This increase will be more pronounced if the new inputs are of higher quality than those previously used. If the production technology exhibits a taste for variety, a larger number of imported inputs will translate into higher output (Halpern, Koren, and Szeidl 2015). This mechanism is likely to underlie the large within-firm productivity gains found in studies that examine the effects of input tariff liberalization in India and Indonesia (Amiti and Konings 2007; Topalova and Khandelwal 2011). In fact, input tariff liberalization led to large increases in the number of imported inputs in India (Goldberg et al. 2009, 2010).

Firms' prices and markups will adjust in response to trade shocks. Trade models with monopolistic competitions and constant elasticity of substitution (CES) preferences render constant markups. Under alternative demand systems, prices and markups tend to respond to trade liberalization (Arkolakis et al. 2019; Feenstra and Weinstein 2017; Mayer, Melitz, and Ottaviano 2014; Melitz and Ottaviano 2008).

Multiproduct firms can improve revenue productivity (TFPR) by reallocating within-firm resources from the production of the least to the most profitable products. This mechanism improves firm-level performance, and it is analogous to the role of reallocation in raising aggregate industry performance. This mechanism only increases TFPR, and this increase is attributed mostly to the reshuffling of resources across products of varying profitability (Bernard, Redding, and Schott 2010).

Effects of Tariff Cuts

Empirical evidence shows that an industry's profitability increases with its exposure to foreign competition. Trade liberalization studies focus on episodes of output and input tariff reductions (Amiti and Konings 2007; Pavcnik 2002). The effects of input tariff cuts are larger than those of output tariff reductions in low- and middle-income countries. They typically operate through two channels—within-firm performance and factor reallocation—and the relative importance of each channel depends on the industry's setting (Melitz and Redding 2014; Melitz and Trefler 2012).

The effects of trade liberalization on performance is heterogeneous across firms. Firms with different characteristics—such as initial profit level, R&D expenditure, and capital intensity, among others—tend to cope differently with trade shocks (Aw, Roberts, and Xu 2011; Bustos 2011; Lileeva and Trefler 2010). "Learning by exporting" (the mechanism by which firms' productivity improves after entering export markets) appears to play an important role when controlling for the fact that entering export markets comes along with higher investment (De Loecker 2013).

High-Productivity Export Firms

High-productivity firms are more likely to enter international markets and continue raising their productivity—as in the case of export firms in nine African countries: Burundi, Cameroon,

(Box continues next page)

BOX 4.2   Trade Liberalization and Within-Firm Changes *(continued)*

Côte d'Ivoire, Ethiopia, Ghana, Kenya, Tanzania, Zambia, and Zimbabwe (Van Biesebroeck 2005). Postexport productivity growth (learning by exporting) for these firms is attributed to the reduction of credit and contract enforcement constraints. However, evidence of postexport growth is not robust. The finding of a positive correlation between exports and firm productivity in Ghana, Kenya, and Tanzania suggests that (a) highly productive firms are more likely to enter export markets, and (b) learning by exporting is not fully supported by the data.

Finally, the destination of exports also matters to productivity among firms engaged in international trade. Firms exporting to other African countries tend to exhibit lower productivity than firms exporting to the rest of the world (Bresnahan et al. 2016; Mengistae and Teal 1998).

---

least to the most profitable firms can still improve *industry-level* performance. This section reviews the evidence of trade policy's impact on misallocation in select African countries.

Trade reforms can contribute to the reallocation of factors of production from the least-productive to the most-productive firms, thus boosting the industry's performance and that of the overall economy. From an individual producer perspective, these reforms are exogenous and can affect the market shares of a particular industry. Changes in market shares toward more-productive firms have the potential to raise aggregate productivity (Collard-Wexler and De Loecker 2015). The reallocation process plays an important role in improving performance, and its impact depends on the initial dispersion of productivity—that is, the dispersion before the reform (Pavcnik 2002).

Tariff policies. Tariff policies have led to distortions in the allocation of resources across manufacturing firms in Sub-Saharan African countries. Changes in output and input tariffs create wedges that lead to a dispersion in marginal revenue products across firms. Output tariffs distort competition, while input tariffs create distortions in capital and other intermediate inputs markets. Alleviating or eliminating these distortions through trade reforms is conducive to a more efficient allocation of factors across firms (De Loecker and Goldberg 2014).

Preferential incentives. Trade policies that support prioritized subsectors and regions may also distort the allocation of factors and hence lower aggregate productivity. In Ethiopia, import substitution policies provided a series of incentives to firms in priority sectors from 1996 to 2002—for example, subsidies such as tax exemptions and loss carry-forwards as well as easier access to credit. These policies led to the entry or survival of inefficient firms, and the later removal of these policies facilitated the exit of the less-productive firms and incentivized firms to grow at a faster pace.

Such policies were followed by export promotion policies from 2003 to 2012, complemented by the 2002 investment proclamation that removed the classification of subsectors as "pioneer" and "promoted."[11] The export promotion policies granted incentives based on the export capability of agroindustry and manufacturing firms (Gebresilasse 2016). The export-based eligibility criteria of the 2003–12 policies could reduce the misallocation of resources by compelling firms to be efficient—because exposure to foreign competition requires a high level of efficiency.

Firms in sectors that had been targeted during the import substitution period (1996–2002) tended to have lower marginal products and lower TFPR than nontargeted firms. Ethiopian firms eligible for these pioneer and promoted sector benefits also exhibited lower physical productivity (TFPQ).

In contrast, the export promotion policies had no significant effects on the firms' TFPR and TFPQ.[12] Still, they had less-distortionary effects on firm productivity as a result of changes in the eligibility criteria as well as the overall export promotion goal (Gebresilasse 2016; Gebrewolde and Rockey 2015).

Trade reforms. The impact of trade reforms on firm-level productivity is mixed. On the one hand, trade reforms have tended to raise firm-level productivity in Ethiopia, but the impact is heterogeneous. Average firm productivity increased by 2 percent after tariffs were cut by 10 percentage points. However, productivity grew faster among exporting firms than nonexporting firms after liberalization. Productivity gains were also higher if input tariffs were cut rather than output tariffs. Resource reallocation as a result of lowering tariffs accounted for 73 percent of the improvement in Ethiopian manufacturing productivity (Zenebe 2018).

On the other hand, the labor productivity of manufacturing plants in Swaziland (renamed Eswatini in 2018) declined, on average, by 3 percent during that country's trade liberalization period (1994–2003). The productivity effects, however, were heterogeneous across sectors: labor productivity increased in the apparel sectors but decreased in pulp and paper and basic metals (Mhlanga and Rankin 2015). The lower productivity of manufacturing firms in Swaziland was attributed to the fact that the positive impact of reallocating resources to higher-activity producers was offset by the lack of complementary investments to enhance production efficiency through innovation and technology adoption.

Infrastructure

In the academic literature and in policy circles, an adequate supply of infrastructure services has long been viewed as a key ingredient for economic development (Aschauer 1989; IMF 2014; World Bank 1994). Over the past 30 years, researchers have devoted considerable effort to theoretical and empirical analyses of the contribution of infrastructure development to growth and productivity.[13] Although there are several methods to assess the infrastructure-growth nexus empirically, a consensus has emerged that, under the right conditions, infrastructure development can play a major role in promoting growth and equity—and, through both channels, help reduce poverty.

Sub-Saharan Africa ranks at the bottom of all low- and middle-income regions in virtually all dimensions of infrastructure performance. It also has inherent characteristics that may enhance the potential importance of infrastructure to its economic development—notably, the large number of landlocked countries (home to a large proportion of the region's total population) and the remoteness of most of the region's economies from global market centers. Sub-Saharan Africa's geographic disadvantages result in high transportation costs that hinder intraregional and interregional trade (Behar and Manners 2008; Elbadawi, Mengistae, and Zeufack 2006; Limao and Venables 2001). Other things being equal, the landlocked countries' limited openness to trade appears to be the main drag on their growth. The region's poor infrastructure only adds to its geographic disadvantages.[14] However, adequate transportation and communication facilities can help to overcome them.

Few academic or policy experts would dispute the view that infrastructure development fosters growth, but there is no consensus on the magnitude of the effect or the factors that shape it. Empirical research initially focused on the long-term effects of infrastructure on aggregate output and productivity.[15] There is ample evidence, for instance, of a long-term relationship between infrastructure and output in Nigeria and South Africa (Ayogu 1999; Kuralatne 2006; Perkins, Fedderke, and Luiz 2005). This might partly reflect more data availability compared with other countries in the region. Panel data evidence also reveals a significant contribution of transportation infrastructure to output (Boopen 2006; Kamara 2006). Finally, roads, power, and telecommunications infrastructure have a significant impact on Africa's long-run growth (Estache 2005).

At the firm level, there are two distinct approaches to assess the growth and productivity effects of infrastructure. The first approach evaluates the impact of infrastructure on the firm's revenues and productivity relative to its counterparts within the industry and in other countries—and this impact is transmitted through differences in the ability to adopt more efficient technologies or to operate technologies efficiently across industries and countries. The second approach examines the effects of infrastructure connectivity (or lack thereof) on resource misallocation and hence on cross-country differences in TFP. Using both approaches, this section looks at the impacts on firm output and productivity of three specific infrastructure sectors: transportation, energy, and the digital economy.

Transportation Infrastructure

Different strands of economic theory have extensively investigated the impact of transportation infrastructure on economic activity. Economic geography suggests that transportation costs play a role in determining the location of economic activities (Weber 1928), especially in a context of imperfect competition and varying degrees of labor mobility across regions (Fujita and Thisse 2002). Endogenous growth theory provides a framework that posits public infrastructure (including transportation infrastructure) as an engine of growth through its contribution to TFP (Garcia-Milà and McGuire 1992; Hulten and Schwab 1991; Munnell 1992).

Transportation improvements, along with lower transportation costs, can potentially reduce firms' input costs and hence increase productivity. The lower production and distribution costs induced by the improvements in the transportation sector can lead to scale effects and enhance competition (Baldwin and Okubo 2006; Melitz and Ottaviano 2008). Transportation infrastructure can also contribute to productivity through agglomeration effects: firms and workers benefit from being close to others. Transportation improvements, therefore, strengthen agglomeration economies if they increase connectivity within the spatial economy (Eberts and McMillen 1999; Graham 2007).

The likely economic benefits of investments in the transportation sector have justified funding for new and improved transportation infrastructure. Inadequate transportation infrastructure adds 30–40 percent to the cost of goods traded among African countries (Sinate et al. 2018). Since Africa is home to 16 landlocked countries, poor and underdeveloped transportation infrastructure limits accessibility to consumers, hampers intraregional trade, and drives up import and export costs. For instance, the expense of moving Africa's imports to customers inland is, on average, 50 percent higher than shipping costs in other low-income regions (Sinate et al. 2018).

A poor road network, in terms of its connectivity and quality, can have deleterious effects on economic activity. Low-quality road networks, along with inefficient transportation and trade services, raise logistical and transaction costs—thus restricting producers' access to markets. Africa's road infrastructure gap, along with high logistics costs, have a detrimental impact on the region's productivity and overall competitiveness (Escribano, Guasch, and Pena 2010). Transportation policies have so far been insufficient to introduce more competition and attract foreign investors, while the region continues to trail the world in both connectivity and quality of road infrastructure (Calderón, Cantú, and Chuhan-Pole 2018).

At the production unit level, there is evidence of the impact of infrastructure on agriculture and manufacturing. The following discusses the impact of transportation infrastructure on manufacturing activity; the effects on agriculture are presented in box 4.3.

Improved transportation networks can spur factor mobility and boost productivity. In Ethiopia, an improved road network can influence the entry decisions and entry sizes of manufacturing firms. The effects of infrastructure on firm decisions were analyzed

---

BOX 4.3 **The Role of Transportation Infrastructure in Agriculture**

The size of subsistence agriculture can be characterized as the outcome of the interplay between sectoral productivities (in agriculture and manufacturing) and transportation productivity. Agriculture takes place in near or remote rural areas, while manufacturing goods are produced in urban areas. Economic models assume that people devoted to subsistence agriculture live in remote areas and that labor is mobile across regions.

The model calibration for Sub-Saharan Africa finds that agricultural productivity improvements and lower costs of intermediate inputs free up labor from the agriculture sector (Gollin and Rogerson 2014). Improved transportation productivity helps individuals move from subsistence agriculture into manufacturing, leaving the share of workers living in the near rural areas unchanged. If productivity improves only in manufacturing, the share of population in subsistence agriculture still declines but more slowly than if the boost were in agricultural or transportation productivity. These findings imply that structural transformation at low levels of development is primarily driven by productivity surges in agriculture and transportation. Economically speaking, a 10 percent increase in agricultural TFP combined with a 10 percent reduction in transportation costs leads to a 14 percentage point reduction in the labor share in subsistence agriculture (Gollin and Rogerson 2014). The welfare effects are significant—comparable to raising consumption per capita in the economy by 62 percent.

The pattern of labor allocation observed in low-income countries (that is, a large share of labor in low-productivity agricultural employment) is influenced by high transportation costs and low

infrastructure spending. In Uganda, high transportation costs are reflected in substantial price dispersion: these high costs incentivize individuals to choose locations that minimize transportation costs for their agricultural goods. This explains the larger share of subsistence agriculture because people live in remote areas to be close to their food source (Gollin and Rogerson 2016). This finding is consistent with evidence that poor transportation facilities constrain agricultural growth (Diao and Yanoma 2003) and that higher transportation costs alter the incentives for agricultural investment (Renkow, Hallstrom, and Karanja 2004; Stifel and Minten 2008).

Improvement in rural road infrastructure can reduce crop prices in rural markets, and these price effects are stronger in markets farther from major urban centers and in low-productivity areas. After the European Union's feeder rehabilitation program in Sierra Leone improved the quality of small rural roads, transportation costs declined for traders purchasing agricultural produce from rural markets as well as for farmers bringing their crops to these markets (Casaburi, Glennerster, and Suri 2013).[a] The better quality of rural roads helped reduce the price of the main staples cultivated domestically in rural markets along the rehabilitated roads—that is, rice and cassava. The price reductions for cassava were larger owing to idiosyncratic factors associated with the crop: (a) cassava sales are less affected by seasonal factors, and (b) cassava is bulkier than other crops to transport.

a. The 2009–11 rehabilitation program targeted four districts in three different provinces: Kambia and Port Loko (Northern Province), Kenema (Eastern Province), and Pujehun (Southern Province). These four districts cover 27 percent of the country's area and 30 percent of its population (Casaburi, Glennerster, and Suri 2013).

---

using geographic information system (GIS)-based panel data on road accessibility of Ethiopian towns and census-based panel data for manufacturing firms from 1996 to 2008 (Shiferaw et al. 2015). Three measures of road infrastructure were considered: (a) total distance traveled during a 60-minute drive, (b) total area accessible during the 60-minute drive, and (c) total travel time from a particular locality to major economic destinations. Local improvements in road infrastructure

are captured in (a) and (b), while (c) measures the connectivity of firms with local or distant markets.

The quality of local road infrastructure was positively associated with the number of firms in the locality. For instance, a 1 percent improvement in road infrastructure was associated with a 1.1–1.2 percent increase in the number of firms. The number of firms had no significant relationship with the connectivity of the road infrastructure. However, the size of new entrants was more strongly associated with connectivity than with the quality of the local road infrastructure.

In sum, better road networks can influence the entry decisions and entry sizes of manufacturing firms. Evidence for Ethiopia shows that higher-quality local road infrastructure enables the entry of firms and that more-extensive market connectivity is important to determine the entry of larger firms. In other words, improved road infrastructure affects aggregate productivity through its impact on the number and size of operating firms—the selection channel (Shiferaw et al. 2015).

Energy Sector

The availability and reliability of electricity services is key for the economic development of the African continent. No country in the world has ever developed without having access to energy. Energy is needed to operate industrial machinery and contributes to human capital productivity by providing power to essential facilities such as schools and hospitals as well as for information and communication technologies (ICTs).

Insufficient and unreliable availability of electric power is one of the biggest challenges facing African firms. According to World Bank Enterprise Surveys, (a) 78 percent of African firms experienced power outages in 2018; (b) 41 percent of African firms (compared with 30 percent worldwide) identified electricity as a major obstacle to business operation; and (c) the average power interruption faced by African firms exceeds 50 hours per month—amounting to a 25-day loss of economic activity per year. The economic cost of the poor energy infrastructure network is sizable. For instance, African firms lose nearly 5 percent of their total annual sales because of power outages (Oseni 2019).

Poor access to a reliable electric power infrastructure hinders manufacturing production in low- and middle-income countries. For instance, manufacturers may have problems connecting to the power grid or, when they do, experience shortages or fluctuations in voltage and frequency (Alby, Dethier, and Straub 2013). An unreliable power supply has direct and indirect impacts on productivity. The lack of access to electricity and the unreliability of its provision directly hamper the manufacturing process (Allcott, Collard-Wexler, and O'Connell 2016; Reinikka and Svensson 2002). Productivity drops even when firms can smooth electricity supply through self-generation. For instance, scheduled blackouts reduce firms' productivity by forcing them to shift resources away from productivity-enhancing activities (Poczter 2017; Reinikka and Svensson 2002).

The unreliable provision of electricity also leads to allocative inefficiencies. Pervasive inefficiency in the allocation of factors is found in Ghanaian manufacturing, as captured by the wide dispersion in revenue and quantity productivity across firms. If these inefficiencies were eliminated, the potential TFP gains of Ghanaian manufacturing firms would be in the range of 35–65 percent. These distortions are partly explained by electricity shortages and insufficient power-generating capacity (Ackah, Asuming, and Abudu 2018; Estache and Vagliasindi 2017). Additional evidence shows that unreliable electricity supply affects firm performance through the reduction of firm-level investments (Lumbila 2005; Reinikka and Svensson 1999).

Power outages have a significant negative impact on productivity. Eliminating power outages could potentially increase the productivity of Ghanaian manufacturing establishments by 10 percent.[16] Firms' various strategies to cope with power outages (such as using generators, switching to less-electricity-intensive production processes, changing production times, and temporarily suspending production) cannot shield them from the negative productivity effects of these outages. If firms are willing to pay a premium for uninterrupted electricity, governments can invest in the electric power sector even if it raises electricity prices. However, that premium is bounded by the additional cost of generating their own electricity relative to purchasing it from the public grid (Abeberese, Ackah, and Asuming 2019).

Access to electric power also increases the ability of poorer households to allocate their labor resources for market production. In postapartheid South Africa, the rural electrification rollout contributed significantly to employment growth in rural communities. The rollout, which expanded rapidly into rural areas and low-capacity household use, had a positive and causal impact on community employment in the rural province of KwaZulu-Natal.[17] The evidence shows a substantial increase of 9.0–9.5 percentage points in female employment—translating into 15,000 more women participating in the labor force. The increase in female employment takes place at the intensive margin: women work about 8.9 more hours per week in districts with an average increase in electrification between 1995 and 2001 (Dinkelman 2011).

Rural electrification has a substantial impact on home production activities as well: there is evidence of a significant shift away from burning wood at home to using electric cooking and lighting in communities that were recently electrified. Household electrification becomes a labor-saving technological shock to home production in rural areas, helping women reallocate their time from home to market production activities. Electricity may have also cut the production costs of new, home-based services for the market and provided individuals with other ways to use their labor in self-employment and microenterprises (Dinkelman 2011).

Digital Infrastructure

Information and communication technologies (ICTs) are key ingredients of a country's development strategy because of their (a) *inclusiveness* (expanding market access to individuals and firms); (b) *efficiency* (boosting the productivity of different inputs); and (c) *innovation capacity* (through the creation of new business models) (Deichmann, Goyal, and Mishra 2016). This subsection focuses on the insertion of digital technologies into agricultural practices and their impact on development through different channels.

The application of digital technologies in finance across African countries will be presented when discussing financial markets.

Agricultural Applications

By lowering transaction costs (both the pecuniary and time costs of access to and exchange of information), ICTs are facilitating the diffusion of information and knowledge in agriculture. Specifically, ICTs can help improve agriculture in low- and middle-income countries—and, notably, in Africa—through three different mechanisms (Deichmann, Goyal, and Mishra 2016):

- *Promotion of market transparency* by reducing informational frictions and increasing the capacity to assess market information. For instance, access to mobile phones reduces information asymmetries resulting from intermediaries with market power. Inexpensive mobile technology enables rural and often marginalized farmers to join regional and national markets.
- *Stimulation of increased demand* for timely, high-quality information on inputs. Agriculture education and extension services can potentially facilitate the technology transfer process by assisting farmers in problem solving and by becoming more inserted within the agricultural knowledge and information systems (Asenso-Okyere and Mekonnen 2012). Information delivery about better agricultural practices, new seeds, or new tools is helping to raise the productivity of other factors of production and thus boosting the efficiency of the production process.
- *Reduction of logistics costs* in the different stages of the agriculture supply chain. The mechanism includes platforms that connect buyers and sellers along the production chain, coordinate product delivery, and facilitate secure payments, among others.

The rapid expansion of digital technologies, as captured by the surge of mobile-phone and internet penetration, has helped reduce farmers' and traders' search costs—even in environments with poor wireline infrastructure or road quality. This lower cost to access knowledge and information can potentially raise rural incomes. Mobile-phone coverage is strongly associated with greater market efficiency because it lowers the price dispersion of agricultural goods. For instance, mobile phones helped reduce grain price dispersion across markets in Niger by at least 6.5 percent and intra-annual price variation by 10 percent (Aker 2008). Specifically, the largest decline in price dispersion across Niger's grain markets occurred in the first four months after getting mobile-phone coverage, and the marginal impact has decreased over time (figure 4.5). The lower price dispersion is partly attributed to reduced search costs because grain traders with mobile-phone coverage had information about and access to more markets (Aker 2008, 2010).

Mobile-phone coverage is more likely to lower the spatial price dispersion of agricultural products that are more perishable (for example, cowpeas), and this reduction is the largest for remote markets in certain periods of the year. In contrast, it has no significant impact on (producer) price dispersion of products that are typically stored by farmers, such as millet and sorghum (Aker and Fafchamps 2015).

Mobile-phone coverage can also help increase the market participation of farmers who are in remote areas and producing perishable goods. After the expansion of mobile-phone coverage, the share of Ugandan farmers selling bananas increased in the communities located more than 20 miles from district centers (Muto and Yamano 2009). Lower price dispersion was also observed among sardine fishers and wholesalers in the Indian state of Kerala because of greater mobile-phone coverage (Jensen 2007), as well as among smallholder Ghanaian farmers who used multiple data sources including open government data provided by Esoko[18] (Schalkwyk, Young, and Verhulst 2017).

In addition, access to digital technologies enables farmers to connect with agents and traders to estimate market demand and the selling price of their products, but the impact on farm gate prices is not conclusive.

FIGURE 4.5 Changes in Price Dispersion before and after Mobile-Phone Coverage in Niger's Grain Markets

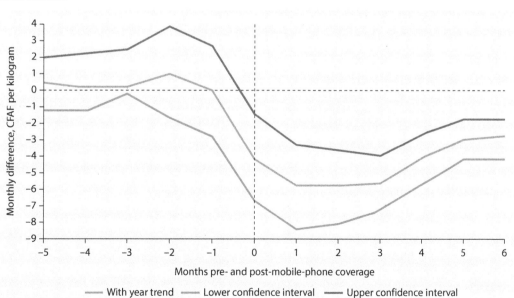

Source: Aker 2008.
Note: Price dispersion is regressed on a series of dummy variables pre- and post-mobile-phone coverage. Upper and lower confidence intervals are shown. CFAF = CFA franc.

On the one hand, access to market information (through radio or mobile phone) was related to higher farm prices in Uganda, especially for more-perishable goods (Muto and Yamano 2009; Svensson and Yanagizawa 2009). On the other hand, there is evidence that access to information did not significantly change average produce prices (Fafchamps and Minten 2012), although the effect could be restricted to specific products (Aker and Fafchamps 2015; Tadesse and Bahiigwa 2015). The lack of robustness in the relationship between farm gate prices and access to market information could be attributed to differences in the degree of information asymmetries, type of information or platform used for delivery, and the presence of other market failures (Deichmann, Goyal, and Mishra 2016).

Access to information may encourage farmers, including poor smallholders, to invest in new technologies. Information on technology transfers and advisory services is communicated by specialists through agricultural extension services. Digital technology has reenergized such advisory services. For example, Digital Green, the Grameen Foundation, and TechnoServe deliver timely, actionable information and advice to farmers in South Asia and Sub-Saharan Africa (Nakasone, Torero, and Minten 2014). Transaction costs associated with traditional agricultural extension services are reduced through a mix of voice, text, videos, and the internet. Governments are also partnering with mobile operators to coordinate the distribution of better seeds and subsidized fertilizers in remote areas through e-vouchers (for example, Nigeria's large-scale e-wallet initiative).

Electronic extension systems differ in their complexity, range of tools, platforms, and devices used to transmit information. Digital Green, a global nongovernmental organization (NGO), used a participatory process to allow farmers' access to agricultural advice by linking them with experts through local social networks in Ethiopia and India (Gandhi et al. 2009). Such ICT approaches have led to greater adoption of agricultural practices by reducing the distance between instructors and farmers.

Digital technologies can also connect farmers with capital goods—especially for those smallholder farmers in remote rural areas who can use machinery to improve productivity but cannot afford to purchase it. For instance, Hello Tractor in Nigeria is an Uber-like service that enables farmers to request, schedule, and prepay for tractor services from nearby owners through short message service (SMS) texts and using mobile money. The smart, two-wheeled tractors are equipped with Global Positioning System (GPS) antennae that collect and transfer necessary data. The prepayment is released to the owner once the service is completed (IFC 2018).

Digital technologies are also used to implement EWS, particularly climate models that provide public information on flood alerts, drought warnings, wildfires, and pest outbreaks. Timely provision of this information can help farmers manage these climate shocks. EWS use data from a wide array of sources, including satellite images and surveys. Satellite images provide climatic parameters in almost real time (for example, rainfall, temperature, evaporation, vegetation, and land cover) that can reach remote areas without measurement stations and allow farmers to manage crop growth. Automated systems provide early warning of deviations from normal growth or other factors. Examples of EWS include the following (Ekekwe 2017):

- *Zenvus,* a Nigerian precision farming start-up, provides soil data (on temperature, nutrients, and vegetative health) to farmers so they can optimally apply fertilizers and irrigate their farms. These data-driven farming practices are improving farm productivity and reducing waste.
- *UjuziKilimo,* a Kenyan start-up, uses big data and analytics to transform farmers into knowledge-based communities and boost productivity by identifying the needs of individual crops.
- *SunCulture,* founded in Kenya and with operations across the region, sells affordable, high-efficiency drip irrigation kits that use solar energy to pump water from any source.

Timely delivery of digital extension services and EWS information on a large scale requires content development and maintenance. The cost is high in low-productivity agricultural areas populated by smallholder farmers with poor infrastructure and low skills. Hence, it is essential to develop low-cost tools to make the delivery of agricultural production advice more efficient. ICT developments that reduced costs for farmers in rural areas lacking appropriate infrastructure improved the efficiency of extension service delivery. However, the returns from ICT for farmers in poorer countries were nearly half of those in richer countries (Lio and Liu 2006).

Digital technologies can potentially improve agriculture supply chain management as well. They enhance the coordination of product transportation and delivery, secure food safety in global agricultural production chains, and facilitate secure payments (Deichmann, Goyal, and Mishra 2016). The nature of food production, along with greater awareness of foodborne diseases, has emphasized the need to guarantee food safety in global food supply chains. Technological products that can trace products from farm to market effectively are being put in place, especially among farmers in low- and middle-income countries trying to reach or expand to new export markets (Karippacheril, Rios, and Srivastava 2011). For example, radio frequency identification (RFID) chips are being placed on crates of produce or in the ears of livestock to collect data on motion, temperature, spoilage, density, and light, among other data. The Namibian Livestock Identification and Traceability System implements a system that facilitates the control, risk management, and eradication of bovine disease. The use of RFID rather than paper-based recording has increased data accuracy and its speed of dissemination, thus contributing to a more dynamic livestock market (World Bank 2012).

Technology may also improve food safety in value chains. For example, IBM, Walmart, and the Chinese retailer JD.com together with Tsinghua University have announced a blockchain food safety alliance to improve food tracking and safety in China. Decentralized ledger technology will be able to trace back the origin of food products in shorter intervals of time, making it easier to prevent food scandals and build trust among domestic food producers and distributors (Aitken 2017).

Aggregate Employment Impacts

Finally, the adoption and use of digital technologies may improve employment rates, shift occupational employment shares, and reduce job inequality across African countries. Recent research compares the economic performance of individuals and firms in African locations that were on the terrestrial network of internet cables with those that were not during the gradual coastal arrival of submarine cables from Europe (Hjort and Poulsen 2019).[19] Employment increased when fast internet arrived, but the higher employment in connected areas did not occur at the expense of jobs in unconnected areas. Access to fast internet also increased the likelihood of individuals being employed in skilled jobs and had no significant impact on the likelihood of individuals being employed in unskilled jobs across African countries.

However, fast internet did shift employment shares to higher-productivity occupations. As a result, job inequality declined: the percentage-point increase in the probability of having a job was comparable between those who only completed primary schooling and those with secondary or tertiary schooling (Hjort and Poulsen 2019). The increase in skilled employment was the largest for those with tertiary education, while those with primary schooling joined the unskilled labor force.

After the arrival of submarine internet cables in Africa, net firm entry increased in sectors that use ICT extensively (for example, finance in South Africa), while productivity grew among operating manufacturing firms (Ethiopia). After getting access to fast internet, firms in Ghana, Kenya, Nigeria, Senegal, and Tanzania tend to export more, increase online communication with clients, and boost employee training (Hjort and Poulsen 2019).

Financial Market Imperfections

Financial systems across the world have become deeper, more efficient, and more stable over recent decades. However, the development of domestic financial systems has been uneven across the world's countries and regions as well as among users within a country. Countries with sound macroeconomic policy frameworks and robust growth have deepened their financial systems considerably (Beck, Demirgüç-Kunt, and Levine 2009). However, low- and lower-middle-income countries still exhibit low levels of financial depth, lower access to formal financial services (such as savings accounts and bank loans), and restricted access to external finance (Banerjee and Duflo 2005; Demirgüç-Kunt, Feyen, and Levine 2013; Lane and Milesi-Ferretti 2007, 2017).

Financial development, in turn, enhances growth at both the country and firm levels. It fosters economic growth through improvements in the allocation of resources and higher TFP growth (Beck, Levine, and Loayza 2000). Financial deepening stimulates the growth of those industries that are more dependent on external finance (Rajan and Zingales 1998) and helps reduce the financing constraints on firms—in particular, small enterprises (Beck, Demirgüç-Kunt, and Maksimovic 2005). It has a transformative impact on economic activity: it shapes the structure of industries, the size distribution of firms, and organizational structures (Demirgüç-Kunt, Love, and Maksimovic 2006). Countries with deeper financial systems also tend to experience faster poverty reduction as the income shares of their poorest quintiles tend to grow at the fastest pace (Beck, Demirgüç-Kunt, and Levine 2007).

Allocative efficiency and productivity growth are enhanced if the financial system (a) enhances the quality of information about firms; (b) exerts sound corporate governance over the resource-borrowing firms; (c) provides effective mechanisms to manage, pool, and diversify risks; (d) mobilizes savings from surplus units toward the most promising projects in the economy; and (e) facilitates trade (Levine 2005).

Financial Frictions and Aggregate Productivity: The Channels of Transmission

Financial frictions play an important role in influencing entrepreneurs' ability to enter the industry or expand their scale of operations. Firms are heterogeneous in their level of productivity (and hence their optimal scale of operation) or in the sector in which they operate. Financial frictions can affect firm-level and aggregate growth dynamics, and their impact on aggregate productivity will depend on the number and type of entrepreneurs as well as their distribution across the different types (Buera, Kaboski, and Shin 2015).

Financial frictions can affect TFP through several different channels. At the intensive margin, financial frictions introduce distortions in the allocation of capital (*capital misallocation*) among heterogeneous operating production units. The inefficient allocation of capital among active entrepreneurs (as captured by the dispersion in their marginal product of capital) would lower TFP. At the extensive margin, financial frictions affect aggregate TFP through two different channels: the number and the composition of entrepreneurs. In other words, financial frictions introduce distortions in (a) the selection into entrepreneurship, as productive but poor individuals delay their entry while rich and low-productivity entrepreneurs remain in business (*misallocation of talent*); and (b) the number of production units for a given distribution of entrepreneurial talent in an economy (Buera, Kaboski, and Shin 2015).

The Intensive Margin

Financial frictions can influence productivity through their impact on the level and dispersion of the marginal product of capital (MPK). Firms' MPK tends to be higher than it would be otherwise amid binding credit constraints (and holding constant wages and rental rates of capital). There is evidence of large returns to capital among small-scale retailers in Mexico—about 20–30 percent per month or three to five times the market interest rates (McKenzie and Woodruff 2008). Similarly, randomized grants to microentrepreneurs in Ghana render very large returns to capital: 7–10 percent and approximately 25 percent per month for cash and in-kind grants, respectively (Fafchamps et al. 2011).

In equilibrium, the MPK is higher if the entrepreneur's productivity is greater (given any amount of capital). In this context, the MPK of constrained entrepreneurs is higher if their levels of productivity increase (for any given amount of wealth), even in cases of pure collateral constraints. The empirical evidence shows a great degree of concentration in the returns of Mexican entrepreneurs who report themselves as financially constrained (McKenzie and Woodruff 2008). In addition, the larger returns of women entrepreneurs in Ghana correspond to those firms that were already more profitable (Fafchamps et al. 2011). These findings suggest that productivity leads to higher returns to capital.

The MPK across firms also varies greatly. Empirical evidence suggests that manufacturing firms in Sub-Saharan Africa with less access to finance have higher MPK and that, conditional on access to finance, small firms have lower MPK. These findings imply that higher efficiency could be attained by allocating more capital to larger firms (Kalemli-Ozcan and Sørensen 2016). Restricted access to finance has important real effects: for instance, moving firms from environments with easy access to finance to those with poor access will increase their MPK by 45 percent. Therefore, financial constraints may help explain resource misallocation within countries, and this misallocation is significantly associated with the strength of property rights. In other words, firms may be reluctant to reinvest their profits in the absence of secure property rights.

The Extensive Margin

Financial frictions can also affect productivity through their impact on individuals' occupational choices. They tend to operate through the occupational choices of low-wealth, marginal-ability entrepreneurs. In partial equilibrium, financial frictions increase the activity of entrepreneurs but lower their

number; hence the impact of tighter credit constraints on firm size is ambiguous.

The shift in the composition of entrepreneurs leads to higher average productivity and, therefore, greater labor demand. However, financial frictions reduce the amount of capital used by entrepreneurs with binding credit constraints. Poor, marginal-ability entrepreneurs will switch their occupations from entrepreneur to worker in the presence of financial constraints. The demand for labor declines while the supply increases, and lower wages will clear the market. The constrained demand for capital declines, thus lowering the interest rate and the cost of capital. Lower labor and capital costs lead to an increase in the firm's profitability as well as in the threshold for entry or survival. Relative to a frictionless environment, some high-wealth, low-productivity individuals will enter and replace poor, marginal-productivity entrepreneurs.

Although financial frictions have an ambiguous net impact on entrepreneurship in partial equilibrium, they unequivocally lead to higher entrepreneurship rates in general equilibrium (Moll 2014). Amid financial constraints, wealthier individuals are more likely to become entrepreneurs while lower wages and capital rental rates translate into higher firm profits. The lower input prices, in turn, lead to a larger unconstrained scale of production for all entrepreneurs. The region of high-productivity, low-wealth entrepreneurs who are capital-constrained expands with lower input prices in general equilibrium. Those high-productivity, low-wealth individuals who remain as entrepreneurs are more constrained than they would be in partial equilibrium, whereas the high-wealth, low-productivity entrepreneurs who enter because of the lower input prices tend to be unconstrained.

Quantitative Analysis of the Channels of Transmission

Financial frictions tend to have sizable effects on labor productivity, aggregate and sector-level TFP, and capital-output ratios.

Financial frictions may lead to an estimated decline of 20–30 percent in aggregate TFP at equilibrium in one-sector, closed economy models (Buera, Kaboski, and Shin 2011; Buera and Shin 2013). The intensive margin (capital misallocation) explains nearly 40 percent of the TFP reduction, and financial frictions tend to reduce entrepreneurship rates (Midrigan and Xu 2014).

Financial frictions have more deleterious effects on manufacturing activities than on services. They tend to reduce the TFP of manufacturing sectors by more than 50 percent, while the TFP of services sectors fall by less than 30 percent. The differential impact across sectors might reflect the higher relative price of manufacturing goods to services in financially underdeveloped economies. At the same time, the capital-output ratio declines by 15 percent in the presence of financial frictions—an effect driven primarily by the higher relative price of manufactured investment goods in financially underdeveloped economies (Buera, Kaboski, and Shin 2011).

Alleviation of financial constraints has dynamic effects on entrepreneurship rates and aggregate TFP. For instance, quadrupling access to financial services will increase entrepreneurship rates in Thailand by 4 percentage points (Giné and Townsend 2004). Financial deepening explains 70 percent of the overall TFP growth in Thailand from 1976 to 1996 (Jeong and Townsend 2007). Financial frictions also have an impact on the transition dynamics after growth-enhancing reforms: output growth converges slowly to a new equilibrium after reforms that trigger an efficient reallocation of resources (at half the speed of a neoclassical Solow model). Additionally, investment rates and TFP tend to be initially low and increase over time, consistent with the experience of miracle economies (Buera and Shin 2013).

Finally, financial market development could ensure that capital is channeled to those firms that are more productive and whose survival is highly dependent on the availability of finance. Technological improvements in financial intermediation may increase understanding of this channel. Costly verification

models enable financial intermediaries to select the amount of labor devoted to monitoring loan activity. In these models, the likelihood of detecting malfeasance depends on this decision and the technology used in the financial sector (Greenwood, Sanchez, and Wang 2010).

Model simulations suggest that technological improvements in financial intermediation account for about 29 percent of US growth (Greenwood, Sanchez, and Wang 2010). Further analysis shows that 45 percent of per capita growth in Taiwan, China, from 1974 to 2004 (6.3 percent per year) is attributed to financial development (and about 16 percent to TFP growth). Finally, the evidence suggests that the output per capita of Uganda could more than double if the country were to adopt global best practices in financial intermediation. However, this impact amounts to only 29 percent of the gap between Uganda's potential and actual output (Greenwood, Sanchez, and Wang 2013).

Wealth, Self-Financing, and Financial Frictions

Wealth is an important driver of occupational choice in the presence of financial frictions. Savings are incentivized by the higher rates of entrepreneurship stemming from financially constrained environments and the role played by wealth in relaxing these constraints. In turn, self-financing motives will depend on the persistence of the firm's productivity. There is ample evidence of highly persistent capital (and other asset) returns in Thailand (Pawasutipaisit and Townsend 2011); among manufacturing firms in the Republic of Korea (Midrigan and Xu 2014); and among industrial plants in Chile and Colombia (Moll 2014).

Financial frictions also play an important role in business entry decisions in low- and middle-income countries. Wealth and access to finance greatly influenced the business entry decisions of individuals in rural and semiurban regions of Thailand before the 1997 Asian financial crisis (Paulson and Townsend 2005). However, wealth did not play a significant role in the occupational choices of Thai individuals in the aftermath of the crisis (Nyshadam 2014). This finding points to a substantial relaxation of financial constraints.

Financial frictions tend to hinder factor reallocation. Self-financing with internal funds or through forward-looking behavior can potentially alleviate these constraints (Buera, Kaboski, and Shin 2011). It can potentially reduce capital misallocation resulting from financial frictions. But its impact may not be as large in sectors with larger-scale, substantial financing needs, such as manufacturing (Buera, Kaboski, and Shin 2015). On average, manufacturing firms are more vulnerable to financial frictions than services firms because the former have larger scale and financing needs, greater misallocation of capital and entrepreneurial talent, and larger distortions on entry and exit decisions. The evidence suggests that capital misallocation accounts for 90 percent of the effect of financial frictions

on services sector TFP (figure 4.6, panel a), while talent misallocation accounts for more than 50 percent of the effect on manufacturing sector TFP (figure 4.6, panel b) (Buera, Kaboski, and Shin 2011).

Financial frictions can act like an adjustment cost that prevents credit-constrained firms from fully adjusting their capital in response to productivity shocks, thus lowering aggregate TFP. The evidence shows that financial frictions can reduce TFP levels by up to 40 percent, and these losses are associated primarily with distortions on entry and technology adoption decisions in the modern sector of the economy (that is, manufacturing). TFP losses attributed to capital misallocation across manufacturing firms are smaller and account for a fraction of the overall efficiency losses related to the tightening of borrowing constraints (Midrigan and Xu 2014).

The inability of financial frictions to generate large losses from misallocation might be attributed to the fact that relatively

FIGURE 4.6 Modeling the Impact of Financial Frictions on Sector-Level TFP

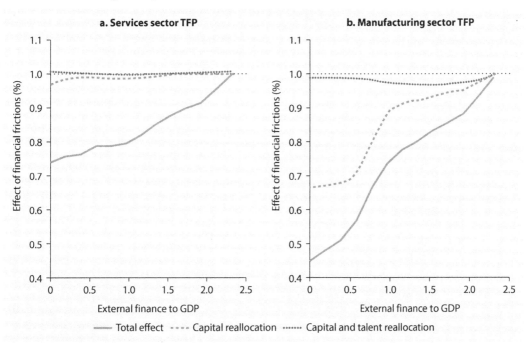

Source: Buera, Kaboski, and Shin 2011.
Note: The solid lines trace the total effect of financial frictions on the measured total factor productivity (TFP) of the service sector (panel a) and the manufacturing sector (panel b). Sector-level TFPs are normalized by their respective levels in the perfect-credit benchmark.

more-productive firms accumulate internal funds over time, enabling them to relax or overcome borrowing constraints. Entry and technology adoption decisions, on the other hand, entail large, long-lived investments with gradual payoffs that are difficult to finance using internal funds. Here, well-developed financial markets play a critical role in generating efficient entry and technology adoption—and thus increasing aggregate productivity.

Self-financing can help eliminate the capital misallocation arising from financial frictions if idiosyncratic productivity shocks are persistent. However, these efficiency gains will depend on the entrepreneurs' productivity levels and asset variation. Entrepreneurs who generate wealth out of previous business success can accumulate enough internal funds to self-finance their investment programs only if their high-productivity episodes are protracted. In the presence of persistent idiosyncratic productivity shocks, capital misallocation and TFP losses from financial frictions are small, but their speed of transition is slow. In fact, it takes a prolonged time to achieve allocative efficiency as the initial capital misallocation slowly unwinds over time (Moll 2014).

Financial Frictions and Poverty Traps

Financial frictions may lead to (individual and aggregate) poverty traps by distorting the entry decisions of entrepreneurs. Poverty traps can be driven by either *lower wages* (as individuals join the labor supply because they cannot afford the fixed costs to become entrepreneurs) or *lower interest rates* (as excess capital supply lowers interest rates and limits individuals' ability to save their way out of poverty over time) (Aghion and Bolton 1997; Banerjee and Newman 1993).

Poverty traps are driven not only by lower input prices but also by the self-financing motive. Initial wealth levels influence how rapidly self-financing materializes, while some individuals might not find it optimal to save for prolonged periods. In a low-interest-rate environment, those not intending to become entrepreneurs would prefer to dissave (Banerjee and Moll 2010; Buera 2008).

Productivity losses and poverty traps resulting from financial frictions have led to several antipoverty policy interventions. Asset grant programs have become commonplace in the policy agenda of low-income countries. Grant programs can help identify potential high-growth entrepreneurs and facilitate their growth.

In Nigeria, for example, grants with a competition component (for example, the You Win! program in 2011) increased entrepreneurial activity, including entry, survival employment, and profits (McKenzie 2017). Nearly 6,000 (out of 24,000 applicants) were selected for a four-day business-plan training course, and each winner received an average award of US$50,000. Grants were provided to both new and existing firms. After three years, new-firm winners were 37 percentage points more likely than the control group to be operating a business and 23 percentage points more likely to employ 10 or more workers. Existing-firm winners were 20 percentage points more likely to have survived and 21 percentage points more likely to employ 10 or more workers. Firms that received these grants tended to innovate more than the control group and earned higher sales and profits. They also acquired more inputs (capital and labor) without changes in business networks, mentors, self-efficacy, or uses of other sources of finance (McKenzie 2017).

On the other hand, the impact of microfinance programs in either urban or rural environments has been widely examined. Evidence comes from countries including *Bangladesh* (Pitt and Khandker 1998); *Ethiopia* (Tarozzi, Desai, and Johnson 2015); *India* (Banerjee et al. 2014; Field et al. 2013); *Kenya, Tanzania,* and *Uganda* (Greaney, Kaboski, and Van Leemput 2013); *the Philippines* (Karlan and Zinman 2010); and *Thailand* (Kaboski and Townsend 2011, 2012). These programs have low take-up rates, and they fail to report large, dramatic, or sustained increases in entrepreneurship, income, investment, or consumption. There is a large variation on the impact across programs, partly attributed to differences in the program design (Attanasio et al. 2015; Field and Pande 2008; Field et al. 2013; Greaney, Kaboski, and Van Leemput 2013). Finally, microloans have a substantial long-run impact on earnings for established entrepreneurs, while entrants tend to be marginal borrowers (Banerjee et al. 2014; Field et al. 2013; Greaney, Kaboski, and Van Leemput 2013).

Introduction of Digital Technologies in Banking and Finance

Mobile money services are an innovation that is boosting financial inclusion in Sub-Saharan Africa as they bring unbanked people into the formal financial system. Kenya's M-Pesa application, now the country's dominant retail payment platform, has been one of the most successful deployments of mobile money in the world.[20] Nearly 70 percent of Kenya's adult population adopted M-Pesa's mobile money services within four years after its launch in 2007.

Africa's Mobile Money Frontier

The rapid adoption of M-Pesa in Kenya has been attributed to the fast expansion of mobile-phone networks and the swift deployment and growth of a dense network of agents (end distributors of the service), which are small business outlets that transform cash into e-money and vice versa for customers (Jack and Suri 2014). The rapid uptake of digital finance in Kenya has also been attributed to the dominant position of the mobile network operator Safaricom, a progressive financial regulator (the Central Bank of Kenya), and multiple densely populated areas (Babcock 2015).

Kenyan households have been able to strengthen their informal risk-sharing networks and respond better to shocks by using mobile money services. For example, in response to an adverse income shock, consumption declined by 7 percent among nonusers of M-Pesa while the consumption of users remained invariant (Jack and Suri 2014). The consumption-smoothing abilities of M-Pesa users were attributed to their greater likelihood of receiving remittances in response to shocks (not only in greater amounts but also from more different types of people). This greater risk-sharing ability translated into increased saving, higher consumption, and occupational changes for user households.

Mobile money services have also led to changes in the composition of household assets in Kenya. Financial savings (that is, self-reported cash plus balances in bank accounts, savings clubs, and mobile money accounts) have increased in areas with a growing network of agents, especially among households headed by women. M-Pesa account holders tend to be less prone to using informal saving mechanisms (such as rotating savings and credit associations [ROSCAs]) and are more likely to access formal banking services (Mbiti and Weil 2016). M-Pesa registered users are also more likely to save than those who are not registered (Demombynes and Thegeya 2012).

In Burkina Faso, mobile money users are more likely to save for health emergencies—especially among the rural population, women, and less-educated individuals. This greater incidence of saving is attributed to the possibility of transferring money within subregions of the country using a secure platform (Ky, Rugemintwari, and Sauviat 2021). Greater access to mobile money services has also raised the likelihood of using a bank account rather than other financial products, possibly because banking institutions started collaborating or competing with M-Pesa. (For example, in 2012, M-Pesa launched the M-Shwari account, a microcredit and microsavings product, further discussed below.)

Saving can help microentrepreneurs increase their ability to respond to unexpected shocks and finance lumpy investments. In Tanzania, policy interventions that promote access to new mobile accounts increased savings and access to finance among women microentrepreneurs (Gautam et al. 2018). The Business Women Connect program, in partnership with an international nonprofit, TechnoServe, was evaluated through two interventions: The first was a registration and training session on M-Pawa—a mobile finance product that enables customers to (a) save money in an interest-bearing mobile savings account, and (b) access microloans based on good savings performance. The second intervention provided microentrepreneurs with intensive business skills training.

One year after the interventions, women saved substantially more through the mobile accounts, had greater access to microloans through the accounts, expanded their business portfolios through the creation of new businesses, and reported higher levels of empowerment and well-being (Gautam et al. 2018). In turn, the women's business and financial literacy has further bolstered the use of mobile savings accounts—thus incentivizing greater capital investment, labor effort, new products, and better business practices. These short-term impacts have yet to translate into greater profits, but the evidence suggests that access to mobile savings accounts has a greater impact on performance if it comes along with measures that alleviate the complementary human capital constraints faced by women.

Ripple Effects of Digital Banking and Finance

Mobile money services may have facilitated occupational choice in Kenya. Individuals living in areas with a larger increase in mobile money agents are more likely to work in business or sales and less likely to work in farming or have a secondary occupation. The expansion of M-Pesa has also enabled women to graduate from subsistence agriculture, cut down their reliance on multiple part-time jobs, and reduce the average household size (Suri and Jack 2016).

Access to mobile money in Kenya has also had a long-term impact on household welfare. Consumption per capita grew substantially among households living in areas with increased access to mobile money agents, and this effect was twice as large for households headed by women. Extreme poverty

also declined in areas with increased access to agents. The diffusion of mobile money services in Kenya helped lift about 194,000 households out of extreme poverty and induced 185,000 women to change their main occupation to business or retail services (Suri and Jack 2016).

Digital credit is also emerging as an option to short-term banking for microfinance loans. Mobile operators are partnering with financial institutions to provide small, short-term loans directly to customers through their existing mobile money ecosystem. M-Pesa partnered with Commercial Bank of Africa Ltd. (CBA) to launch M-Shwari products in November 2012. M-Shwari users can earn interest on savings products and qualify for CBA-backed loans. Digital loans have not only led to an expansion of credit for eligible households but also have strengthened household resilience. In response to a negative shock, households eligible for M-Shwari are less likely to forgo expenditures (Bharadwaj, Jack, and Suri 2019). The successful update of M-Shwari in Kenya has led to the development of similar products in other African countries—say, M-Pawa in Tanzania, which serviced 4.9 million borrowers in the first two years (Aglionby 2015), and MoKash in Uganda, which registered 1 million users in the first three months of its launch in 2016.

Digital credit has some advantages relative to traditional loans. It is approved more quickly and is readily available to customers without requiring an in-person vetting by the banking institution. Telecommunications data are used to develop alternative credit scores, thus facilitating the extension of loans without collateral or the traditional credit scores computed by credit bureaus. Digital-based credit scores may grant financial inclusion to individuals without credit scores in environments that lack verifiable credit history data or have nonexistent or ineffective credit bureaus.

On the other hand, digital credit also poses some challenges. The size of these loans is not as large, and they often have relatively high interest rates, multiple fees, and short repayment periods. For example, the average

M-Shwari loan is about US$12 with maturity of no more than 30 days (Cook and McKay 2015). Users are charged a fixed facilitation fee (instead of an interest rate). These fees are typically high—for instance, a monthly fee of 7.5 percent for M-Shwari (or 138 percent annually), or 10 percent per week for some Malawian digital loans (an annualized rate of 1,000 percent). Repayment of digital loans on time raises the probability of the user being granted larger loans with lower fees and longer maturity. It remains an open question whether the uptake of digital loans would decline if borrowers had more information on these products or were already fully informed about their costs (Francis, Blumenstock, and Robinson 2017).

Access to credit among women entrepreneurs is more restricted than among men because of inequality in the ownership of fixed assets (say, land or property) to serve as collateral to secure loans. However, developments in the financial technology industry can be harnessed to unlock the collateral challenge facing women entrepreneurs. Psychometric loan appraisal technologies—which predict the likelihood of loan repayment by entrepreneurs—have been used as an alternative to traditional collateral in Ethiopia (Alibhai et al. 2018). Specifically, they test the ability (business skills and intelligence) and willingness (ethics, honesty, attitudes, and beliefs) to repay a loan. Borrowers take an interactive, tablet-based test consisting of games, puzzles, and questions. If they score above a certain cutoff, they can obtain an uncollateralized loan of up to US$7,500. Customers scoring at a high threshold on the psychometric test were seven times more likely than lower-performing customers to repay their loans. This pilot is being currently scaled up in Madagascar and Zimbabwe and will be implemented next in Côte d'Ivoire, Nigeria, and Zambia. In the absence of collateral, and with limited information available on the creditworthiness of women borrowers, psychometric testing is a promising solution.

Finally, cash still dominates the transactions of many of the world's poor despite the increased use of digital financial services. In this context, efforts to foster digital literacy would help potential users to understand the interface with digital financial systems. Training sessions to understand the benefits of digital financial products and, more importantly, how to use them will increase the uptake of digital accounts and deposits (Holloway, Niazi, and Rouse 2017).

Notes

1. The selection channel also involves distortions that can affect individuals' occupational choices, such as (a) joining the formal sector as an entrepreneur (instead of as an informal entrepreneur or worker); and (b) agriculture versus nonagriculture jobs.
2. So far, the academic literature has identified some factors that can account for large effects of misallocation in agriculture; however, that is not the case for the extent of misallocation found in manufacturing (Restuccia and Rogerson 2017).
3. Revenue total factor productivity (TFPR) is typically defined as the ratio of firms' sales (or revenues) to input costs (appropriately weighted by their production elasticities). The marginal product of land is the additional output gained from adding another unit of land. This might apply to a farmer who purchases a field adjacent to the existing property or to a factory owner who increases the square footage of a facility.
4. Restuccia and Santaeulàlia-Llopis (2017) use the 2010–11 Malawi Integrated Survey of Agriculture (ISA). This survey has ample information on agricultural production (physical amounts by drop and plot) and the inputs used in all agricultural activities at the plot level. The data are representative at the national level, with a sampling frame based on the census and an original sample that includes 12,271 households (56,397 individuals), of whom 81 percent live in rural areas. Household land is measured as the sum of the size of each cultivated household plot, including rented-in land (about 12.5 percent of all cultivated land). Household farms, on average, cultivate 1.8 plots. Plot size is recorded in acres using the Global Positioning System (GPS) for 98 percent of plots. For each household, the amount of the land used for

agricultural production is measured regardless of the tenure status. The operational scale of farms is small: 78.3 percent of households operate less than 1 hectare, 96.1 percent of households operate less than 2 hectares, and only 0.3 percent of households operate more than 4 hectares. The average farm size is 0.83 hectares. The data contain detailed information on the quality of land for each plot used in every household. It distinguishes up to 11 dimensions of land, thus enabling the control for land quality when measuring household-farm productivity.

5. Chen (2017) builds a two-sector general equilibrium model where untitled land cannot be rented or traded across farmers, and it can only be used by those who were originally assigned to the plot. Simulations of the model show that titling all of the land raises agricultural productivity by 51.8 percent. About 42.5 percent of this productivity gain arises from land reallocation, while 57.5 percent reflects lower distortions in occupational choice.

6. An increase in average temperature of 2 degrees Celsius is expected to reduce agricultural production by almost 25 percent (IPCC 2015). Attenuating the collateral effects of climatic shocks (such as migration, occupational change, and land changes) will require reallocation of land and labor.

7. Data from satellite images can provide a range of climatic parameters in almost real time (such as rainfall, temperature, and so on) that can reach farmers in remote areas without measurement stations and enable them to better manage crop growth.

8. Fertilizer implementation features that have weakened the impacts of targeted ISPs include frequent late delivery of vouchers, politicized voucher allocation, and illegal collusion between leaders and agrodealers, among others.

9. At the Second Ordinary Assembly of the African Union in July 2003 in Maputo, Mozambique, African heads of state and government endorsed the "Maputo Declaration on Agriculture and Food Security in Africa." The Declaration's important provisions included a "commitment to the allocation of at least 10 percent of national budgetary resources to agriculture and rural development policy implementation within five years."

10. The 10 countries in the region with the largest ISPs (Burkina Faso, Ethiopia, Ghana, Kenya, Malawi, Mali, Nigeria, Senegal, Tanzania, and Zambia) spent US$1.02 billion on fertilizer subsidy programs in 2014 (Goyal and Nash 2017).

11. The main criteria for the distinction between "promoted" and "pioneer" are a sector's labor intensiveness and linkage to the agriculture sector. "Pioneer" activities are the top tier of activities that are agriculture-based and require a large outlay or have strong linkage effects. "Promoted" activities are of secondary priority and include rainfed agriculture, livestock development, nonbasic industries, and contracting.

12. Bigsten, Gebreeyesus, and Söderbom (2016) also found that output tariff reductions had no impact on firms' productivity in Ethiopia.

13. Increasing attention has been paid recently to the impact of infrastructure on poverty and inequality (Calderón and Servén 2004, 2010; De Ferranti et al. 2004; Estache 2005; World Bank 2005).

14. Infrastructure gaps in the Africa region are driven by a host of issues beyond the financing gap—for instance, the lack of commitment to sustainable tariffs in infrastructure services such as electric power, transportation, and water. Yet there is heavy reliance on public subsidies. The gap is also attributed to the poor performance of public utilities, characterized by weak management and political interference. There is also weak political support for sector reforms that can crowd-in private infrastructure investment, such as the opposition of state-owned enterprises to public-private partnerships. An in-depth discussion of the issues mentioned above—although highly relevant to understand infrastructure gaps in the region—goes beyond the scope of this report.

15. See Ndulu (2006) and Ayogu (2007) for diagnostic views on infrastructure and its long-term impact in Africa.

16. The estimation of a causal relationship exploits exogenous variation in outages, induced by an electricity rationing program, across small- and medium-size Ghanaian manufacturing firms.

17. Accounting for the likely endogeneity in the relationship between electrification and employment growth can be affected by endogenous criteria to place infrastructure

projects in certain regions. For instance, performance criteria can introduce biases in the comparison between electrified and nonelectrified areas (Dinkelman 2011).
18. Esoko is an agricultural profiling and messaging service, managed on the internet, that delivers market data via mobile phone. It is headquartered in Accra, Ghana.
19. Submarine internet cables at landing points on the African coast arrived gradually in the late 2000s and early 2010s.
20. "M-Pesa" is derived from M for mobile and "pesa" (Swahili for cash).

References

Abeberese, Ama Baafra, Charles Godfred Ackah, and Patrick Opoku Asuming. 2019. "Productivity Losses and Firm Responses to Electricity Shortages: Evidence from Ghana." *World Bank Economic Review* 35 (1): 1–18.

Ackah, Charles Godfred, Patrick Opoku Asuming, and Derrick Abudu. 2018. "Misallocation of Resources and Productivity: The Case of Ghana." Unpublished manuscript, Institute of Statistical, Social and Economic Research, University of Ghana.

Aghion, Philippe, and Patrick Bolton. 1997. "A Theory of Trickle-Down Growth and Development." *Review of Economic Studies* 64 (2): 151–72.

Aglionby, John. 2015. "New Payments Service to Launch in Kenya." *Financial Times*, October 27, 2015.

Aitken, Roger. 2017. "IBM & Walmart Launching Blockchain Food Safety Alliance in China with Fortune 500's JD.com." *Forbes*, December 14, 2017.

Aker, Jenny C. 2008. "Does Digital Divide or Provide? The Impact of Cell Phones on Grain Markets in Niger." Working Paper 177, Bureau for Research and Economic Analysis of Development (BREAD), London, UK.

Aker, Jenny C. 2010. "Information from Markets Near and Far: Mobile Phones and Agricultural Markets in Niger." *American Economic Journal: Applied Economics* 2 (3): 46–59.

Aker, Jenny C., and Marcel Fafchamps. 2015. "Mobile Phone Coverage and Producer Markets: Evidence from West Africa." *World Bank Economic Review* 29 (2): 262–92.

Alby, Philippe, Jean-Jacques Dethier, and Stéphane Straub. 2013. "Firms Operating under Electricity Constraints in Developing Countries." *World Bank Economic Review* 27 (1): 109–32.

Alibhai, Salman, Niklas Buehren, Rachel Coleman, Markus Goldstein, and Francesco Strobbe. 2018. "Disruptive Finance: Using Psychometrics to Overcome Collateral Constraints in Ethiopia." Working paper, World Bank, Washington, DC.

Allcott, Hunt, Allan Collard-Wexler, and Stephen D. O'Connell. 2016. "How Do Electricity Shortages Affect Industry? Evidence from India." *American Economic Review* 106 (3): 587–624.

Amiti, Mary, and Jozef Konings. 2007. "Trade Liberalization, Intermediate Inputs, and Productivity: Evidence from Indonesia." *American Economic Review* 97 (5): 1611–38.

Aragón, Fernando M., Francisco Oteiza, and Juan Pablo Rud. 2018. "Climate Change and Agriculture: Farmer Adaptation to Extreme Heat." Working Paper W18/06, Institute for Fiscal Studies, London.

Aragón, Fernando M., and Juan Pablo Rud. 2018. "Weather, Productivity, and Factor Misallocation: Evidence from Ugandan Farmers." Background paper, World Bank, Washington, DC.

Arkolakis, Costas, Arnaud Costinot, Dave Donaldson, and Andrés Rodríguez-Clare. 2019. "The Elusive Pro-Competitive Effects of Trade." *Review of Economic Studies* 86 (1): 46–80.

Asatryan, Zareh, and Andreas Peichl. 2017. "Responses of Firms to Tax, Administrative and Accounting Rules: Evidence from Armenia." Working Paper 6754, Center for Economic Studies and ifo Institute (CESifo), Munich.

Aschauer, David A. 1989. "Is Public Expenditure Productive?" *Journal of Monetary Economics* 23 (2): 177–200.

Asenso-Okyere, Kwadwo, and Daniel Ayalew Mekonnen. 2012. "The Importance of ICTs in the Provision of Information for Improving Agricultural Productivity and Rural Incomes in Africa." Working Paper 2012-015, United Nations Development Programme, Regional Bureau for Africa, New York.

Attanasio, Orazio, Britta Augsburg, Ralph De Haas, Emla Fitzsimons, and Heike Harmgart. 2015. "The Impacts of Microfinance: Evidence from Joint-Liability Lending in Mongolia." *American Economic Journal: Applied Economics* 7 (1): 90–122.

Aw, Bee Yan, Mark J. Roberts, and Daniel Yi Xu. 2011. "R&D Investment, Exporting, and Productivity Dynamics." *American Economic Review* 101 (4): 1312–44.

Ayogu, Melvin D. 1999. "Before Prebendalism: A Positive Analysis of Core Infrastructure Investment in a Developing Fiscal Federalism." *African Development Review* 11 (2): 169–98.

Ayogu, Melvin D. 2007. "Infrastructure and Economic Development in Africa: A Review." *Journal of African Economies* 16 (Suppl. 1): 75–126.

Babcock, Bruce A. 2015. "Using Cumulative Prospect Theory to Explain Anomalous Crop Insurance Coverage Choice." *American Journal of Agricultural Economics* 97 (5): 1371–84.

Bachas, Pierre, Roberto N. Fattal-Jaef, and Anders Jensen. 2018. "Size-Dependent Tax Enforcement and Compliance: Global Evidence and Aggregate Implications." Policy Research Working Paper 8363, World Bank, Washington, DC.

Baldwin, Richard E., and Toshihiro Okubo. 2006. "Heterogeneous Firms, Agglomeration and Economic Geography: Spatial Selection and Sorting." *Journal of Economic Geography* 6 (3): 323–46.

Banerjee, Abhijit V., and Esther Duflo. 2005. "Growth Theory through the Lens of Development Economics." In *Handbook of Economic Growth, Vol. 1A,* edited by Philippe Aghion and Steven N. Durlauf, 473–552. Amsterdam: Elsevier.

Banerjee, Abhijit V., Emily Breza, Esther Duflo, Rachel Glennerster, and Cynthia G. Kinnan. 2014. "Does Microfinance Foster Business Growth? The Importance of Entrepreneurial Heterogeneity." Unpublished manuscript, Massachusetts Institute of Technology, Cambridge, MA.

Banerjee, Abhijit V., and Andrew F. Newman. 1993. "Occupational Choice and the Process of Development." *Journal of Political Economy* 101 (2): 274–98.

Banerjee, Abhijit V., and Benjamin Moll. 2010. "Why Does Misallocation Persist?" *American Economic Journal: Macroeconomics* 2 (1): 189–206.

Beck, Thorsten, Asli Demirgüç-Kunt, and Ross Levine. 2007. "Finance, Inequality and the Poor." *Journal of Economic Growth* 12: 27–49.

Beck, Thorsten, Asli Demirgüç-Kunt, and Ross Levine. 2009. "Financial Institutions and Markets across Countries and over Time: Data and Analysis." Policy Research Working Paper 4943, World Bank, Washington, DC.

Beck, Thorsten, Asli Demirgüç-Kunt, and Vladimir Maksimovic. 2005. "Financial and Legal Constraints to Firm Growth: Does Firm Size Matter?" *Journal of Finance* 60 (1): 137–77.

Beck, Thorsten, Ross Levine, and Norman Loayza. 2000. "Finance and the Sources of Growth." *Journal of Financial Economics* 58 (1–2): 261–300.

Behar, Alberto, and Phil Manners. 2008. "Logistics and Exports." Working Paper 2008-13, Centre for the Study of African Economies (CSAE), Oxford University.

Bento, Pedro, and Diego Restuccia. 2017. "Misallocation, Establishment Size, and Productivity." *American Economic Journal: Macroeconomics* 9 (3): 267–303.

Bernard, Andrew B., Stephen J. Redding, and Peter K. Schott. 2010. "Multiple-Product Firms and Product Switching." *American Economic Review* 100 (1): 70–97.

Bharadwaj, Prashant, William Jack, and Tavneet Suri. 2019. "Fintech and Household Resilience to Shocks: Evidence from Digital Loans in Kenya." Working Paper 25604, National Bureau of Economic Research, Cambridge, MA.

Bigsten, Arne, Mulu Gebreeyesus, and Måns Söderbom. 2016. "Tariffs and Firm Performance in Ethiopia." *Journal of Development Studies* 52 (7): 986–1001.

Bloom, Nicholas, Benn Eifert, Aprajit Mahajan, David McKenzie, and John Roberts. 2013. "Does Management Matter? Evidence from India." *Quarterly Journal of Economics* 128 (1): 1–51.

Boopen, Seetanah. 2006. "Transport Infrastructure and Economic Growth: Evidence from Africa Using Dynamic Panel Estimates." *Empirical Economics Letters* 5 (1): 37–52.

Bresnahan, Lauren, Ian Coxhead, Jeremy Foltz, and Tewodaj Mogues. 2016. "Does Freer Trade *Really* Lead to Productivity Growth? Evidence from Africa." *World Development* 86: 18–29.

Brockmeyer, Anne, and Marco Hernandez. 2016. "Taxation, Information, and Withholding: Evidence from Costa Rica." Policy Research

Working Paper 7600, World Bank, Washington, DC.

Buera, Francisco J. 2008. "Persistency of Poverty, Financial Frictions, and Entrepreneurship." Unpublished manuscript, Northwestern University, Evanston, IL.

Buera, Francisco J., Joseph P. Kaboski, and Yongseok Shin. 2011. "Finance and Development: A Tale of Two Sectors." *American Economic Review* 101 (5): 1964–2002.

Buera, Francisco J., Joseph P. Kaboski, and Yongseok Shin. 2015. "Entrepreneurship and Financial Frictions: A Macrodevelopment Perspective." *Annual Review of Economics* 7 (1): 409–36.

Buera, Francisco J., Benjamin Moll, and Yongseok Shin. 2013. "Well-Intended Policies." *Review of Economic Dynamics* 16 (1): 216–30.

Buera, Francisco J., and Yongseok Shin. 2013. "Financial Frictions and the Persistence of History: A Quantitative Exploration." *Journal of Political Economy* 121 (2): 221–72.

Bustos, Paula. 2011. "Trade Liberalization, Exports, and Technology Upgrading: Evidence on the Impact of MERCOSUR on Argentinian Firms." *American Economic Review* 101 (1): 304–40.

Calderón, César, Catalina Cantú, and Punam Chuhan-Pole. 2018. "Infrastructure Development in Sub-Saharan Africa: A Scorecard." Policy Research Working Paper 8425, World Bank, Washington, DC.

Calderón, César, and Luis Servén. 2004. "The Effects of Infrastructure Development on Growth and Income Distribution." Policy Research Working Paper 270, World Bank, Washington, DC.

Calderón, César, and Luis Servén. 2010. "Infrastructure and Economic Development in Sub-Saharan Africa." *Journal of African Economies* 19 (Suppl. 1): i13–i87.

Carleton, Tamma A., and Solomon M. Hsiang. 2016. "Social and Economic Impacts of Climate." *Science* 353 (6304): aad9837.

Carter, Michael R., Rachid Laajaj, and Dean Yang. 2014. "Subsidies and the Persistence of Technology Adoption: Field Experimental Evidence from Mozambique." Working Paper 20465, National Bureau of Economic Research, Cambridge, MA.

Casaburi, Lorenzo, Rachel Glennerster, and Tavneet Suri. 2013. "Rural Roads and Intermediated Trade: Regression Discontinuity Evidence from Sierra Leone." Unpublished manuscript, Harvard University, Cambridge, MA.

Chen, Chaoran. 2017. "Untitled Land, Occupational Choice, and Agricultural Productivity." *American Economic Journal: Macroeconomics* 9 (4): 91–121.

Chen, Chaoran. 2020. "Technology Adoption, Capital Deepening, and International Productivity Differences." *Journal of Development Economics* 143: 10238.

Chen, Chaoran, and Diego Restuccia. 2018. "Agricultural Productivity Growth in Africa." Background paper, World Bank, Washington, DC.

Chen, Chaoran, Diego Restuccia, and Raül Santaeulàlia-Llopis. 2017. "The Effects of Land Markets on Resource Allocation and Agricultural Productivity." Working Paper 24034, National Bureau of Economic Research, Cambridge, MA.

Chen, Shuai, Xiaoguang Chen, and Jintao Xu. 2016. "Impacts of Climate Change on Agriculture: Evidence from China." *Journal of Environmental Economics and Management* 76: 105–24.

Cirera, Xavier, Roberto Fattal-Jaef, Nicolas P. P. Gonne, and Hibret Maemir. 2018. "Elusive Missing Middle: The Size Distribution of Firms in Sub-Saharan Africa." Unpublished manuscript, World Bank, Washington, DC.

Cirera, Xavier, Roberto Fattal-Jaef, and Hibret Maemir. 2018. "Taxing the Good? Distortions, Misallocation, and Productivity in Sub-Saharan Africa." *World Bank Economic Review* 34 (1): 75–100.

Coldham, Simon. 2000. "Land Reform and Customary Rights: The Case of Uganda." *Journal of African Law* 44 (1): 65–77.

Collard-Wexler, Allan, and Jan De Loecker. 2015. "Reallocation and Technology: Evidence from the US Steel Industry." *American Economic Review* 105(1): 131–71.

Cook, Tamara, and Claudia McKay. 2015. "How M-Shwari Works: The Story So Far." Access to Finance Forum Report No. 10, Consultative Group to Assist the Poor (CGAP), Washington, DC.

De Ferranti, David, Guillermo E. Perry, Francisco H. G. Ferreira, and Michael Walton. 2004. *Inequality in Latin America: Breaking with History?* Washington, DC: World Bank.

Deichmann, Uwe, Aparajita Goyal, and Deepak Mishra. 2016. "Will Digital Technologies Transform Agriculture in Developing Countries?" *Agricultural Economics* 47 (S1): 67–100.

Deininger, Klaus, Daniel Ayalew Ali, and Tekie Alemu. 2008. "Assessing the Functioning of Land Rental Markets in Ethiopia. *Economic Development and Cultural Change* 57 (1): 21–33.

De Loecker, Jan. 2013. "Detecting Learning by Exporting." *American Economic Journal: Microeconomics* 5 (3): 1–21.

De Loecker, Jan, and Pinelopi Koujianou Goldberg. 2014. "Firm Performance in a Global Market." *Annual Review of Economics* 6 (1): 201–27.

Demirgüç-Kunt, Asli, Erik Feyen, and Ross Levine. 2013. "The Evolving Importance of Banks and Securities Markets." *World Bank Economic Review* 27 (3): 476–90.

Demirgüç-Kunt, Asli, Inessa Love, and Vladimir Maksimovic. 2006. "Business Environment and the Incorporation Decision." *Journal of Banking and Finance* 30 (11): 2967–93.

Demombynes, Gabriel, and Aaron Thegeya. 2012. "Kenya's Mobile Revolution and the Promise of Mobile Savings." Policy Research Working Paper 5988, World Bank, Washington, DC.

D'Erasmo, Pablo, and Hernan Moscoso Boedo. 2012. "Financial Structure, Informality and Development." *Journal of Monetary Economics* 59 (3): 286–302.

Diao, Xinshen, and Yukitsugu Yanoma. 2003. "Exploring Regional Dynamics in Sub-Saharan African Agriculture." Discussion Paper No. 2, Development Strategy and Governance Division, International Food Policy Research Institute, Washington, DC.

Dinkelman, Taryn. 2011. "The Effects of Rural Electrification on Employment: New Evidence from South Africa." *American Economic Review* 101 (7): 3078–3108.

Eberts, Randall W., and Daniel P. McMillen. 1999. "Agglomeration Economies and Urban Public Infrastructure." In *Handbook of Regional and Urban Economics, Volume 3: Applied Urban Economics*, edited by Paul C. Cheshire and Edwin S. Mills, 1455–95. Amsterdam: Elsevier Science B.V.

Ekekwe, Ndubuisi. 2017. "How Digital Technology Is Changing Farming in Africa." *Harvard Business Review*, May 18, 2017.

Elbadawi, Ibrahim, Taye Mengistae, and Albert G. Zeufack. 2006. "Market Access, Supplier Access, and Africa's Manufactured Exports: A Firm Level Analysis." *Journal of International Trade & Economic Development* 15 (4): 493–523.

Escribano, Alvaro, J. Luis Guasch, and Jorge Pena. 2010. "Assessing the Impact of Infrastructure Quality on Firm Productivity in Africa Cross-Country Comparisons Based on Investment: Climate Surveys from 1999 to 2005." Policy Research Working Paper 5191, World Bank, Washington, DC.

Estache, Antonio. 2005. "What Do We Know about Sub-Saharan Africa's Infrastructure and the Impact of Its 1990s Reforms?" Working paper, World Bank, Washington, DC.

Estache, Antonio, and Maria Vagliasindi. 2007. "Infrastructure for Accelerated Growth for Ghana: Needs and Challenges." Background paper for "Ghana: Meeting the Challenge of Accelerated and Shared Growth." Ghana Country Economic Memorandum, Report No. 40934-GH, World Bank, Washington, DC.

Fafchamps, Marcel, David McKenzie, Simon R. Quinn, and Christopher Woodruff. 2011. "When Is Capital Enough to Get Female Microenterprises Growing? Evidence from a Randomized Experiment in Ghana." Working Paper 17207, National Bureau of Economic Research, Cambridge, MA.

Fafchamps, Marcel, and Bart Minten. 2012. "Impact of SMS-Based Agricultural Information on Indian Farmers." *World Bank Economic Review* 26 (3): 383–414.

Fajnzylber, Pablo. 2007. "Informality, Productivity, and the Firm." In *Informality: Exit and Exclusion*, edited by Guillermo E. Perry, William F. Maloney, Omar S. Arias, Pablo Fajnzylber, Andrew D. Mason, and Jaime Saavedra-Chanduvi, 157–78. Washington, DC: World Bank.

Feenstra, Robert C., and David E. Weinstein. 2017. "Globalization, Markups, and the U.S. Price Level." *Journal of Political Economy* 125 (4): 1040–74.

Field, Erica, and Rohini Pande. 2008. "Repayment Frequency and Default in Microfinance: Evidence from India." *Journal of the European Economic Association* 6 (2–3): 501–09.

Field, Erica, Rohini Pande, John Papp, and Natalia Rigol. 2013. "Does the Classic Microfinance Model Discourage Entrepreneurship among the Poor? Experimental Evidence from

India." *American Economic Review* 103 (6): 2196–2226.

Francis, Eilin, Joshua Blumenstock, and Jonathan Robinson. 2017. "Digital Credit: A Snapshot of the Current Landscape and Open Research Questions." Working Paper No. 516, BREAD, London.

Fujita, Masahisa, and Jacques-François Thisse. 2002. *Economics of Agglomeration: Cities, Industrial Location, and Regional Growth.* Cambridge: Cambridge University Press.

Gabler, Alain, and Markus Poschke. 2013. "Experimentation by Firms, Distortions, and Aggregate Productivity." *Review of Economic Dynamics* 16 (1): 26–38.

Gandhi, Rikin, Rajesh Veeraraghavan, Kentaro Toyama, and Vanaja Ramprasad. 2009. "Digital Green: Participatory Video and Mediated Instruction for Agricultural Extension." *Information Technologies & International Development* 5 (1): 1–15.

Garcia-Milà, Teresa, and Therese J. McGuire. 1992. "The Contribution of Publicly Provided Inputs to States' Economies." *Regional Science and Urban Economics* 22 (2): 229–41.

Gautam, Bastian, Iacopo Bianchi, Markus Goldstein, and Joao Montalvao. 2018. "Short-Term Impacts of Improved Access to Mobile Savings, with and without Business Training: Experimental Evidence from Tanzania." Working Paper 478, Center for Global Development, Washington, DC.

Gebresilasse, Mesay M. 2016. "Industrial Policy and Misallocation in the Ethiopian Manufacturing Sector." Unpublished manuscript, Boston University.

Gebrewolde, Tewodros Makonnen, and James Rockey. 2015. "The Global Gender Gap in Labor Income." Discussion Papers in Economics 17/14, Division of Economics, School of Business, University of Leicester.

Giné, Xavier, and Robert Townsend. 2004. "Evaluation of Financial Liberalization: A General Equilibrium Model with Constrained Occupation Choice." *Journal of Development Economics* 74 (2): 269–307.

Goldberg, Pinelopi K., Amit Khandelwal, Nina Pavcnik, and Petia Topalova. 2009. "Trade Liberalization and New Imported Inputs." *American Economic Review* 99: 494–500.

Goldberg, Pinelopi K., Amit Khandelwal, Nina Pavcnik, and Petia Topalova. 2010. "Imported Intermediate Inputs and Domestic Product Growth: Evidence from India." *Quarterly Journal of Economics* 125 (4): 1727–67.

Gollin, Douglas. 2006. "Do Taxes on Large Firms Impede Growth? Evidence from Ghana." *Bulletins* No. 7488, Center for Economic Development, University of Minnesota, Duluth.

Gollin, Douglas, and Richard Rogerson. 2014. "Productivity, Transport Costs and Subsistence Agriculture." *Journal of Development Economics* 107: 38–48.

Gollin, Douglas, and Richard Rogerson. 2016. "Agriculture, Roads, and Economic Development in Uganda." In *African Successes, Volume IV: Sustainable Growth,* edited by Sebastian Edwards, Simon Johnson, and David N. Weil, 69–110. Chicago: University of Chicago Press for the National Bureau of Economic Research.

Goyal, Aparajita. 2018. "Subsidies and Productivity." Background note for the Boosting Productivity in Sub-Saharan Africa project, World Bank, Washington, DC.

Goyal, Aparajita, and John Nash. 2017. *Reaping Richer Returns: Public Spending Priorities for African Agriculture Productivity Growth.* Africa Development Forum Series. Washington, DC: World Bank.

Graham, Daniel J. 2007. "Agglomeration, Productivity and Transport Investment." *Journal of Transport Economics and Policy* 41 (3): 317–43.

Greaney, Brian, Joseph P. Kaboski, and Eva Van Leemput. 2013. "Can Self-Help Groups Really Be 'Self-Help'?" Working Paper 18970, National Bureau of Economic Research, Cambridge, MA.

Greenwood, Jeremy, Juan M. Sanchez, and Cheng Wang. 2010. "Financing Development: The Role of Information Costs." *American Economic Review* 100 (4): 1875–91.

Greenwood, Jeremy, Juan M. Sanchez, and Cheng Wang. 2013. "Quantifying the Impact of Financial Development on Economic Development." *Review of Economic Dynamics* 16 (1): 194–215.

Guner, Nezih, Gustavo Ventura, and Yi Xu. 2008. "Macroeconomic Implications of Size-Dependent Policies." *Review of Economic Dynamics* 11 (4): 721–44.

Halpern, László, Miklós Koren, and Adam Szeidl. 2015. "Imported Inputs and Productivity." *American Economic Review* 105 (12): 3660–3703.

Hjort, Jonas, and Jonas Poulsen. 2019. "The Arrival of Fast Internet and Employment in Africa." *American Economic Review* 109 (3): 1032–79.

Holloway, Kyle, Zarah Niazi, and Rebecca Rouse. 2017. "Women's Economic Empowerment Through Financial Inclusion: A Review of Existing Evidence and Remaining Knowledge Gaps." Paper, Financial Inclusion Program, Innovations for Poverty Action, New Haven, CT.

Hulten, Charles R., and Robert M. Schwab. 1991. "Public Capital Formation and the Growth of Regional Manufacturing Industries." *National Tax Journal* 44 (4): 121–34.

IFC (International Finance Corporation). 2018. *Working with Smallholders: A Handbook for Firms Building Sustainable Supply Chains.* Washington, DC: World Bank.

IMF (International Monetary Fund). 2014. *World Economic Outlook, October.* Washington, DC: IMF.

IMF (International Monetary Fund). 2017. *Fiscal Monitor, April 2017: Achieving More with Less.* Washington, DC: IMF.

IPCC (Intergovernmental Panel on Climate Change). 2015. *Climate Change 2014: Synthesis Report. Contribution of Working Groups I, II and III to the Fifth Assessment Report of the Intergovernmental Panel on Climate Change.* Geneva: IPCC.

Jack, William, and Tavneet Suri. 2014. "Risk Sharing and Transactions Costs: Evidence from Kenya's Mobile Money Revolution." *American Economic Review* 104 (1): 183–223.

Jensen, Robert. 2007. "The Digital Provide: Information (Technology), Market Performance, and Welfare in the South Indian Fisheries Sector." *Quarterly Journal of Economics* 122 (3): 879–924.

Jeong, Hyeok, and Robert M. Townsend. 2007. "Sources of TFP Growth: Occupational Choice and Financial Deepening." *Economic Theory* 32 (1): 179–221.

Kaboski, Joseph P., and Robert M. Townsend. 2011. "A Structural Evaluation of a Large-Scale Quasi-Experimental Microfinance Initiative." *Econometrica* 79 (5): 1357–1406.

Kaboski, Joseph P., and Robert M. Townsend. 2012. "The Impact of Credit on Village Economies." *American Economic Journal: Applied Economics* 4 (2): 98–133.

Kamara, Ibrahim B. 2006. "Economic Growth and Government Infrastructure Expenditure in Sub-Saharan Africa." Unpublished manuscript, University of Cape Town, South Africa.

Kalemli-Ozcan, Sebnem, and Bent E. Sørensen. 2016. "Misallocation, Property Rights, and Access to Finance: Evidence from within and across Africa." In *African Successes, Volume III: Modernization and Development*, edited by Sebastian Edwards, Simon Johnson, and David N. Weil, 183–211. Chicago: University of Chicago Press for the National Bureau for Economic Research.

Karippacheril, Tina George, Luz Diaz Rios, and Lara Srivastava. 2011. "Module 12: Improving Food Safety and Traceability." In e-sourcebook, "ICT in Agriculture: Connecting Smallholders to Knowledge, Networks, and Institutions." Report No. 64605, World Bank, Washington, DC.

Karlan, Dean, and Jonathan Zinman. 2010. "Expanding Credit Access: Using Randomized Supply Decisions to Estimate the Impacts." *Review of Financial Studies* 23 (1): 433–64.

Kherallah, Mylene, Christopher L. Delgado, Eleni Zaude Gabre-Madhin, Nicholas Minot, and Michael Johnson. 2002. *Reforming Agricultural Markets in Africa: Achievements and Challenges.* Washington, DC: International Food Policy Research Institute.

Kishindo, Paul. 2011. "The Village Head and the Problem of Role Relevance in the Context of Declining Rural Land Availability in Malawi." Working Paper No. 2, Centre for Social Research, Chancellor College, Zomba, Malawi.

Kuralatne, Chandi. 2006. "Social and Economic Infrastructure Impacts on Economic Growth in South Africa." Paper presented at the Development Policy Research Unit (DPRU) Conference, Johannesburg, South Africa, October 18–20.

Ky, Serge, Clovis Rugemintwari, and Alain Sauviat. 2021. "Friends or Foes? Mobile Money Interaction with Formal and Informal Finance." *Telecommunications Policy* 45 (1): 102057.

Lane, Philip R., and Gian-Maria Milesi-Ferretti. 2007. "The External Wealth of Nations Mark II: Revised and Extended Estimates of Foreign Assets and Liabilities, 1970–2004." *Journal of International Economics* 73 (2): 223–50.

Lane, Philip R., and Gian-Maria Milesi-Ferretti. 2017. "International Financial Integration in the Aftermath of the Global Financial Crisis." Working Paper 17/115, International Monetary Fund, Washington, DC.

Lagakos, David, and Michael E. Waugh. 2013. "Selection, Agriculture, and Cross-Country Productivity Differences." *American Economic Review* 103 (2): 948–80.

Leal Ordóñez, Julio C. 2014. "Tax Collection, the Informal Sector, and Productivity." *Review of Economic Dynamics* 17 (2): 262–86.

Levine, Ross. 2005. "Finance and Growth: Theory and Evidence." In *Handbook of Economic Growth, Vol. 1A*, edited by Philippe Aghion and Steven Durlauf, 865–934. Amsterdam: Elsevier.

Lileeva, Alla, and Daniel Trefler. 2010. "Improved Access to Foreign Markets Raises Plant-Level Productivity . . . for Some Plants." *Quarterly Journal of Economics* 125 (3): 1051–99.

Limao, Nuno, and Anthony J. Venables. 2001. "Infrastructure, Geographical Disadvantage, Transport Costs, and Trade." *World Bank Economic Review* 15 (3): 451–79.

Lio, Monchi, and Meng-Chun Liu. 2006. "ICT and Agricultural Productivity: Evidence from Cross-Country Data." *Agricultural Economics* 34 (3): 221–28.

Lucas, Robert E., Jr. 1978. "On the Size Distribution of Business Firms." *Bell Journal of Economics* 9 (2): 508–23.

Lumbila, K. N. 2005. "What Makes DFI Work? A Panel Analysis of the Growth Effects of FDI in Africa." African Region Working Paper Series, No. 80, World Bank, Washington, DC.

Mayer, Thierry, Marc J. Melitz, and Gianmarco I. P. Ottaviano. 2014. "Market Size, Competition, and the Product Mix of Exporters." *American Economic Review* 104 (2): 495–536.

Mbiti, Isaac, and David N. Weil. 2016. "Mobile Banking: The Impact of M-Pesa in Kenya." In *African Successes, Volume III: Modernization and Development*, edited by Sebastian Edwards, Simon Johnson, and David N. Weil, 247–93. Chicago: University of Chicago Press.

McKenzie, David J. 2017. "Identifying and Spurring High-Growth Entrepreneurship: Experimental Evidence from a Business Plan Competition." *American Economic Review* 107 (8): 2278–2307.

McKenzie, David J., and Christopher Woodruff. 2008. "Experimental Evidence on Returns to Capital and Access to Finance in Mexico." *World Bank Economic Review* 22 (3): 457–82.

Melitz, Marc J., and Gianmarco I. P. Ottaviano. 2008. "Market Size, Trade, and Productivity." *Review of Economic Studies* 75 (1): 295–316.

Melitz, Marc J., and Stephen J. Redding. 2014. "Heterogenous Firms and Trade." In *Handbook of International Economics, Vol. 4*, edited by Gita Gopinath, Elhanan Helpman, and Kenneth Rogoff, 1–54. Amsterdam: Elsevier.

Melitz, Marc J., and Daniel Trefler. 2012. "Gains from Trade When Firms Matter." *Journal of Economic Perspectives* 26 (2): 91–118.

Mengistae, Taye A., and Francis Teal. 1998. "Trade Liberalization, Regional Integration and Firm Performance in Africa's Manufacturing Sector: A Report to European Commission." REP98-1, Centre for the Study of African Economies, University of Oxford.

Mhlanga, Samuel V., and Neil A. Rankin. 2015. "Does Technical Efficiency Dominate Resource Reallocation in Aggregate Productivity Growth? Firm-Level Evidence from the Manufacturing Sector in Swaziland." Unpublished manuscript, Department of Economics, University of Stellenbosch, South Africa.

Midrigan, Virgiliu, and Daniel Y. Xu. 2014. "Finance and Misallocation: Evidence from Plant-Level Data." *American Economic Review* 104 (2): 422–58.

Moll, Benjamin. 2014. "Productivity Losses from Financial Frictions: Can Self-Financing Undo Capital Misallocation?" *American Economic Review* 104 (10): 3186–3221.

Morris, Brian. 2016. *An Environmental History of Southern Malawi: Land and People of the Shire Highlands*. Cham, Switzerland: Palgrave Macmillan.

Morris, Michael, Valerie A. Kelly, Ron J. Kopicki, and Derek Byerlee. 2007. *Fertilizer Use in African Agriculture: Lessons Learned and Good Practice Guidelines*. Directions in Development Series. Washington, DC: World Bank.

Munnell, Alicia H. 1992. "Policy Watch: Infrastructure Investment and Economic Growth." *Journal of Economic Perspectives* 6 (4): 189–98.

Muto, Megumi, and Takashi Yamano. 2009. "The Impact of Mobile Phone Coverage Expansion on Market Participation: Panel Data Evidence from Uganda." *World Development* 37 (12): 1887–96.

Nakasone, Eduardo, Maximo Torero, and Bart Minten. 2014. "The Power of Information: The ICT Revolution in Agricultural Development." *Annual Review of Resource Economics* 6 (1): 533–50.

Ndulu, Benno J. 2006. "Infrastructure, Regional Integration and Growth in Sub-Saharan Africa: Dealing with the Disadvantages of Geography and Sovereign Fragmentation." *Journal of African Economies* 15 (suppl 2): 212–44.

Nguimkeu, Pierre E. 2015. "An Estimated Model of Informality with Constrained Entrepreneurship." Unpublished manuscript, Department of Economics, Georgia State University, Atlanta.

Nyshadam, Anant. 2014. "Learning about Comparative Advantage in Entrepreneurship: Evidence from Thailand." Unpublished manuscript, Department of Economics, University of Southern California, Los Angeles.

Oseni, Musiliu O. 2019. "Costs of Unreliable Electricity to African Firms." Brief, Energy Hub for Growth, Nigerian Electricity Regulatory Commission.

Paulson, Anna L., and Robert M. Townsend. 2005. "Financial Constraints and Entrepreneurship: Evidence from the Thai Financial Crisis." Federal Reserve Bank of Chicago, *Economic Perspectives* 3Q/2005: 34–48.

Pavcnik, Nina. 2002. "Trade Liberalization, Exit, and Productivity Improvements: Evidence from Chilean Plants." *Review of Economic Studies* 69 (1): 245–76.

Pawasutipaisit, Anan, and Robert M. Townsend. 2011. "Wealth Accumulation and Factors Accounting for Success." *Journal of Econometrics* 161 (1): 56-81.

Perkins, Peter, Johann Fedderke, and John Luiz. 2005. "An Analysis of Economic Infrastructure Investment in South Africa." *South African Journal of Economics* 73 (2): 211–28.

Pitt, Mark M., and Shahidur R. Khandker. 1998. "The Impact of Group-Based Credit Programs on Poor Households in Bangladesh: Does the Gender of Participants Matter?" *Journal of Political Economy* 106 (5): 958–96.

Place, Frank, and Keijiro Otsuka. 2002. "Land Tenure Systems and Their Impacts on Agricultural Investments and Productivity in Uganda." *Journal of Development Studies* 38 (6): 105–28.

Poczter, Sharon. 2017. "You Can't Count on Me: The Impact of Electricity Unreliability on Productivity." *Agricultural and Resource Economics Review* 46 (3): 579–602.

Rajan, Raghuram G., and Luigi Zingales. 1998. "Power in a Theory of the Firm." *Quarterly Journal of Economics* 113 (2): 387–432.

Ranasinghe, Ashantha. 2014. "Impact of Policy Distortions on Firm-Level Innovation, Productivity Dynamics and TFP." *Journal of Economic Dynamics & Control* 46 (3): 114–29.

Reinikka, Ritva, and Jakkob Svensson. 1999. "How Inadequate Provision of Public Infrastructure and Services Affects Private Investment." Policy Research Working Paper 2262, World Bank, Washington, DC, December.

Reinikka, Ritva, and Jakob Svensson. 2002. "Coping with Poor Public Capital." *Journal of Development Economics* 69 (1): 51–69.

Renkow, Mitch, Daniel G. Hallstrom, and Daniel D. Karanja. 2004. "Rural Infrastructure, Transactions Costs and Market Participation in Kenya." *Journal of Development Economics* 73 (1): 349–67.

Restuccia, Diego. 2016. "Resource Allocation and Productivity in Agriculture." Unpublished manuscript, University of Toronto.

Restuccia, Diego, and Richard Rogerson. 2017. "The Causes and Costs of Misallocation." *Journal of Economic Perspectives* 31 (3): 151–74.

Restuccia, Diego, and Raül Santaeulàlia-Llopis. 2017. "Land Misallocation and Productivity." Working Paper 23128, National Bureau of Economic Research, Cambridge, MA.

Ricker-Gilbert, Jacob, Nicole M. Mason, Francis A. Darko, and Solomon T. Tembo. 2013. "What Are the Effects of Input Subsidy Programs on Maize Prices? Evidence from Malawi and Zambia." *Agricultural Economics* 44 (6): 671–86.

Ricker-Gilbert, Jacob, and Thomas S. Jayne. 2012. "Do Fertilizer Subsidies Boost Staple Crop Production and Reduce Poverty across the Distribution of Smallholders in Africa? Quantile Regression Results from Malawi." Selected Paper for the Triennial Meeting of the International Association of Agricultural Economists, Foz Do Iguaçu, Brazil, August 18–24.

Schalkwyk, Francois van, Andrew Young, and Stefaan Verhulst. 2017. "Ghana. Esoko: Leveling the Information Playing Field for Smallholder Farmers in Ghana." Open Data's Impact case study, The Governance Lab, Tandon School of Engineering, New York University.

Schmidt, Klaus M. 1997. "Managerial Incentives and Product Market Competition." *Review of Economic Studies* 64 (2): 191–213.

Shiferaw, Admasu, Måns Söderbom, Eyerusalem Siba, and Getnet Alemu. 2015. "Road Infrastructure and Enterprise Dynamics in Ethiopia." *Journal of Development Studies* 51 (11): 1541–58.

Sinate, David, Vanlalruata Fanai, Snehal Bangera, and Sara Joy. 2018. "Connecting Africa: Role of Transport Infrastructure." Working Paper No. 72, Export-Import Bank of India, Mumbai.

Stifel, David, and Bart Minten. 2008. "Isolation and Agricultural Productivity." *Agricultural Economics* 39 (1): 1–15.

Suri, Tavneet, and William Jack. 2016. "The Long-Run Poverty and Gender Impacts of Mobile Money." *Science* 354 (6317): 1288–92.

Svensson, Jakob, and David Yanagizawa. 2009. "Getting Prices Right: The Impact of the Market Information Service in Uganda." *Journal of the European Economic Association* 7 (2–3): 435–45.

Swistak, Arthur, L. Liu, and Ricardo Varsano. 2017. "Towards More Efficient Non-Resource Taxation: A Strategy for Reform." Technical Assistance Report, Fiscal Affairs Department, International Monetary Fund, Washington, DC.

Tadesse, Getaw, and Godfrey Bahiigwa. 2015. "Mobile Phones and Farmers' Marketing Decisions in Ethiopia." *World Development* 68: 296–307.

Tarozzi, Alessandro, Jaikishan Desai, and Kristin Johnson. 2015. "The Impacts of Microcredit: Evidence from Ethiopia." *American Economic Journal: Applied Economics* 7 (1): 54–89.

Topalova, Petia and Amit Khandelwal. 2011. "Trade Liberalization and Firm Productivity: The Case of India." *Review of Economics and Statistics* 93 (3): 995–1009.

Van Biesebroeck, Johannes. 2005. "Exporting Raises Productivity in Sub-Saharan African Manufacturing Firms." *Journal of International Economics* 67 (2): 373–91.

Weber, M. 1928. *Theory of the Location of Industries.* Chicago: University of Chicago.

World Bank. 1994. *World Development Report 1994: Infrastructure for Development.* New York: Oxford University Press for the World Bank.

World Bank. 2005. *World Development Report 2006: Equity and Development.* Washington, DC: World Bank.

World Bank. 2008. *World Development Report 2008: Agriculture for Development.* Washington, DC: World Bank.

World Bank. 2012. "Agriculture Sector Report." In "Transformation-Ready: The Strategic Application of Information and Communication Technologies in Africa." World Bank, Washington, DC.

Zenebe, Dawit. 2018. "Trade Liberalization, Productivity, and Resource Allocation in Manufacturing Firms in Ethiopia." Unpublished manuscript, University of Wisconsin–Madison.

Zhang, Peng, Junjie Zhang, and Minpeng Chen. 2017. "Economic Impacts of Climate Change on Agriculture: The Importance of Additional Climatic Variables Other than Temperature and Precipitation." *Journal of Environmental Economics and Management* 83: 8–31.

Agenda for Future Research | 5

The report has documented the low aggregate labor productivity of Sub-Saharan Africa relative to other world regions. The region's scarce resources, compounded by inefficiencies in their allocation, have exacerbated the problem, as reflected by

- *Cross-country differences in total factor productivity (TFP)*, which overwhelmingly explain the cross-country differences in income per worker at the aggregate level;
- *Marked delays in structural transformation*, as captured by the agriculture sector's high employment share and low productivity; and
- *Pervasive misallocation of resources across farms and firms*, with deleterious consequences for aggregate output and productivity.

Although this report has focused on the role played by misallocation in explaining the low productivity of Sub-Saharan Africa, several avenues of research could provide further insights on the dynamics of productivity in the region as well as different channels of policy transmission to boost productivity.

Impacts of productivity shocks versus demand shocks. Future work needs to distinguish productivity shocks (or technical efficiency) from demand shocks in the measures of revenue productivity (TFPR) among Sub-Saharan African production establishments. This research requires the timely availability and recurrent production of high-quality data on output and input prices at the establishment level. This does not preclude improving the country coverage as well as the methodology and periodicity of firm-level censuses. However, the quest for new and more data faces other challenges:

- Output price data is more widely available than input price data at the establishment level.
- The reported output prices are, in most cases, unit values.
- Surveys should be undertaken at the product level if most of a specific sector's manufacturing establishments are multiproduct.

Having greater data availability on output and input prices does not prevent the need to impose more structure in identifying the role played by demand shocks in the measured TFPR. Recent research using firm-level censuses with price data shows that there is still a large dispersion of TFPR across manufacturing firms in Ethiopia, and this is mirrored by large differences in physical productivity (TFPQ). Prices tend to vary significantly less than productivity levels and do not constitute a major driving factor of TFPR differences (Söderbom 2018).

Policy impact at the firm level. Further analysis should be undertaken on the impact of policies on the *within* rather than the *between* component of aggregate productivity growth using longitudinal data.[1] Trade liberalization, for instance, may affect both components of aggregate productivity. However, the elements that may boost productivity at the firm level (rather than at the industry level) have not been adequately discussed—for example, the reduction of X-inefficiencies,[2] investment in new technologies, quality upgrade of products and inputs, and locational decisions, among others. In Sub-Saharan Africa, recent work has estimated these different components or sources of productivity growth in manufacturing (Dennis et al. 2016; Jones et al. 2019).

Drivers of productivity improvements from managerial practices. Finally, there is greater need to deepen research in the region on the internal drivers of productivity at the establishment level in Sub-Saharan Africa. A growing field of research focuses on the productivity improvements of adopting better managerial practices. For instance, firms with better management practices tend to perform better along several dimensions: they are larger and grow faster, they are more productive, and they have higher survival rates (Bloom and Van Reenen 2007). And better-managed firms also recruit and retain workers with higher average human capital (Bender et al. 2018).

To those ends, more-flexible labor market regulations are associated with better use of incentives by management (Bloom and Van Reenen 2010). Increased product competition also tends to improve firm management, including through the reallocation of economic activity toward better-managed firms (Bloom, Sadun, and Van Reenen 2016).

Other internal drivers to explore include greater input quality, product innovation and research and development (R&D) investments, and firm structure decisions.

Notes

1. Cusolito and Maloney (2018) provide evidence on the policy impacts on the "within" component of aggregate productivity growth in emerging markets outside Africa—namely, Chile, Colombia, and Malaysia. (As chapter 1 discusses further, the "within" component accounts for the productivity growth within firms. The "between" component reflects the role of factor reallocation across firms in aggregate productivity growth.)
2. X-inefficiency is the divergence of a firm's observed behavior in practice (influenced by a lack of competitive pressure) from efficient behavior assumed or implied by economic theory. The concept, introduced by Leibenstein (1966), refers to the result of inputs not producing their maximum output as a consequence of an "X" factor. This translates into failures of both cost minimization and production maximization and, hence, implies a loss of efficiency and refers to all nonallocative inefficiencies.

References

Bender, Stefan, Nicholas Bloom, David Card, John Van Reenen, and Stefanie Wolter. 2018. "Management Practices, Workforce Selection, and Productivity." *Journal of Labor Economics* 36 (S1): S371–S409.

Bloom, Nicholas, Raffaella Sadun, and John Van Reenen. 2016. "Management as a Technology?" Working Paper 22327, National Bureau of Economic Research, Cambridge, MA.

Bloom, Nicholas, and John Van Reenen. 2007. "Measuring and Explaining Management Practices across Firms and Countries." *Quarterly Journal of Economics* 122 (4): 1351–1408.

Bloom, Nicholas, and John Van Reenen. 2010. "Why Do Management Practices Differ across Firms and Countries?" *Journal of Economic Perspectives* 24 (1): 203–24.

Cusolito, Ana Paula, and William F. Maloney. 2018. *Productivity Revisited: Shifting Paradigms in Analysis and Policy*. Washington, DC: World Bank.

Dennis, Allen, Taye Mengistae, Yutaka Yoshino, and Albert Zeufack. 2016. "Sources of Productivity Growth in Uganda: The Role of Interindustry and Intraindustry Misallocation in the 2000s." Policy Research Working Paper 7909, World Bank, Washington, DC.

Jones, Patricia, Emmanuel K. K. Lartey, Taye Mengistae, and Albert Zeufack. 2019. "Sources of Manufacturing Productivity Growth in Africa." Policy Research Working Paper 8980, World Bank, Washington, DC.

Leibenstein, Harvey. 1966. "Allocative Efficiency vs. 'X-Efficiency.'" *American Economic Review* 56 (3): 392–415.

Söderbom, Måns. 2018. "Productivity Dispersion and Firm Dynamics in Ethiopia's Manufacturing Sector." Unpublished manuscript, University of Gothenburg, Sweden.

Output per Worker, Factor Accumulation, and Total Productivity | A

This appendix describes the concepts, data, and methodologies used to generate the statistics reported in appendix B ("Country Productivity Analysis"), which presents factor accumulation, output, and productivity for a wide array of Sub-Saharan countries from 1960 to 2017.[1] Appendix B reports the evolution of output per worker, factor accumulation, and total factor productivity (TFP) from three different dimensions: (a) *latest data* on output, population, and sectoral shares of employment and output; (b) *trends* in labor productivity, capital-output ratios, and human capital; and (c) *growth decompositions* under different assumptions.

Latest data. First, each country reports the latest figures on (a) output and population, and (b) sectoral shares in value added and employment. The data on output and population are collected from Penn World Table (PWT) 9.0 (which contains annual information from 1950 to 2014, at best), and these series were updated using PWT 9.1 data from 2015 to 2017. Additionally, each country reports the output and employment shares across five sectors of economic activity in 2016: agriculture, manufacturing, nonmanufacturing industry, market services, and nonmarket services.

Trends. Second, the study tracks the evolution over time of output per worker, the capital-output ratio, and the PWT index of human capital from 1960 to 2017 (or from a later starting year according to data availability across countries). All these series are expressed relative to the benchmark country that approximates the world technological frontier—that is, the United States. The time series are used to conduct a basic development accounting exercise: it computes the share of factor accumulation and the share of TFP that explain the output differences between any Sub-Saharan African country and the global efficiency benchmark (the United States).

Decompositions. Third, the results are computed for three different growth account exercises—a traditional Solow decomposition, a Solow decomposition that incorporates the accumulation of public and private physical capital, and a Solow decomposition that includes natural capital—for each country in the Sub-Saharan Africa sample.

This report gathered data on output per worker for a sample of 45 Sub-Saharan African countries; however, the data availability of the different inputs of production (employment, physical capital, human capital, and natural capital) was more limited. Thirty-seven of the countries had data on gross domestic product (GDP), physical, and human capital, while only 24 of the countries had data on natural capital (the stock of all extractable resources such as geology, soils, air, water, and living organisms). Finally, the report gathered data on sectoral shares of output and employment for only 29 countries in the region.

Development Accounting

Development accounting exercises have been undertaken as early as the late 1960s, albeit for a limited number of countries (Denison 1967; Walters 1968). Subsequent efforts integrated Jorgenson's growth accounting framework with the work of structure proposed by Griliches and Christensen[2] to compare the levels of output per worker between the United States and other high-income countries (Christensen, Cummings, and Jorgenson 1981; Jorgenson and Nishimizu 1978).

More-recent applications of this framework have calculated the sources of the large and persistent income differences observed between the world's richest and poorest countries (Hall and Jones 1999; Hsieh and Klenow 2010; Jones 2016; Klenow and Rodríguez-Clare 1997).

Exposition of the Framework

The development accounting framework assumes that the relationship between output and the factors of production is captured by the following production function (Caselli 2005; Hall and Jones 1999):

$$Y_t = A_t K_t^\alpha \left(hL\right)_t^{1-\alpha}, \quad \text{(A.1)}$$

where Y is the country's GDP in the period t, K is the aggregate capital stock, and hL is the "quality adjusted" labor force—that is, the number of workers L multiplied by their average human capital h. Furthermore, α is the sensitivity of output with respect to capital, and A represents the efficiency with which the factors of production are used. Finally, it is assumed that there are no adjustment costs in the accumulation of capital and that there is perfect competition in the markets of production factors so that their remuneration is equal to their social marginal products.

In the spirit of Klenow and Rodríguez-Clare (1997), the production function in equation (A.1) is expressed in its *intensive form*:

$$y_t = Z_t \left(\frac{K_t}{Y_t}\right)^{\frac{\alpha}{1-\alpha}} h_t, \quad \text{(A.2)}$$

where y is the real output per worker $(y = Y/L)$, $\frac{K_t}{Y_t}$ is the capital-output ratio, and $Z_t \equiv \left(A_t\right)^{\frac{1}{1-\alpha}}$ is TFP measured in labor augmenting units.

Equation (A.2) is at the core of the development accounting framework. It is compatible with the steady state of a neoclassical growth model where (a) the capital output ratio, $\frac{K_t}{Y_t}$, is proportional to the investment rate; and (b) the level of human capital or TFP has no direct effects on the steady-state capital-output ratio (Mankiw, Romer, and Weil 1992). When expressing the production function in per worker terms, changes in effective labor per worker or residual TFP are accompanied by changes in capital per worker (Hsieh and Klenow 2010; Klenow and Rodríguez-Clare 1997).

The development accounting framework uses equation (A.2) to decompose the distance of the different Sub-Saharan African countries to the United States (the benchmark typically used in the literature to proxy the frontier of production possibilities) into two distinct components—(a) the distance to the frontier in terms of physical and human capital (that is, factor accumulation); and (b) the distance in terms of TFP—as described in equation (A.3):

$$\frac{y_t^j}{y_t^{US}} = \left(\frac{Z_t^j}{Z_t^{US}}\right)\left(\frac{\kappa_t^j}{\kappa_t^{US}}\right)^{\frac{\alpha}{1-\alpha}}\left(\frac{h_t^j}{h_t^{US}}\right), \quad \text{(A.3)}$$

where $\frac{y_t^j}{y_t^{US}}$ is the output per worker of Sub-Saharan African country j relative to that of the United States in period t. This measure of distance to the frontier can be decomposed into (a) a composite factor that accounts for the differences in the stock of physical and human capital, $\left(\frac{\kappa_t^j}{\kappa_t^{US}}\right)^{\frac{\alpha}{1-\alpha}}\left(\frac{h_t^j}{h_t^{US}}\right)$; and (b) a portion of the differences in output per worker that are attributed to the relative distance in TFP, $\left(\frac{Z_t^j}{Z_t^{US}}\right)$. The comparison of large and persistent cross-country differences in productivity per worker may require a steady-state approximation. The larger exponent on human capital and TFP (relative to the per worker expression of the production function) reflects the impact of these variables on output both directly and indirectly through capital per worker.

Development Accounting for Sub-Saharan Africa

Sub-Saharan Africa and the group of low- and middle-income countries in non-African regions show diverging paths in real output per worker over time in spite of quite similar initial conditions in the 1960s (table A.1):

- The gap in output per worker in Sub-Saharan Africa relative to the United States is 0.12 from 1960 to 1969; that is, the region's labor productivity is about 12 percent that of the United States (column [1] of table A.1). This gap is the product of the contribution of the gap in capital-output ratios, human capital, and TFP (columns [2], [3], and [4], respectively).
- The capital-output ratio in Sub-Saharan Africa relative to that of the United States is approximately 0.4, and the difference in capital-output ratio that matters for output per worker is about 0.51 in 1960–69 (column [2] of table A.1). This implies that differences in physical capital help explain about 44 percent of the differences in output per worker between

Sub-Saharan Africa and the United States. Given the differences in years of schooling for adults over 15 years old and differences in the returns to education, the relative human capital index for Sub-Saharan Africa is 0.42 in 1960–69 (column [3]). That is, human capital in the region is about 42 percent of that in the United States.

- Sub-Saharan Africa's TFP relative to the United States is about 0.56 (column [4] of table A.1). This implies that productive processes in the region are slightly more than half as productive as those in the United States.
- In other words, the table shows that real output per worker in the United States was about 18 times higher than that of Sub-Saharan Africa (17.7) in 1960–69.[3] A factor of 8.8 of this difference is due to inputs, and a factor of 2 is due to TFP. This implies that the distance to the frontier in terms of output per worker is 8.8 parts due to inputs and 2 parts due to TFP. Hence, the share due to TFP is 25 percent (column [5] of table A.1).
- In 2010–17, real output per worker in Sub-Saharan Africa was about 8 percent that of the United States (0.083). The relative gap in terms of the region's capital-output ratio has narrowed significantly; in fact, its relative capital-output ratio increased from 0.4 in 1960–69 to 0.85 in 2010–17. In terms of human capital, the relative h index increased only from 0.42 in 1960–69 to 0.47 in 2010–17. This is a small improvement in reducing the gap in human capital. The (implied) TFP differences between Sub-Saharan Africa and the United States in 2010–17 are even larger than those in 1960–69; that is, production processes are not even one-tenth as efficient as those in the United States (0.06). In other words, real output per worker in the United States was about 23 times more productive than in Sub-Saharan Africa, with more than 75 percent of the distance to the frontier attributed to differences in TFP levels (0.781).

TABLE A.1 Development Accounting in Sub-Saharan Africa and in Non-African Developing Countries, Relative to the United States, 1960–2017

		Output per worker [1]	Contribution Capital-GDP [2]	Human Capital [3]	TFP [4]	Share due to TFP [5]
Sub-Saharan Africa	1960–69	0.118	0.511	0.416	0.554	0.251
(SSA)	1970–79	0.136	0.742	0.381	0.481	0.285
	1980–89	0.103	1.070	0.382	0.253	0.483
	1990–99	0.062	1.344	0.409	0.113	0.663
	2000–09	0.067	1.407	0.442	0.108	0.758
	2010–17	0.083	2.842	0.474	0.061	0.781
Developing Countries	1960–69	0.088	0.773	0.455	0.250	0.553
excluding SSA	1970–79	0.111	0.743	0.469	0.317	0.503
	1980–89	0.110	0.899	0.503	0.243	0.577
	1990–99	0.130	1.776	0.569	0.128	0.663
	2000–09	0.149	1.244	0.616	0.194	0.703
	2010–17	0.215	1.647	0.653	0.200	0.674

Source: Penn World Table (PWT) 9.0 and PWT9.1 updates (Feenstra, Inklaar, and Timmer 2015).
Note: Output per worker, contribution of capital-GDP ratios, human capital, and total factor productivity (TFP) are expressed in terms relative to US efficiency benchmarks, following equation (A.3) in the text. Regional or group figures are employment-weighted averages. "Developing" countries are low- and middle-income countries according to World Bank country income classifications.

The Diverging Path of Non-African Low- and Middle-Income Countries

In spite of having similar starting labor productivity levels in the 1960s, low- and middle-income countries in non-African regions evolved differently from those in Sub-Saharan Africa (table A.1). From 1960 to 1969, the relative output per worker in Sub-Saharan Africa was 12 percent that of the United States, while that of the other regions' low- and middle-income countries was about 9 percent (table A.1). The latter group had a lower gap in capital-output and human capital relative to the United States during this period.

Although relative labor productivity in Sub-Saharan Africa declined over the past 50 years, it increased among the low- and middle-income countries in other regions—especially over the past two decades. Relative output per worker of such countries increased from 0.09 in 1960–69 to 0.22 in 2010–17. In addition, their capital-output ratios caught up with those of the United States (increasing from 0.61 in 1960–69 to 1.12 in 2010–17).

In these non-African countries, relative human capital grew much faster than in Sub-Saharan Africa: the relative h index of non-African low- and middle-income countries increased from 0.45 in 1960–69 to 0.65 in 2010–17. The implied TFP difference between such countries and the United States is 0.2 in 2010–17 (down from 0.25 in 1960–69); that is, production processes are about one-fifth as efficient across these low- and middle-income countries as in the United States. About half of output per worker differences between these countries and the United States were attributed to TFP differences in 1960–69. The efficiency narrative became more marked in 2010–17: differences in TFP levels now explain two-thirds of the output per worker gap (0.674).

Appendix B in this report shows the trends of the different factors that make up the development accounting analysis for each Sub-Saharan African country: the time series of the real output per worker, the capital-output ratio, the human capital index, and TFP. All these series are expressed as a ratio of the corresponding series for the efficiency benchmark. (In practice, the United States benchmark is equal to 1.) Appendix B also presents the evolution of the share of labor productivity differences explained by factor accumulation and TFP as well as the TFP gaps for each Sub-Saharan African country by decade.

Growth Accounting

Assessing the sources of economic growth dates back to the late 1950s. Growth in real output was decomposed as the weighted average of the growth rate of labor and capital as well as a residual labeled total factor productivity (TFP) growth (Abramovitz 1956; Solow 1957; Tinbergen 1942). The so-called *Solow residual* was nothing but the unexplained part of economic growth that was interpreted as a measure of technological change. Subsequent contributions in the 1960s and 1970s led to the application of more general production functions and more accurate measurement of inputs and outputs (Denison 1962; Denison, Griliches, and Jorgenson 1972; Jorgenson and Griliches 1967)—for instance, accounting for changes in both the quantity and quality of labor and capital inputs (Denison 1962).[4] In spite of these adjustments, from 1947 to 1973, the estimated contribution of TFP to economic growth was still about one-third of GDP growth in the United States, 42 percent in Japan, and more than half in several European economies (Christensen, Cummings, and Jorgenson 1981).

The differences in output per worker across the world's countries—especially the large and protracted differences documented in the literature between high-income countries and low- to middle-income countries— are overwhelmingly attributed to differences in TFP rather than to differences in the levels of physical or human capital (see, among others, Caselli 2005; Hall and Jones 1999; Hsieh and Klenow 2010; Klenow and Rodríguez-Clare 1997).[5] The consensus in the literature points to 20 percent of country income differences being explained by the

accumulation of physical capital and 10–30 percent by human capital. Hence, differences in TFP may account for 50–70 percent of country income differences (Hsieh and Klenow 2010).

This appendix conducts the growth accounting analysis under different technological specifications. Hence, it computes the TFP growth using the traditional Solow decomposition, a decomposition accounting for public and private capital accumulation, and a decomposition including natural capital. The appendix shows the estimation of TFP growth for Sub-Saharan African countries using these three different specifications provided that there is data availability.

The technology of production function is represented by a Cobb-Douglas production function with constant returns to scale (Caselli 2005; Hall and Jones 1999):

$$Y_t = A_t K_t^\alpha (hL)_t^{(1-\alpha)}, \qquad (A.4)$$

where Y is the country's GDP, K is the aggregate capital stock, and hL is the "quality adjusted" labor force—that is, the number of workers L multiplied by their average human capital h. Furthermore, α is the (constant) sensitivity of output with respect to capital, and A represents the level of TFP or the efficiency with which factors of production are used or combined. In addition, it is assumed that there are no adjustment costs in capital accumulation and that there is perfect competition in the markets of production factors, so that they are paid their social marginal products.

Traditional Solow Decomposition

The technology described in equation (A.4) can be expressed in per worker terms:

$$y_t = A_t k_t^\alpha h_t^{(1-\alpha)}, \qquad (A.5)$$

where k is the capital labor ratio ($k = K/L$).

If we define $\hat{x}_t = \dfrac{dx_t}{x_t}$, then TFP growth is

$$\hat{A}_t = \hat{y}_t - \alpha \hat{k}_t - (1-\alpha)\hat{h}_t \qquad (A.6)$$

The definition and the construction of human capital are explained in the next section.

Solow Decomposition Accounting for Private and Public Capital Stock

The stock of capital of the economy is decomposed into the stocks of private and public capital (denoted by the subindexes p and g, respectively). The production function in equation (A.1) now becomes

$$Y_t = A_t K_{pt}^{\alpha_p} K_{gt}^{\alpha_g} \left(h_t L_t \right)^{1-\alpha_p-\alpha_g}, \quad (A.7)$$

where K_p and K_g represent the private and public capital stock, respectively.

TFP growth can be expressed as

$$\hat{A}_t = \hat{y}_t - \alpha_p \left(\hat{K}_{pt} - \hat{L}_t \right) - \alpha_g \left(\hat{K}_{gt} - \hat{L}_t \right)$$
$$- \left(1 - \alpha_p - \alpha_g \right) \hat{h}_t \quad (A.8)$$

The values of α_p and α_g are calibrated following Lowe, Papageorgiou, and Pérez-Sebastián (2012): α_p and α_g cannot be directly derived from national income and product accounts data. However, the share of reproducible capital, $\alpha_g + \alpha_p$, can be calculated from the labor share of income of the economy (*labsh* in the PWT) as (1-*labsh*).[6]

The estimation of the composition of capital is not trivial: this report uses estimates of the production function augmented by public capital for high-income economies (Kamps 2004) as well as for low- and middle-income

countries (Gupta et al. 2011). The estimated output elasticities of private capital and public capital are summarized in columns [1] and [2] of table A.2. These estimated elasticities are used to compute the relative income shares of private and public capital for high-income countries, middle-income countries, and low-income countries. The relative income share of private capital is computed as $\alpha_p/(\alpha_g + \alpha_p)$, as shown in the last column of table A.2. The income shares for private and public capital (α_p and α_g, respectively) are then computed using the estimated relative income shares (which varies across groups) and the PWT 9.0 labor share (which may vary across countries and over time).

Solow Decomposition Accounting for Natural Capital

The technology described in equation (A.1) now incorporates the use of natural resources (Monge-Naranjo, Sánchez, and Santaeulàlia-Llopis 2019):

$$Y_t = A_t \left(K_t^\gamma T_t^{1-\gamma} \right)^\alpha \left(h_t L_t \right)^{1-\alpha}, \quad (A.9)$$

where K is the aggregate stock of capital, T represents the service flows of the natural capital, and $\alpha(1-\gamma)$ represents the natural resource share in GDP.

The income share of natural resources is computed using data on the rents from natural resources. These data are collected from the World Bank's World Development Indicators database. In this context, TFP growth is

---

TABLE A.2   Estimated Output Elasticities to Private and Public Capital, by Country Income Group

Sample	Elasticities		Relative share of private capital
	Private capital	Public capital	
	[1]	[2]	[1]/([1]+[2])
Low-Income Countries	0.23	0.25	0.48
Middle-Income Countries	0.29	0.17	0.63
High-Income Countries	0.26	0.22	0.54

Sources: Gupta et al. 2011 (low- and middle-income countries); Kamps 2004 (high-income countries).

$$\hat{A}_t = \hat{y}_t - \alpha\gamma\left(\hat{K}_t - \hat{L}_t\right) - \left\{\alpha(1-\gamma)\right\}\left(\hat{T}_t - \hat{L}_t\right) - (1-\alpha)\hat{h}_t.$$

(A.10)

With information on α (from the share of labor force) and $\alpha(1-\gamma)$ (as computed by the ratio of natural resource rents to GDP), we can implicitly compute γ. For the purposes of our calculation, assume a natural-resource-augmented production function similar to equation (A.7): $Y_t = A_t K_t^\alpha T_t^\gamma \left(h_t L_t\right)^{1-\alpha-\gamma}$, where α and γ represent the share of reproducible and natural capital in GDP. Equation (A.6) defines $\hat{A}_t$ as TFP growth without accounting for natural resources. Then, TFP growth in a technology that accounts for natural capital, $\hat{A}_t^{NR}$, is equal to

$$\hat{A}_t^{NR} = \hat{A}_t + \gamma\left[\left(\alpha\hat{k}_t + (1-\alpha)\hat{h}_t\right) - \hat{T}_t\right], \quad (A.11)$$

where the difference between the traditional TFP growth (equation [A.3]) and the measure of TFP growth including natural capital (equation [A.11]) depends on the growth rate of the composite input index from the classical model, the growth in the use of natural capital T, and the share of natural capital rents in production (see Brandt, Schreyer, and Zipperer 2017).

Definitions and Data Description

The comparison of productivity levels and sources of productivity growth in Sub-Saharan Africa relative to other world regions requires a dataset with ample coverage across countries and over time. To conduct this analysis at the aggregate level, this report uses PWT 9.0 data with annual information from 1960 to 2014 for a wide array of countries in the world. This information is updated using the PWT 9.1 with information for the years 2015 to 2017.[7] This discussion of the data, presented as a preamble to appendix B (the country-specific data analyses), relies

heavily on the dataset's companion paper by Feenstra, Inklaar, and Timmer (2015).

One of the goals of this appendix is to compare differences in aggregate labor productivity and TFP across countries and over time, with emphasis on the productivity and growth performance of Sub-Saharan African countries. Labor productivity is an indicator that is related to economic growth, competitiveness, and living standards in an economy. It is typically defined as the total volume of output (as measured by GDP) produced per unit of labor (or number of people employed) during a period of time. GDP captures the monetary value of goods and services produced in a determined country during a period of time. Employment consists of all working-age people who either have paid employment or are self-employed.[8]

Labor productivity only partially reflects the productivity of labor in terms of workers' personal capacity or intensity of effort. TFP, on the other hand, is the ratio of aggregate output to aggregate inputs (Sickles and Zelenyuk 2019). It measures the impact of technological change and changes in worker knowledge on the long-term output of an economy. It is derived from increases in the levels of efficiency and technology. It is considered to be that portion of the growth of an economy that is not explained by the amount of inputs used (say, labor and capital).

Output. The levels of *output* are proxied using the data on real GDP estimated from the output side (GDP^O) from the PWT. This indicator is a better approximation of the total production of the economy. Additionally, the PWT uses the expenditure approach to measure the level of economic activity (GDP^E). In contrast, GDP^E captures the standards of living of the different countries in the world. According to the PWT methodology, countries with strong terms of trade will have a higher real GDP^E than GDP^O.

Real output. The PWT distinguishes *real output* measures that are constant across countries but depend on the current year (CGDP^O) from those that are constant across countries and also constant over time (RGDP^O). The former indicator, also known as *current price* real GDP (CGDP^O), is used to conduct country comparisons in a particular year, whereas the latter one, known as *constant price* real GDP (RGDP^O), is used for comparisons across countries and over time. CGDP^O—the output-side real GDP at current purchasing power parities (PPPs) (in US\$, millions, at 2011 prices)—is used to conduct development accounting exercises. Finally, the PWT uses the real GDP at constant national prices (RGDP^{NA}) (also expressed in US\$, millions, at 2011 prices) to conduct growth accounting exercises.

Physical capital. The stock of *physical capital* is estimated based on the accumulation and depreciation of past investments using the *perpetual inventory method* (PIM). One of the novel aspects of the estimation of the aggregate capital stock in PWT 9.0 is the use of investments disaggregated by type of asset. The data on investments by asset type is obtained from either the national accounts or partly estimated using the commodity-flow method in the spirit of Caselli and Wilson (2004). The average depreciation rate in PWT 9.0 varies across countries and over time because the asset composition differs across countries and the depreciation rate is not similar across assets. In addition, PWT 9.0 uses information on the asset composition of the capital stock to compute the relative price of investment.

Human capital per worker. The index of *human capital* per worker, *h*, is constructed using the average years of schooling in the population over 25 years old (Barro and Lee 2013). Following Hall and Jones (1999), the years of schooling are converted into a measure of *h* through the formula $h = exp\{\phi(s)\}$, with *s* representing the average years of schooling and $\phi(s)$ being

a piece-wise linear function (as in Caselli 2005):

$$\phi(s) = \begin{cases} 0.134 \cdot s & \text{if } s \leq 4 \\ 0.134 \cdot 4 + 0.101 \cdot (s-4) & \text{if } 4 < s \leq 8 \\ 0.134 \cdot 4 + 0.101 \cdot 4 + 0.068 \cdot (s-8) & \text{if } s > 8. \end{cases}$$

$$(A.12)$$

If we assume that the wage-schooling relationship is log-linear (as in the empirical literature), then the relationship between *h* and *s* should also be log-linear. The PWT constructs the *h* index for 150 countries using data on schooling years from Barro and Lee (2013) for 95 countries, and from Cohen and Soto (2007) and Cohen and Leker (2014) for an additional 55 countries.

International data on education-wage profiles suggest that the return to an additional year of education in Sub-Saharan Africa, the region with the lowest level of education, is about 13.4 percent. In contrast, the return to an additional year of education is 10.1 percent for the world and 6.8 percent for the Organisation for Economic Co-operation and Development (OECD) countries (Psacharopoulos 1994). This measure of human capital tries to reconcile the properties of a log-linear relationship between education and income at the country level with the concavity of that relationship across countries. The *h* index from the PWT assumes homogeneous returns across countries.

The relationship between *h* and *s* has also been characterized in the empirical literature as $\phi(s_{it}) = \phi_i s_{it}$ for each country *i* in period *t*. This specification assumes that the returns to education are heterogeneous across countries. This report has used two different sets of country estimates for the returns to education to construct the human capital index: (a) the estimated Mincerian returns from Caselli, Ponticelli, and Rossi (2017) and Caselli (2017);[9] and (b) the estimated Mincerian returns from Montenegro and Patrinos (2014).[10] These two sets of country estimates of Mincerian returns lead to two different human capital indexes with heterogeneous returns to education across countries.

The degree of association between the indexes with homogeneous and heterogeneous returns to education—expressed in five-year growth rates, $\phi(s_{it})-\phi(s_{it-5})$—is quite high, and it fluctuates between 0.75 and 0.80. Note that the correlation among the three indexes of human capital expressed in 10-year growth rates, $\phi(s_{it})-\phi(s_{it-10})$, fluctuates between 0.73 and 0.77.

Labor share of income. Finally, the PWT has estimated the *labor share* (or the share of labor income in economic activity) for a wide array of countries and years. There is broad availability of information on labor compensation of employees; however, a separate estimation is needed for the labor compensation of self-employed workers. The cross-country estimates of the labor share yield some stylized facts (Feenstra, Inklaar, and Timmer 2015):

• The global average of the labor share in income is about 0.52 (significantly lower than the two-thirds typically assumed in the macroeconomic literature).
• There is no systematic relationship between labor shares and income per capita levels.
• Labor shares have declined over time in most of the countries covered.[11]

Sectoral Productivity: Sources of Data

This report has assembled a large database of value-added, employment, and productivity indicators at the sectoral level for a wide array of countries from 1990 to 2016. This dataset allows for the examination of trends in labor productivity and employment shares across sectors in Sub-Saharan Africa relative to other regions. In other words, it helps to document the patterns of structural transformation among countries in the region.

The main sources of sectoral data are the United Nations National Accounts (UN-NAC) database, the World Bank's World Development Indicators (WDI) database, and International Labour Organization (ILO) statistics. The value-added data at the sector level are first obtained from UN-NAC from 1990 to 2016. It is expressed in US dollars at current prices and at 2010 prices. Economic activity is disaggregated into seven large sectors: agriculture, mining and utilities, construction, manufacturing, trade and hospitality, transport and communication, and other activities. For the purposes of the analysis conducted in this report, the International Standard Industrial Classification (ISIC) Revision 3.0 data are reclassified into five larger sectors (table A.3): agriculture, manufacturing, nonmanufacturing, market services, and nonmarket services.

Second, we obtain disaggregated sector-level data on total workers from the ILO and grouped the data using the same five-sector classification outlined in table A.3. The sector-level data on employment from the ILO range from 1990 to 2016. Hence, employment data constitute the most binding constraint in terms of data availability over time.

The list of 28 Sub-Saharan African countries with sectoral data is presented in table A.4. The analysis of sectoral productivity in the main text of the report is undertaken not only for Sub-Saharan Africa but also for country groups within the region, classified as follows:

• *Income level:* Low- and lower-middle-income countries (LLMCs) and upper-middle-income countries (UMICs)
• *Degree of natural resource abundance:* 0 for non-resource abundance, 1 for non-oil resource abundance, and 2 for oil abundance
• *Geographical subregion:* West, East, Central, and Southern African countries.

TABLE A.3   **Classification of Sectors of Economic Activity**

ISIC sector of economic activity	Sector group for analysis
A. Agriculture, hunting, and forestry	Agriculture
B. Fishing	Agriculture
C. Mining and quarrying	Nonmanufacturing
D. Manufacturing	Manufacturing
E. Electricity, gas, and water supply	Nonmanufacturing
F. Construction	Nonmanufacturing
G. Wholesale and retail trade; repair of motor vehicles, motorcycles	Market services
H. Hotels and restaurants	Market services
I. Transport, storage, and communications	Market services
J. Financial intermediation	Market services
K. Real estate, renting, and business activities	Market services
L. Public administration and defense; compulsory social security	Nonmarket services
M. Education	Nonmarket services
N. Health and social work	Nonmarket services
O. Other community, social, and personal service activities	Nonmarket services
P. Private households with employed persons	Nonmarket services

Source: Original table for this publication.
Note: ISIC = International Standard Industrial Classification provided by UNIDO.

TABLE A.4   **Classification of Sub-Saharan African Countries**

Code	Name	Income	Resources	Subregion
AGO	Angola	LLMC	2	Southern Africa
BEN	Benin	LLMC	0	West Africa
BWA	Botswana	UMIC	1	Southern Africa
BFA	Burkina Faso	LLMC	0	West Africa
BDI	Burundi	LLMC	0	East Africa
CMR	Cameroon	LLMC	2	Central Africa
CAF	Central African Republic	LLMC	0	Central Africa
COG	Congo, Rep.	LLMC	2	Central Africa
GAB	Gabon	UMIC	2	Central Africa
GMB	Gambia, The	LLMC	0	West Africa
KEN	Kenya	LLMC	0	East Africa
LSO	Lesotho	LLMC	0	Southern Africa
MDG	Madagascar	LLMC	0	Southern Africa
MWI	Malawi	LLMC	0	Southern Africa
MLI	Mali	LLMC	1	West Africa
MRT	Mauritania	LLMC	1	West Africa
MUS	Mauritius	UMIC	0	East Africa
MOZ	Mozambique	LLMC	1	Southern Africa
NAM	Namibia	UMIC	1	Southern Africa
NER	Niger	LLMC	0	West Africa

Table continued next page

TABLE A.4   **Classification of Sub-Saharan African Countries** *(Continued)*

Code	Name	Income	Resources	subregion
NGA	Nigeria	LLMC	2	West Africa
RWA	Rwanda	LLMC	0	East Africa
SLE	Sierra Leone	LLMC	1	West Africa
ZAF	South Africa	UMIC	0	Southern Africa
SWZ	Eswatini	LLMC	0	Southern Africa
TGO	Togo	LLMC	0	West Africa
UGA	Uganda	LLMC	0	East Africa
ZMB	Zambia	LLMC	1	Southern Africa

Source: Barrot, Calderón, and Servén 2018.
Note: The indicator variable under "Resources" classifies countries into oil-rich countries (2); non-oil-rich countries (1); and resource-poor countries (0).
LLMC = low- or lower-middle-income country; UMIC = upper-middle-income country.

Notes

1. The start and end of the time series for each country will depend on data availability.

2. Discussion of this framework refers to the work of Christensen and Jorgenson (1970); Christensen, Jorgenson, and Lau (1973); Griliches and Jorgenson (1966); and Jorgenson and Griliches (1967).

3. This corresponds to the ratio of output per worker in the United States to that of each Sub-Saharan African country and aggregated using labor-force weighted averages.

4. Denison (1962) adjusted the measurement of the labor input for changes in the size of the labor force and shifts related to age, gender, hours worked, and unemployment. These improvements, as well as others in the basic growth-accounting methodology, led to estimates of the contribution of TFP to US growth that were much lower than Solow's.

5. In a comprehensive survey, Caselli (2005) finds that factor accumulation cannot explain more than half of the differences in income per capita across countries.

6. Note that *labsh* is heterogeneous across countries and displays some time variation within each country.

7. The data can be downloaded from the PWT 9.1 website: https://www.rug.nl/ggdc/productivity/pwt/.

8. Labor productivity can also be measured as GDP per hour worked. The labor input here is defined as total hours worked of all people engaged in employment. Empirically, the availability of hours worked of people employed in the economy is more limited for low- and lower-middle-income countries.

9. The data on Mincerian returns collected by Caselli, Ponticelli, and Rossi (2017) are available for download from http://personal.lse.ac.uk/casellif/papers/references_table.pdf.

10. In both cases, whenever there are data on years of schooling and no data on returns for a specific country, we input the average returns to education of its corresponding region.

11. The labor share in income for many countries has been declining over the past two decades (IMF 2017). In industrial countries, technological progress accounts for about half of the overall decline in the labor share. This progress is manifested by sharp reductions in the relative price of investment goods and varying exposure to routine-based occupations. For instance, 47 percent of US workers are at risk of automation over the next two decades (Frey and Osborne 2017), while that percentage increases to 57 percent of jobs in the OECD (World Bank 2016). This reduces the earnings of middle-skilled workers. In low- and middle-income countries, the declining labor share is mainly driven by global integration forces—in particular, the expansion of global value chains that have contributed to increasing the overall capital intensity in production. Trade and financial integration grew sharply over the past quarter century, thanks to the removal of restrictions on international trade and capital mobility and the decline in transportation and communication costs—the latter being facilitated by technological progress. In the short term, policy makers should implement policies to provide workers access to growth opportunities and design mechanisms to share growth benefits more broadly.

References

Abramovitz, Moses. 1956. "Resource and Output Trends in the United States Since 1870." *American Economic Review* 46 (2): 5–23.

Barro, Robert J., and Jong-Wha Lee. 2013. "A New Data Set of Educational Attainment in the World, 1950–2010." *Journal of Development Economics* 104: 184–98.

Barrot, Luis-Diego, César Calderón, and Luis Servén. 2018. "Sectoral Productivity Shifts in Sub-Saharan Africa." Background paper, World Bank, Washington, DC.

Brandt, Nicola, Paul Schreyer, and Vera Zipperer. 2017. "Productivity Measurement with Natural Capital." *Review of Income and Wealth* 63 (S1): S7–S21.

Caselli, Francesco. 2005. "Accounting for Cross-Country Income Differences." In *Handbook of Economic Growth*, Vol. 1, Part A, edited by Philippe Aghion and Steven Durlauf, 679–741. Amsterdam: Elsevier.

Caselli, Francesco. 2017. *Technology Differences over Space and Time*. Princeton, NJ: University Press.

Caselli, Francesco, Jacopo Ponticelli, and Federico Rossi. 2017. "A New Dataset on Mincerian Returns." In *Technology Differences over Space and Time*, by Francesco Caselli, 108–18. Princeton, NJ: Princeton University Press.

Caselli, Francesco, and Daniel J. Wilson. 2004. "Importing Technology." *Journal of Monetary Economics* 51 (1): 1–32.

Christensen, Laurits R., Dianne Cummings, and Dale W. Jorgenson. 1981. "Relative Productivity Levels, 1947–1973: An International Comparison." *European Economic Review* 16 (1): 61–94.

Christensen, Laurits R., and Dale W. Jorgenson. 1970. "U.S. Real Product and Real Factor Input, 1929–1967." *Review of Income and Wealth* 16 (1): 19–50.

Christensen, Laurits R., Dale W. Jorgenson, and Lawrence J. Lau. 1973. "Transcendental Logarithmic Production Frontiers." *Review of Economics and Statistics* 55 (1): 28–45.

Cohen, Daniel, and Laura Leker. 2014. "Health and Education: Another Look with the Proper Data." Discussion Paper 9940, Centre for Economic Policy Research, London.

Cohen, Daniel, and Marcelo Soto. 2007. "Growth and Human Capital: Good Data, Good Results." *Journal of Economic Growth* 12 (1): 51–76.

Denison, Edward F. 1962. "Sources of Growth in the United States and the Alternatives before Us." Supplement Paper No. 13, Committee for Economic Development, New York.

Denison, Edward F. 1967. *Why Growth Rates Differ: Postwar Experience in Nine Western Countries*. Washington, DC: Brookings Institution Press.

Denison, Edward F., Zvi Griliches, and Dale W. Jorgenson. 1972. "The Measurement of Productivity." *Survey of Current Business* 52 (5) Part II: 3–111.

Feenstra, Robert C., Robert Inklaar, and Marcel P. Timmer. 2015. "The Next Generation of the Penn World Table." *American Economic Review* 105 (10): 3150–82.

Frey, Carl Benedikt, and Michael A. Osborne. 2017. "The Future of Employment: How Susceptible Are Jobs to Computerisation?" *Technological Forecasting and Social Change* 114: 254–80.

Griliches, Zvi, and Dale W. Jorgenson. 1966. "Sources of Measured Productivity Change: Capital Input." *American Economic Review* 56 (1/2): 50–61.

Gupta, Sanjeev, Alvar Kangur, Chris Papageorgiou, and Abdoul Wane. 2011. "Efficiency-Adjusted Public Capital and Growth." Working Paper No. 11/217, International Monetary Fund, Washington, DC.

Hall, Robert E., and Charles I. Jones. 1999. "Why Do Some Countries Produce So Much More Output per Worker than Others?" *Quarterly Journal of Economics* 114 (1): 83–116.

Hsieh, Chang-Tai, and Peter J. Klenow. 2010. "Development Accounting." *American Economic Journal: Macroeconomics* 2 (1): 207–23.

IMF (International Monetary Fund). 2017. "Understanding the Downward Trend in Labor Income Shares." In *World Economic Outlook, April 2017: Gaining Momentum?*, 121–72. Washington, DC: IMF.

Jones, Charles I. 2016. "The Facts of Economic Growth." In *Handbook of Macroeconomics, Vol. 2A*, edited by John B. Taylor and Harald Uhlig, 3–69. Amsterdam: Elsevier.

Jorgenson, Dale W., and Zvi Griliches. 1967. "The Explanation of Productivity Change." *Review of Economic Studies* 34 (3): 249–83.

Jorgenson, Dale W., and Mieko Nishimizu. 1978. "U.S. and Japanese Economic Growth, 1952–1974: An International Comparison." *Economic Journal* 88 (352): 707–26.

Kamps, Christophe. 2004. "New Estimates of Government Net Capital Stocks for 22 OECD Countries, 1960–2001." Working Paper No. 04/67, International Monetary Fund, Washington, DC.

Klenow, Peter J., and Andrés Rodríguez-Clare. 1997. "The Neoclassical Revival in Growth Economics: Has It Gone Too Far?" In *NBER Macroeconomics Annual 1997*, edited by Ben S. Bernanke and Julio J. Rotemberg, 73–103. Cambridge, MA: MIT Press.

Lowe, Matt, Chris Papageorgiou, and Fidel Pérez-Sebastián. 2012. "The Public and Private MPK." Paper No. c017_021, International Conference on Dynamics, Economic Growth, and International Trade (DEGIT), Milan, September 13–14.

Mankiw, N. Gregory, David Romer, and David N. Weil. 1992. "A Contribution to the Empirics of Economic Growth." *Quarterly Journal of Economics* 107 (2): 407–37.

Monge-Naranjo, Alexander, Juan M. Sánchez, and Raül Santaeulàlia-Llopis. 2019. "Natural Resources and Global Misallocation." *American Economic Journal: Macroeconomics* 11 (2): 79–126.

Montenegro, Claudio E., and Harry Anthony Patrinos. 2014. "Comparable Estimates of Returns to Schooling Around the World." Policy Research Working Paper 7020, World Bank, Washington, DC.

Psacharopoulos, George. 1994. "Returns to Investment in Education: A Global Update." *World Development* 22 (9): 1325–43.

Sickles, Robin C., and Valentin Zelenyuk. 2019. *Measurement of Productivity and Efficiency: Theory and Practice.* Cambridge: Cambridge University Press.

Solow, Robert M. 1957. "Technical Change and the Aggregate Production Function." *Review of Economics and Statistics* 39 (3): 312–20.

Tinbergen, Jan. 1942. "Zur Theorie der Langfristigen Wirtschaftsentwicklung." *Weltwirtschaftliches Archiv* 55 (1): 511–49.

Walters, Dorothy. 1968. "Canadian Income Levels and Growth: An International Perspective." Staff Study No. 23, Economic Council of Canada, Ottawa.

World Bank. 2016. *World Development 2016: Digital Dividends.* Washington, DC: World Bank.

Country Productivity Analysis in Sub-Saharan Africa $\Big|$ B

ANGOLA

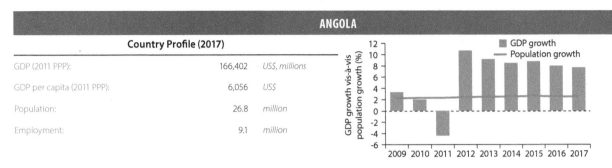

Country Profile (2017)

GDP (2011 PPP):	166,402	US$, millions
GDP per capita (2011 PPP):	6,056	US$
Population:	26.8	million
Employment:	9.1	million

Sectoral shares, 2016 (%)

	Agriculture	Manufacturing	Nonmanufacturing activities	Market services	Nonmarket services
Value added	8.3	5.8	53.1	14.7	18.2
Employment	51.1	1.5	7.4	24.1	15.9

Development accounting

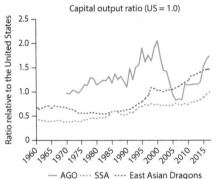

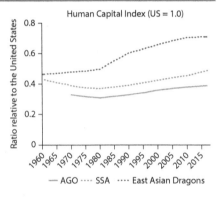

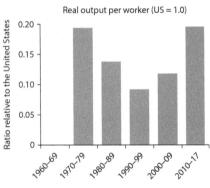

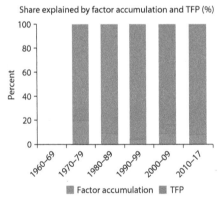

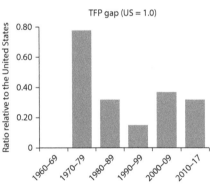

Growth accounting (% per year)

	Observed annual growth rates				Contribution to output growth per worker			
	1961–2017	1961–1977	1978–1995	1996–2017	1961–2017	1961–1977	1978–1995	1996–2017
I. Traditional growth accounting								
Output	0.39	−1.30	−1.95	2.84	0.39	−1.30	−1.95	2.84
Physical capital	0.26	1.24	−1.13	1.10	0.19	0.88	−0.81	0.78
Human capital	0.79	0.25	0.90	0.86	0.23	0.07	0.26	0.25
TFP	..	..	..	..	−0.02	−2.26	−1.40	1.81
II. Growth accounting: private and public capital accumulation								
Output	0.39	−1.30	−1.95	2.84	0.39	−1.30	−1.95	2.84
Physical capital	..	..	..	..	..	..	..	..
- Public	1.61	1.47	−0.64	3.48	0.42	0.39	−0.17	0.92
- Private	−1.52	1.09	−1.48	−2.38	−0.68	0.49	−0.67	−1.07
Human capital	0.79	0.25	0.90	0.86	0.23	0.07	0.26	0.25
TFP	..	..	..	..	0.43	−2.25	−1.38	2.75
III. Growth accounting including the natural capital								
Output	..	..	..	2.84	..	..	..	2.84
Physical capital	..	..	..	1.10	..	..	..	0.22
Natural capital	..	..	..	5.14	..	..	..	1.60
Human capital	..	..	..	0.86	..	..	..	0.18
TFP	..	..	..	..	..	..	..	0.84

Note: .. = insufficient or no data to perform the calculation.
East Asian Dragons = five East Asian economic "dragons": Indonesia, the Republic of Korea, Malaysia, Singapore, and Thailand; PPP = purchasing power parity; PPP = public-private partnerships; SSA = Sub-Saharan Africa; TFP = total factor productivity.

BENIN

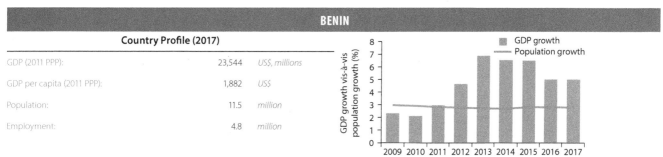

Country Profile (2017)

GDP (2011 PPP):	23,544	US$, millions
GDP per capita (2011 PPP):	1,882	US$
Population:	11.5	million
Employment:	4.8	million

Sectoral shares, 2016 (%)

	Agriculture	Manufacturing	Nonmanufacturing activities	Market services	Nonmarket services
Value added	24.5	14.5	8.8	24.3	27.9
Employment	40.9	15.7	3.5	28.1	11.8

Development accounting

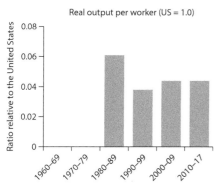
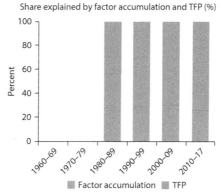
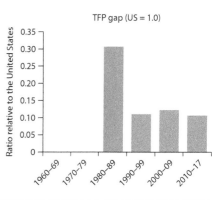

Growth accounting (% per year)

	Observed annual growth rates				Contribution to output growth per worker			
	1961–2017	1961–1977	1978–1995	1996–2017	1961–2017	1961–1977	1978–1995	1996–2017
I. Traditional growth accounting								
Output	1.21	..	1.03	1.33	1.21	..	1.03	1.33
Physical capital	−0.75	..	−1.96	0.07	−0.27	..	−0.71	0.03
Human capital	0.97	..	1.13	1.48	0.91	..	0.86	0.94
TFP	..	..	..	..	0.57	..	0.88	0.36
II. Growth accounting: private and public capital accumulation								
Output	1.21	..	1.03	1.33	1.21	..	1.03	1.33
Physical capital	..	..	..	..	..	..	..	..
- Public	−2.33	..	−2.74	−2.05	−0.58	..	−0.60	−0.39
- Private	1.49	..	−0.07	2.56	0.34	..	−0.01	0.44
Human capital	0.97	..	1.13	1.48	0.81	..	0.83	0.94
TFP	..	..	..	..	0.64	..	0.81	0.34
III. Growth accounting including the natural capital								
Output	..	..	..	1.33	..	..	..	1.33
Physical capital	..	..	..	0.07	..	..	..	0.03
Natural capital	..	..	..	−3.66	..	..	..	0.00
Human capital	..	..	..	1.48	..	..	..	0.95
TFP	..	..	..	..	..	..	..	0.36

Note: .. = insufficient or no data to perform the calculation.
East Asian Dragons = five East Asian economic "dragons": Indonesia, the Republic of Korea, Malaysia, Singapore, and Thailand; PPP = purchasing power parity; PPP = public-private partnerships; SSA = Sub-Saharan Africa; TFP = total factor productivity.

BOTSWANA

Country Profile (2017)

GDP (2011 PPP):	35,951	*US$, millions*
GDP per capita (2011 PPP):	15,896	*US$*
Population:	2.3	*million*
Employment:	1.0	*million*

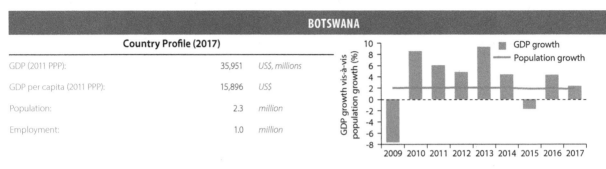

Sectoral shares, 2016 (%)

	Agriculture	Manufacturing	Nonmanufacturing activities	Market services	Nonmarket services
Value added	1.9	7.0	22.2	28.4	40.4
Employment	27.2	1.3	11.5	24.6	35.4

Development accounting

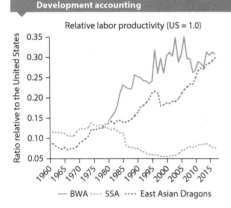

Relative labor productivity (US = 1.0)

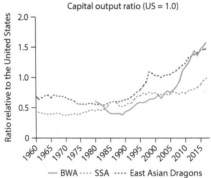

Capital output ratio (US = 1.0)

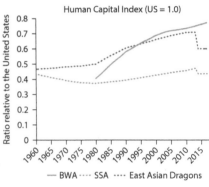

Human Capital Index (US = 1.0)

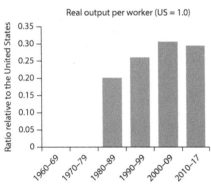

Real output per worker (US = 1.0)

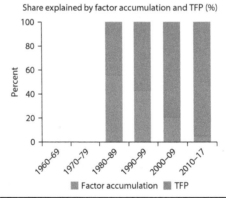

Share explained by factor accumulation and TFP (%)

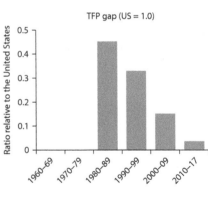

TFP gap (US = 1.0)

Growth accounting (% per year)

	Observed annual growth rates				Contribution to output growth per worker			
	1961–2017	*1961–1977*	*1978–1995*	*1996–2017*	*1961–2017*	*1961–1977*	*1978–1995*	*1996–2017*
I. Traditional growth accounting								
Output	2.74	..	3.79	2.02	2.74	..	3.79	2.02
Physical capital	4.25	..	3.03	5.09	2.88	..	2.05	3.44
Human capital	1.57	..	2.88	1.14	0.67	..	1.10	0.37
TFP	..	..	..	..	−0.81	..	0.64	−1.79
II. Growth accounting: private and public capital accumulation								
Output	2.74	..	3.79	2.02	2.74	..	3.79	2.02
Physical capital	..	..	..	..	..	..	..	..
- Public	4.36	..	3.65	4.84	1.15	..	0.95	1.21
- Private	4.15	..	2.62	5.20	1.88	..	1.17	2.22
Human capital	1.57	..	2.88	1.14	0.54	..	0.98	0.37
TFP	..	..	..	..	−0.84	..	0.69	−1.78
III. Growth accounting including the natural capital								
Output	..	..	..	2.02	..	..	..	2.02
Physical capital	..	..	..	5.09	..	..	..	2.68
Natural capital	..	..	..	17.81	..	..	..	0.82
Human capital	..	..	..	1.14	..	..	..	0.31
TFP	..	..	..	..	..	..	..	−1.80

Note: .. = insufficient or no data to perform the calculation.
East Asian Dragons = five East Asian economic "dragons": Indonesia, the Republic of Korea, Malaysia, Singapore, and Thailand; PPP = purchasing power parity; PPP = public-private partnerships; SSA = Sub-Saharan Africa; TFP = total factor productivity.

BURKINA FASO

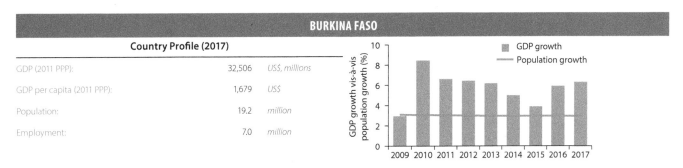

Country Profile (2017)

GDP (2011 PPP):	32,506	*US$, millions*
GDP per capita (2011 PPP):	1,679	*US$*
Population:	19.2	*million*
Employment:	7.0	*million*

Sectoral shares, 2016 (%)

	Agriculture	Manufacturing	Nonmanufacturing activities	Market services	Nonmarket services
Value added	28.6	8.3	14.3	18.8	30.0
Employment	26.3	15.8	16.1	29.9	11.9

Development accounting

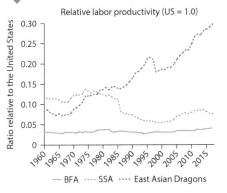
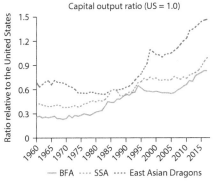
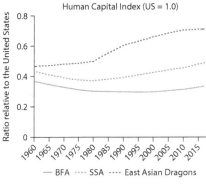

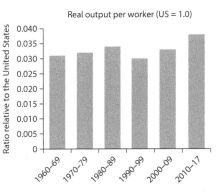
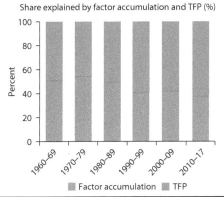
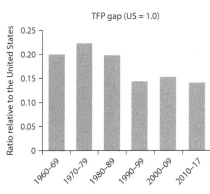

Growth accounting (% per year)

	Observed annual growth rates				Contribution to output growth per worker			
	1961–2017	*1961–1977*	*1978–1995*	*1996–2017*	*1961–2017*	*1961–1977*	*1978–1995*	*1996–2017*
I. Traditional growth accounting								
Output	2.00	1.57	0.87	3.26	2.00	1.57	0.87	3.26
Physical capital	3.67	2.55	4.45	3.91	1.35	0.94	1.63	1.44
Human capital	0.39	0.03	0.20	0.83	0.25	0.02	0.13	0.52
TFP	..	..	..	..	0.40	0.61	−0.89	1.29
II. Growth accounting: private and public capital accumulation								
Output	2.00	1.57	0.87	3.26	2.00	1.57	0.87	3.26
Physical capital	..	..	..	..	..	..	..	..
- Public	3.65	2.59	3.63	4.49	0.70	0.50	0.70	0.86
- Private	3.81	2.51	5.13	3.73	0.67	0.44	0.90	0.65
Human capital	0.39	0.03	0.20	0.83	0.25	0.02	0.13	0.52
TFP	..	..	..	..	0.38	0.61	−0.85	1.21
III. Growth accounting including the natural capital								
Output	..	..	..	..	..	..	..	..
Physical capital	..	..	..	..	..	..	..	..
Natural capital	..	..	..	..	..	..	..	..
Human capital	..	..	..	..	..	..	..	..
TFP	..	..	..	..	..	..	..	..

Note: .. = insufficient or no data to perform the calculation.
East Asian Dragons = five East Asian economic "dragons": Indonesia, the Republic of Korea, Malaysia, Singapore, and Thailand; PPP = purchasing power parity; PPP = public-private partnerships; SSA = Sub-Saharan Africa; TFP = total factor productivity.

BURUNDI

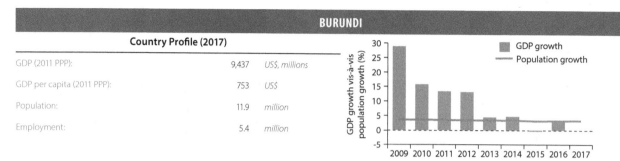

Country Profile (2017)

GDP (2011 PPP):	9,437	*US$, millions*
GDP per capita (2011 PPP):	753	*US$*
Population:	11.9	*million*
Employment:	5.4	*million*

Sectoral shares, 2016 (%)

	Agriculture	Manufacturing	Nonmanufacturing activities	Market services	Nonmarket services
Value added	32.4	11.6	3.3	13.7	39.0
Employment	91.3	1.8	0.7	2.8	3.5

Development accounting

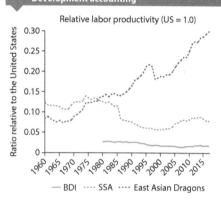

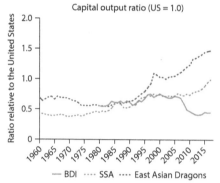

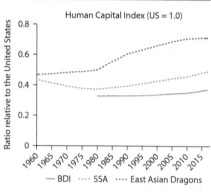

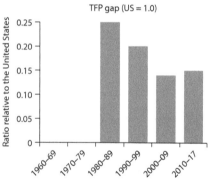

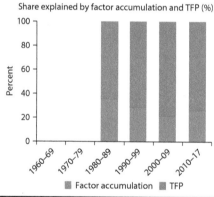

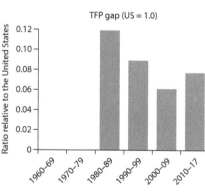

Growth accounting (% per year)

	Observed annual growth rates				Contribution to output growth per worker			
	1961–2017	1961–1977	1978–1995	1996–2017	1961–2017	1961–1977	1978–1995	1996–2017
I. Traditional growth accounting								
Output	1.00	..	−0.16	1.80	1.00	..	−0.16	1.80
Physical capital	0.01	..	0.19	−0.11	0.00	..	0.05	−0.03
Human capital	0.42	..	0.36	0.78	0.47	..	0.31	0.57
TFP	..	..	..	..	0.54	..	−0.53	1.26
II. Growth accounting: private and public capital accumulation								
Output	1.00	..	−0.16	1.80	1.00	..	−0.16	1.80
Physical capital	..	..	..	..	..	..	..	..
- Public	2.55	..	0.75	3.77	0.43	..	0.08	0.54
- Private	−0.97	..	0.04	−1.66	−0.15	..	0.00	−0.22
Human capital	0.42	..	0.36	0.78	0.36	..	0.20	0.57
TFP	..	..	..	..	0.36	..	−0.45	0.91
III. Growth accounting including the natural capital								
Output	..	..	..	1.80	..	..	..	1.80
Physical capital	..	..	..	−0.11	..	..	..	−0.02
Natural capital	..	..	..	126.99	..	..	..	0.34
Human capital	..	..	..	0.78	..	..	..	0.30
TFP	..	..	..	..	..	..	..	1.17

Note: .. = insufficient or no data to perform the calculation.
East Asian Dragons = five East Asian economic "dragons": Indonesia, the Republic of Korea, Malaysia, Singapore, and Thailand; PPP = purchasing power parity; PPP = public-private partnerships; SSA = Sub-Saharan Africa; TFP = total factor productivity.

CABO VERDE

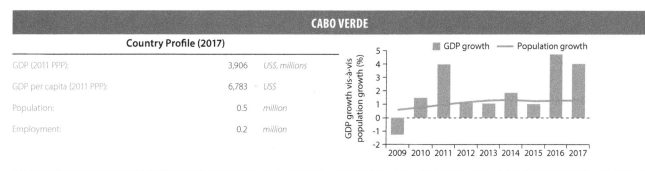

Country Profile (2017)

GDP (2011 PPP):	3,906	US$, millions
GDP per capita (2011 PPP):	6,783	US$
Population:	0.5	million
Employment:	0.2	million

Sectoral shares (%)

	Agriculture	Manufacturing	Nonmanufacturing activities	Market services	Nonmarket services
Value added	..	..	..	..	..
Employment	..	..	..	..	..

Development accounting

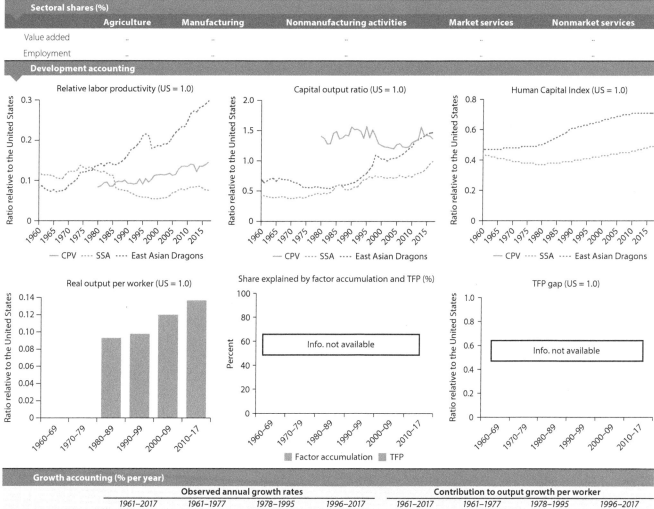

Growth accounting (% per year)

	Observed annual growth rates				Contribution to output growth per worker			
	1961–2017	*1961–1977*	*1978–1995*	*1996–2017*	*1961–2017*	*1961–1977*	*1978–1995*	*1996–2017*
I. Traditional growth accounting								
Output	..	..	..	..	..	..	..	..
Physical capital	..	..	..	..	..	..	..	..
Human capital	..	..	..	..	..	..	..	..
TFP	..	..	..	..	..	..	..	..
II. Growth accounting: private and public capital accumulation								
Output	..	..	..	..	..	..	..	..
Physical capital	..	..	..	..	..	..	..	..
- Public	..	..	..	..	..	..	..	..
- Private	..	..	..	..	..	..	..	..
Human capital	..	..	..	..	..	..	..	..
TFP	..	..	..	..	..	..	..	..
III. Growth accounting including the natural capital								
Output	..	..	..	..	..	..	..	..
Physical capital	..	..	..	..	..	..	..	..
Natural capital	..	..	..	..	..	..	..	..
Human capital	..	..	..	..	..	..	..	..
TFP	..	..	..	..	..	..	..	..

Note: .. = insufficient or no data to perform the calculation.
East Asian Dragons = five East Asian economic "dragons": Indonesia, the Republic of Korea, Malaysia, Singapore, and Thailand; PPP = purchasing power parity; PPP = public-private partnerships;
SSA = Sub-Saharan Africa; TFP = total factor productivity.

CAMEROON

Country Profile (2017)

GDP (2011 PPP):	69,451	US$, millions
GDP per capita (2011 PPP):	2,785	US$
Population:	24.6	million
Employment:	10.9	million

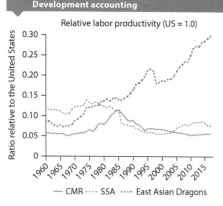

Sectoral shares, 2016 (%)

	Agriculture	Manufacturing	Nonmanufacturing activities	Market services	Nonmarket services
Value added	15.4	15.3	15.0	29.1	25.2
Employment	62.4	5.8	3.4	22.9	5.5

Development accounting

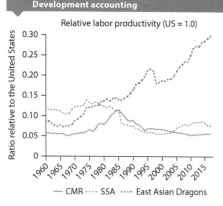
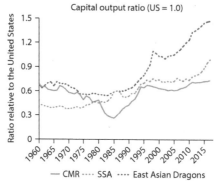
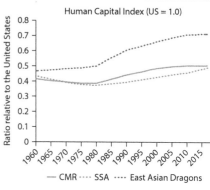

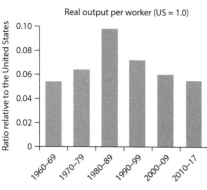
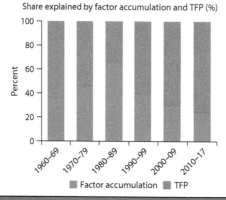
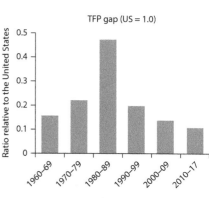

Growth accounting (% per year)

	Observed annual growth rates				Contribution to output growth per worker			
	1961–2017	1961–1977	1978–1995	1996–2017	1961–2017	1961–1977	1978–1995	1996–2017
I. Traditional growth accounting								
Output	0.77	2.37	−0.42	0.50	0.77	2.37	−0.42	0.50
Physical capital	0.48	0.96	0.91	−0.24	0.22	0.45	0.42	−0.11
Human capital	0.90	0.67	1.41	0.67	0.48	0.36	0.75	0.36
TFP	..	..	..	..	0.06	1.57	−1.60	0.26
II. Growth accounting: private and public capital accumulation								
Output	0.77	2.37	−0.42	0.50	0.77	2.37	−0.42	0.50
Physical capital	..	..	..	..	..	..	..	..
- Public	0.90	0.90	0.85	0.94	0.22	0.22	0.21	0.23
- Private	0.33	0.97	0.93	−0.66	0.07	0.22	0.21	−0.15
Human capital	0.90	0.67	1.41	0.67	0.48	0.36	0.75	0.36
TFP	..	..	..	..	−0.01	1.58	−1.59	0.06
III. Growth accounting including the natural capital								
Output	..	..	..	0.50	..	..	..	0.50
Physical capital	..	..	..	−0.24	..	..	..	−0.11
Natural capital	..	..	..	0.39	..	..	..	0.03
Human capital	..	..	..	0.67	..	..	..	0.42
TFP	..	..	..	..	..	..	..	0.17

Note: .. = insufficient or no data to perform the calculation.
East Asian Dragons = five East Asian economic "dragons": Indonesia, the Republic of Korea, Malaysia, Singapore, and Thailand; PPP = purchasing power parity; PPP = public-private partnerships; SSA = Sub-Saharan Africa; TFP = total factor productivity.

CENTRAL AFRICAN REPUBLIC

Country Profile (2017)

GDP (2011 PPP):	3,544	*US$, millions*
GDP per capita (2011 PPP):	707	*US$*
Population:	5.0	*million*
Employment:	2.2	*million*

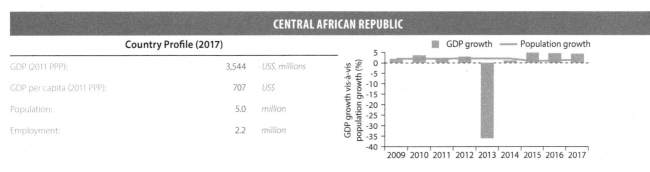

Sectoral shares, 2016 (%)

	Agriculture	Manufacturing	Nonmanufacturing activities	Market services	Nonmarket services
Value added	31.2	23.0	4.3	20.9	20.6
Employment	85.6	7.5	0.5	3.4	3.0

Development accounting

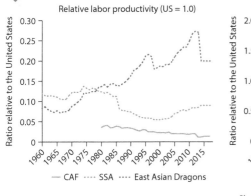
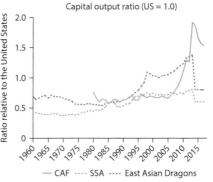
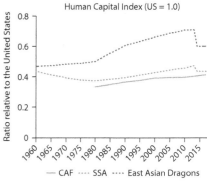

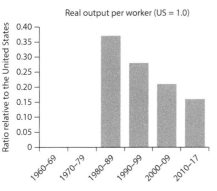
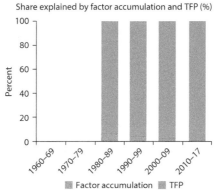
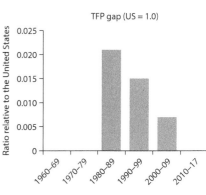

Growth accounting (% per year)

	Observed annual growth rates				Contribution to output growth per worker			
	1961–2017	*1961–1977*	*1978–1995*	*1996–2017*	*1961–2017*	*1961–1977*	*1978–1995*	*1996–2017*
I. Traditional growth accounting								
Output	−1.44	..	−1.23	−1.58	−1.44	..	−1.23	−1.58
Physical capital	−1.80	..	−1.78	−1.82	−1.41	..	−1.39	−1.42
Human capital	0.64	..	1.03	0.69	0.19	..	0.25	0.15
TFP	..	..	..	..	−0.22	..	−0.09	−0.31
II. Growth accounting: private and public capital accumulation								
Output	−1.44	..	−1.23	−1.58	−1.44	..	−1.23	−1.58
Physical capital	..	..	..	..	..	..	..	..
- Public	−1.96	..	−1.61	−2.20	−0.77	..	−0.64	−0.90
- Private	−1.64	..	−2.11	−1.32	−0.59	..	−0.77	−0.49
Human capital	0.64	..	1.03	0.69	0.13	..	0.22	0.15
TFP	..	..	..	..	−0.21	..	−0.04	−0.34
III. Growth accounting including the natural capital								
Output	..	..	..	..	..	..	..	..
Physical capital	..	..	..	..	..	..	..	..
Natural capital	..	..	..	..	..	..	..	..
Human capital	..	..	..	..	..	..	..	..
TFP	..	..	..	..	..	..	..	..

Note: .. = insufficient or no data to perform the calculation.
East Asian Dragons = five East Asian economic "dragons": Indonesia, the Republic of Korea, Malaysia, Singapore, and Thailand; PPP = purchasing power parity; PPP = public-private partnerships; SSA = Sub-Saharan Africa; TFP = total factor productivity.

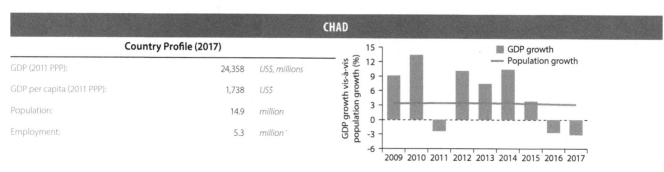

CHAD

Country Profile (2017)

GDP (2011 PPP):	24,358	US$, millions
GDP per capita (2011 PPP):	1,738	US$
Population:	14.9	million
Employment:	5.3	million

Sectoral shares (%)

	Agriculture	Manufacturing	Nonmanufacturing activities	Market services	Nonmarket services
Value added	..	..	..	..	..
Employment	..	..	..	..	..

Development accounting

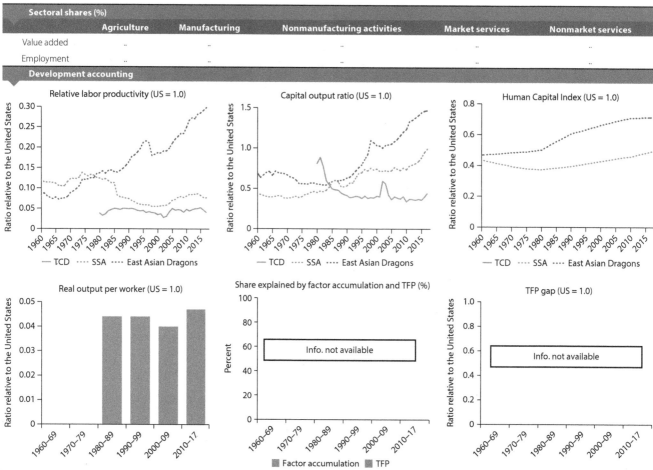

Growth accounting (% per year)

	Observed annual growth rates				Contribution to output growth per worker			
	1961–2017	1961–1977	1978–1995	1996–2017	1961–2017	1961–1977	1978–1995	1996–2017
I. Traditional growth accounting								
Output	..	..	..	..	..	..	..	..
Physical capital	..	..	..	..	..	..	..	..
Human capital	..	..	..	..	..	..	..	..
TFP	..	..	..	..	..	..	..	..
II. Growth accounting: private and public capital accumulation								
Output	..	..	..	..	..	..	..	..
Physical capital	..	..	..	..	..	..	..	..
- Public	..	..	..	..	..	..	..	..
- Private	..	..	..	..	..	..	..	..
Human capital	..	..	..	..	..	..	..	..
TFP	..	..	..	..	..	..	..	..
III. Growth accounting including the natural capital								
Output	..	..	..	..	..	..	..	..
Physical capital	..	..	..	..	..	..	..	..
Natural capital	..	..	..	..	..	..	..	..
Human capital	..	..	..	..	..	..	..	..
TFP	..	..	..	..	..	..	..	..

Note: .. = insufficient or no data to perform the calculation.
East Asian Dragons = five East Asian economic "dragons": Indonesia, the Republic of Korea, Malaysia, Singapore, and Thailand; PPP = purchasing power parity; PPP = public-private partnerships; SSA = Sub-Saharan Africa; TFP = total factor productivity.

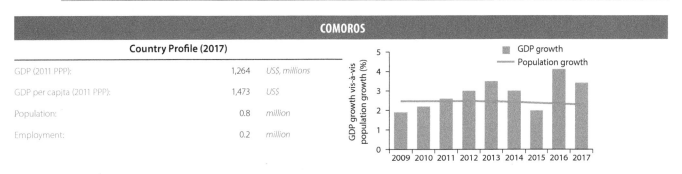

COMOROS

Country Profile (2017)

GDP (2011 PPP):	1,264	US$, millions
GDP per capita (2011 PPP):	1,473	US$
Population:	0.8	million
Employment:	0.2	million

Sectoral shares (%)

	Agriculture	Manufacturing	Nonmanufacturing activities	Market services	Nonmarket services
Value added	..	..	..	..	..
Employment	..	..	..	..	..

Development accounting

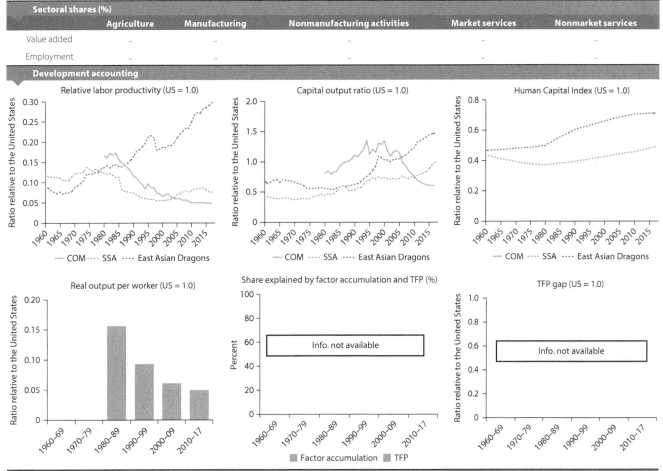

Growth accounting (% per year)

	Observed annual growth rates				Contribution to output growth per worker			
	1961–2017	*1961–1977*	*1978–1995*	*1996–2017*	*1961–2017*	*1961–1977*	*1978–1995*	*1996–2017*
I. Traditional growth accounting								
Output	..	..	..	..	..	..	..	..
Physical capital	..	..	..	..	..	..	..	..
Human capital	..	..	..	..	..	..	..	..
TFP	..	..	..	..	..	..	..	..
II. Growth accounting: private and public capital accumulation								
Output	..	..	..	..	..	..	..	..
Physical capital	..	..	..	..	..	..	..	..
- Public	..	..	..	..	..	..	..	..
- Private	..	..	..	..	..	..	..	..
Human capital	..	..	..	..	..	..	..	..
TFP	..	..	..	..	..	..	..	..
III. Growth accounting including the natural capital								
Output	..	..	..	..	..	..	..	..
Physical capital	..	..	..	..	..	..	..	..
Natural capital	..	..	..	..	..	..	..	..
Human capital	..	..	..	..	..	..	..	..
TFP	..	..	..	..	..	..	..	..

Note: .. = insufficient or no data to perform the calculation.
East Asian Dragons = five East Asian economic "dragons": Indonesia, the Republic of Korea, Malaysia, Singapore, and Thailand; PPP = purchasing power parity; PPP = public-private partnerships;
SSA = Sub-Saharan Africa; TFP = total factor productivity.

DEMOCRATIC REPUBLIC OF CONGO

Country Profile (2017)

GDP (2011 PPP):	92,195	US$, millions
GDP per capita (2011 PPP):	1,157	US$
Population:	82.6	million
Employment:	27.5	million

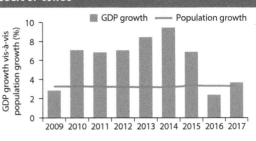

Sectoral shares (%)

	Agriculture	Manufacturing	Nonmanufacturing activities	Market services	Nonmarket services
Value added	..	..	..	..	..
Employment	..	..	..	..	..

Development accounting

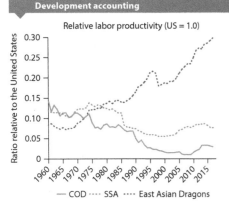
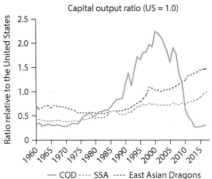
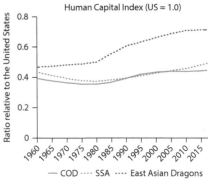

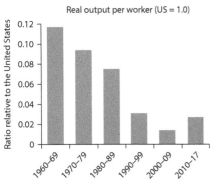
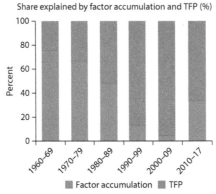
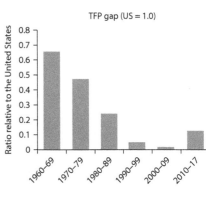

Growth accounting (% per year)

	Observed annual growth rates				Contribution to output growth per worker			
	1961–2017	1961–1977	1978–1995	1996–2017	1961–2017	1961–1977	1978–1995	1996–2017
I. Traditional growth accounting								
Output	−1.53	−0.57	−4.20	−0.08	−1.53	−0.57	−4.20	−0.08
Physical capital	0.20	1.13	1.31	−1.43	0.09	0.49	0.57	−0.62
Human capital	0.78	0.48	1.35	0.54	0.44	0.28	0.77	0.31
TFP	..	..	..	..	−2.06	−1.34	−5.53	0.23
II. Growth accounting: private and public capital accumulation								
Output	−1.53	−0.57	−4.20	−0.08	−1.53	−0.57	−4.20	−0.08
Physical capital	..	..	..	..	..	..	..	..
- Public	4.28	1.16	1.36	9.09	0.97	0.26	0.31	2.05
- Private	−0.17	1.13	1.31	−2.40	−0.04	0.23	0.27	−0.49
Human capital	0.78	0.48	1.35	0.54	0.44	0.28	0.77	0.31
TFP	..	..	..	..	−2.90	−1.34	−5.54	−1.94
III. Growth accounting including the natural capital								
Output	..	..	..	−0.08	..	..	..	−0.08
Physical capital	..	..	..	−1.43	..	..	..	−0.99
Natural capital	..	..	..	12.52	..	..	..	3.39
Human capital	..	..	..	0.54	..	..	..	0.66
TFP	..	..	..	..	..	..	..	−3.13

Note: .. = insufficient or no data to perform the calculation.
East Asian Dragons = five East Asian economic "dragons": Indonesia, the Republic of Korea, Malaysia, Singapore, and Thailand; PPP = purchasing power parity; PPP = public-private partnerships; SSA = Sub-Saharan Africa; TFP = total factor productivity.

REPUBLIC OF CONGO

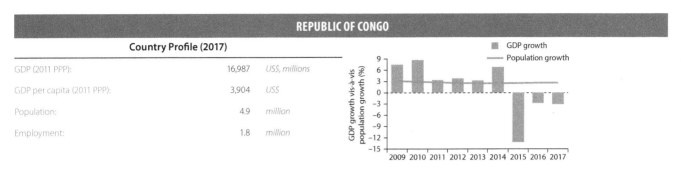

Country Profile (2017)

GDP (2011 PPP):	16,987	US$, millions
GDP per capita (2011 PPP):	3,904	US$
Population:	4.9	million
Employment:	1.8	million

Sectoral shares (%)

	Agriculture	Manufacturing	Nonmanufacturing activities	Market services	Nonmarket services
Value added	5.3	4.6	65.3	13.5	11.4
Employment	37.3	19.9	5.3	28.1	9.5

Development accounting

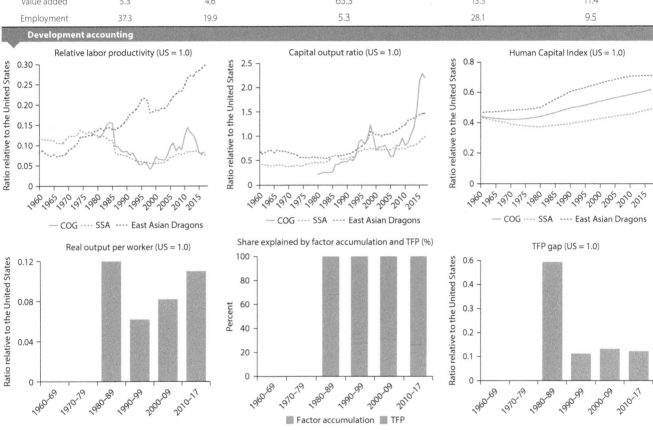

Growth accounting (% per year)

	Observed annual growth rates				Contribution to output growth per worker			
	1961–2017	*1961–1977*	*1978–1995*	*1996–2017*	*1961–2017*	*1961–1977*	*1978–1995*	*1996–2017*
I. Traditional growth accounting								
Output	0.10	..	0.64	−0.27	0.10	..	0.64	−0.27
Physical capital	2.72	..	3.18	2.40	1.79	..	2.10	1.58
Human capital	1.13	..	2.19	0.32	0.36	..	0.72	0.11
TFP	..	..	..	..	−2.05	..	−2.18	−1.96
II. Growth accounting: private and public capital accumulation								
Output	0.10	..	0.64	−0.27	0.10	..	0.64	−0.27
Physical capital	..	..	..	..	..	..	..	..
- Public	4.47	..	1.03	6.81	1.22	..	0.34	2.35
- Private	1.75	..	4.10	0.15	0.44	..	1.24	0.05
Human capital	1.13	..	2.19	0.32	0.31	..	0.72	0.11
TFP	..	..	..	..	−1.87	..	−1.66	−2.77
III. Growth accounting including the natural capital								
Output	..	..	..	−0.27	..	..	..	−0.27
Physical capital	..	..	..	2.40	..	..	..	0.21
Natural capital	..	..	..	4.77	..	..	..	1.57
Human capital	..	..	..	0.32	..	..	..	0.12
TFP	..	..	..	..	..	..	..	−2.17

Note: .. = insufficient or no data to perform the calculation.
East Asian Dragons = five East Asian economic "dragons": Indonesia, the Republic of Korea, Malaysia, Singapore, and Thailand; PPP = purchasing power parity; PPP = public-private partnerships;
SSA = Sub-Saharan Africa; TFP = total factor productivity.

CÔTE D'IVOIRE

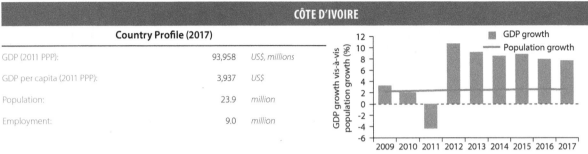

Country Profile (2017)

GDP (2011 PPP):	93,958	US$, millions
GDP per capita (2011 PPP):	3,937	US$
Population:	23.9	million
Employment:	9.0	million

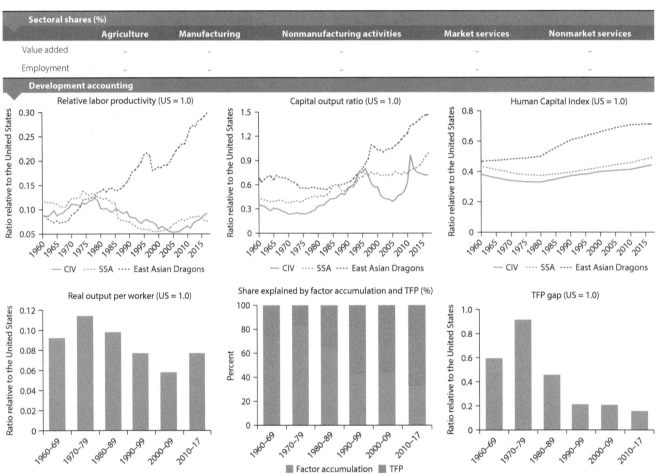

Sectoral shares (%)

	Agriculture	Manufacturing	Nonmanufacturing activities	Market services	Nonmarket services
Value added	..	..	..	..	..
Employment	..	..	..	..	..

Development accounting

Relative labor productivity (US = 1.0)

Capital output ratio (US = 1.0)

Human Capital Index (US = 1.0)

— CIV ···· SSA ···· East Asian Dragons

Real output per worker (US = 1.0)

Share explained by factor accumulation and TFP (%)

■ Factor accumulation ■ TFP

TFP gap (US = 1.0)

Growth accounting (% per year)

	Observed annual growth rates				Contribution to output growth per worker			
	1961–2017	1961–1977	1978–1995	1996–2017	1961–2017	1961–1977	1978–1995	1996–2017
I. Traditional growth accounting								
Output	0.93	4.17	−2.10	0.89	0.93	4.17	−2.10	0.89
Physical capital	−0.32	1.60	−1.39	−0.93	−0.16	0.80	−0.69	−0.46
Human capital	0.82	0.26	1.22	0.94	0.42	0.13	0.61	0.47
TFP	..	..	..	..	0.67	3.24	−2.02	0.88
II. Growth accounting: private and public capital accumulation								
Output	0.93	4.17	−2.10	0.89	0.93	4.17	−2.10	0.89
Physical capital	..	..	..	..	..	..	..	..
- Public	0.54	2.15	1.73	−1.67	0.14	0.56	0.45	−0.43
- Private	−0.93	1.37	−3.63	−0.50	−0.22	0.32	−0.86	−0.12
Human capital	0.82	0.26	1.22	0.94	0.42	0.13	0.61	0.47
TFP	..	..	..	..	0.59	3.16	−2.30	0.97
III. Growth accounting including the natural capital								
Output	..	..	..	0.89	..	..	..	0.89
Physical capital	..	..	..	−0.93	..	..	..	−0.59
Natural capital	..	..	..	15.47	..	..	..	0.95
Human capital	..	..	..	0.94	..	..	..	0.66
TFP	..	..	..	..	..	..	..	−0.13

Note: .. = insufficient or no data to perform the calculation.
East Asian Dragons = five East Asian economic "dragons": Indonesia, the Republic of Korea, Malaysia, Singapore, and Thailand; PPP = purchasing power parity; PPP = public-private partnerships; SSA = Sub-Saharan Africa; TFP = total factor productivity.

EQUATORIAL GUINEA

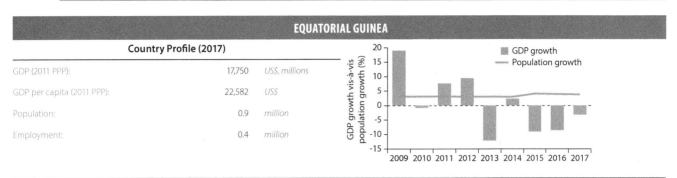

Country Profile (2017)

GDP (2011 PPP):	17,750	US$, millions
GDP per capita (2011 PPP):	22,582	US$
Population:	0.9	million
Employment:	0.4	million

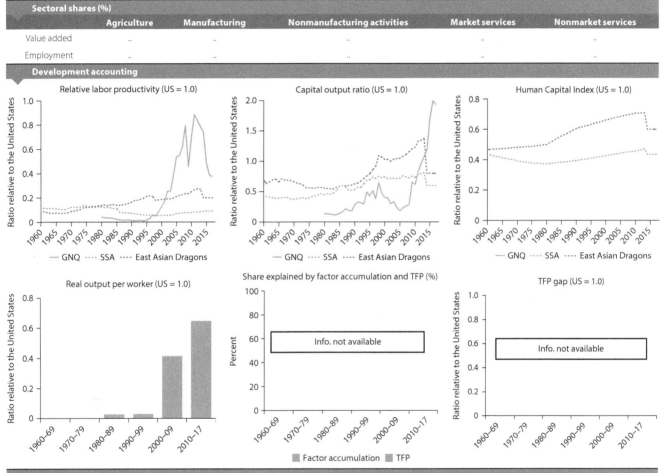

Sectoral shares (%)

	Agriculture	Manufacturing	Nonmanufacturing activities	Market services	Nonmarket services
Value added	..	..	..	..	..
Employment	..	..	..	..	..

Development accounting

Relative labor productivity (US = 1.0)

Capital output ratio (US = 1.0)

Human Capital Index (US = 1.0)

Real output per worker (US = 1.0)

Share explained by factor accumulation and TFP (%)

Info. not available

TFP gap (US = 1.0)

Info. not available

Growth accounting (% per year)

	Observed annual growth rates				Contribution to output growth per worker			
	1961–2017	*1961–1977*	*1978–1995*	*1996–2017*	*1961–2017*	*1961–1977*	*1978–1995*	*1996–2017*
I. Traditional growth accounting								
Output	..	..	..	..	..	..	..	..
Physical capital	..	..	..	..	..	..	..	..
Human capital	..	..	..	..	..	..	..	..
TFP	..	..	..	..	..	..	..	..
II. Growth accounting: private and public capital accumulation								
Output	..	..	..	..	..	..	..	..
Physical capital	..	..	..	..	..	..	..	..
- Public	..	..	..	..	..	..	..	..
- Private	..	..	..	..	..	..	..	..
Human capital	..	..	..	..	..	..	..	..
TFP	..	..	..	..	..	..	..	..
III. Growth accounting including the natural capital								
Output	..	..	..	..	..	..	..	..
Physical capital	..	..	..	..	..	..	..	..
Natural capital	..	..	..	..	..	..	..	..
Human capital	..	..	..	..	..	..	..	..
TFP	..	..	..	..	..	..	..	..

Note: .. = insufficient or no data to perform the calculation.
East Asian Dragons = five East Asian economic "dragons": Indonesia, the Republic of Korea, Malaysia, Singapore, and Thailand; PPP = purchasing power parity; PPP = public-private partnerships; SSA = Sub-Saharan Africa; TFP = total factor productivity.

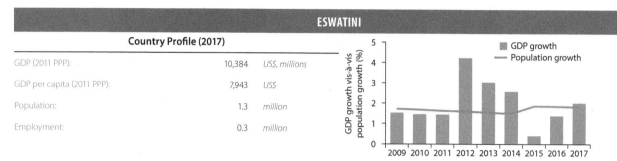

ESWATINI

Country Profile (2017)

GDP (2011 PPP):	10,384	US$, millions
GDP per capita (2011 PPP):	7,943	US$
Population:	1.3	million
Employment:	0.3	million

Sectoral shares, 2016 (%)

	Agriculture	Manufacturing	Nonmanufacturing activities	Market services	Nonmarket services
Value added	7.3	37.0	3.7	21.6	30.3
Employment	68.2	11.0	1.8	11.5	7.4

Development accounting

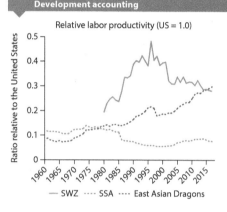

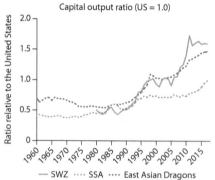

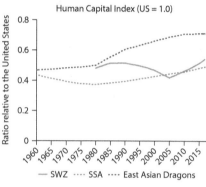

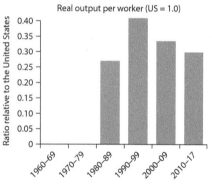

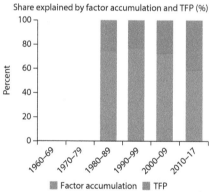

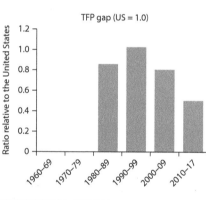

Growth accounting (% per year)

	Observed annual growth rates				Contribution to output growth per worker			
	1961–2017	1961–1977	1978–1995	1996–2017	1961–2017	1961–1977	1978–1995	1996–2017
I. Traditional growth accounting								
Output	0.96	..	0.76	1.10	0.96	..	0.76	1.10
Physical capital	1.13	..	3.52	−0.50	0.40	..	1.24	−0.18
Human capital	0.90	..	0.79	0.69	0.41	..	0.37	0.45
TFP	..	..	..	..	0.15	..	−0.85	0.83
II. Growth accounting: private and public capital accumulation								
Output	0.96	..	0.76	1.10	0.96	..	0.76	1.10
Physical capital	..	..	..	..	..	..	..	..
- Public	3.38	..	4.76	2.44	0.38	..	0.52	0.32
- Private	0.23	..	3.26	−1.84	0.04	..	0.61	−0.41
Human capital	0.90	..	0.79	0.69	0.50	..	0.43	0.45
TFP	..	..	..	..	0.05	..	−0.81	0.75
III. Growth accounting including the natural capital								
Output	..	..	..	..	..	..	..	..
Physical capital	..	..	..	..	..	..	..	..
Natual capital	..	..	..	..	..	..	..	..
Human capital	..	..	..	..	..	..	..	..
TFP	..	..	..	..	..	..	..	..

Note: .. = insufficient or no data to perform the calculation.
East Asian Dragons = five East Asian economic "dragons": Indonesia, the Republic of Korea, Malaysia, Singapore, and Thailand; PPP = purchasing power parity; PPP = public-private partnerships; SSA = Sub-Saharan Africa; TFP = total factor productivity.

ETHIOPIA

Country Profile (2017)

GDP (2011 PPP):	160,054	US$, millions
GDP per capita (2011 PPP):	1,444	US$
Population:	104.5	million
Employment:	49.2	million

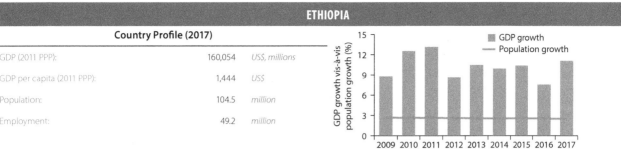

Sectoral shares (%)

	Agriculture	Manufacturing	Nonmanufacturing activities	Market services	Nonmarket services
Value added	..	..	..	..	..
Employment	..	..	..	..	..

Development accounting

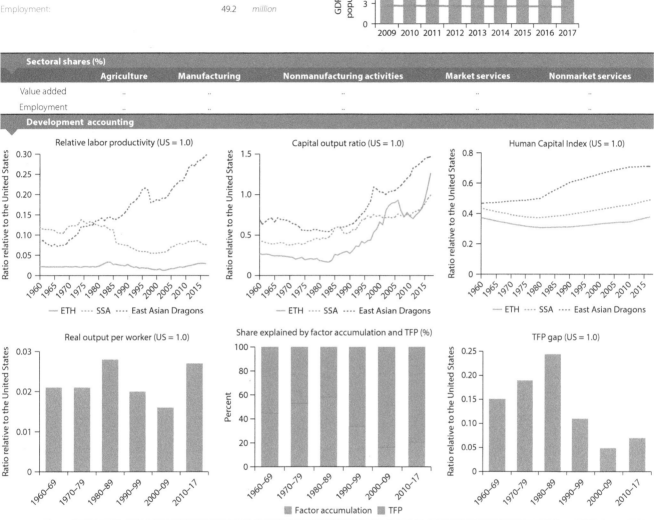

Growth accounting (% per year)

	Observed annual growth rates				Contribution to output growth per worker			
	1961–2017	*1961–1977*	*1978–1995*	*1996–2017*	*1961–2017*	*1961–1977*	*1978–1995*	*1996–2017*
I. Traditional growth accounting								
Output	1.54	−0.05	−0.90	4.77	1.54	−0.05	−0.90	4.77
Physical capital	1.06	0.40	−2.07	4.14	0.46	0.17	−0.89	1.79
Human capital	0.58	0.06	0.54	1.03	0.33	0.03	0.31	0.58
TFP	..	..	..	..	0.75	−0.25	−0.32	2.40
II. Growth accounting: private and public capital accumulation								
Output	1.54	−0.05	−0.90	4.77	1.54	−0.05	−0.90	4.77
Physical capital	..	..	..	..	..	..	..	..
- Public	1.11	0.40	−1.91	4.13	0.25	0.09	−0.43	0.93
- Private	1.12	0.40	−2.26	4.45	0.23	0.08	−0.47	0.92
Human capital	0.58	0.06	0.54	1.03	0.33	0.03	0.31	0.58
TFP	..	..	..	..	0.73	−0.25	−0.31	2.34
III. Growth accounting including the natural capital								
Output	..	..	..	4.77	..	..	..	4.77
Physical capital	..	..	..	4.14	..	..	..	1.61
Natural capital	..	..	..	125.11	..	..	..	0.64
Human capital	..	..	..	1.03	..	..	..	0.53
TFP	..	..	..	..	..	..	..	1.99

Note: .. = insufficient or no data to perform the calculation.
East Asian Dragons = five East Asian economic "dragons": Indonesia, the Republic of Korea, Malaysia, Singapore, and Thailand; PPP = purchasing power parity; PPP = public-private partnerships; SSA = Sub-Saharan Africa; TFP = total factor productivity.

GABON

Country Profile (2017)

GDP (2011 PPP):	23,004	US$, millions
GDP per capita (2011 PPP):	12,108	US$
Population:	1.8	million
Employment:	0.5	million

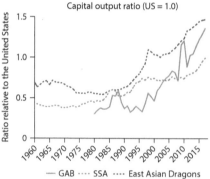

Sectoral shares, 2016 (%)

	Agriculture	Manufacturing	Nonmanufacturing activities	Market services	Nonmarket services
Value added	4.7	4.9	43.3	12.5	34.6
Employment	41.3	3.7	9.2	31.7	14.0

Development accounting

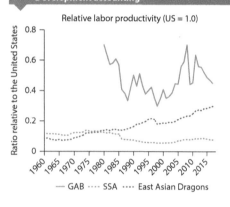

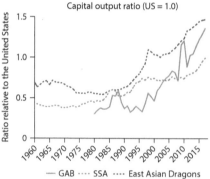

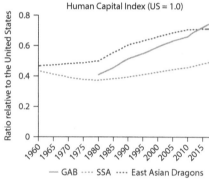

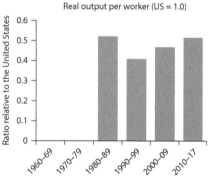

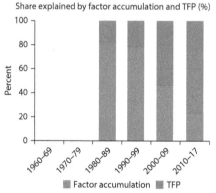

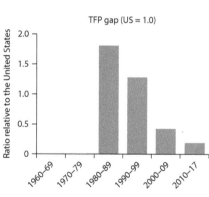

Growth accounting (% per year)

	Observed annual growth rates				Contribution to output growth per worker			
	1961–2017	1961–1977	1978–1995	1996–2017	1961–2017	1961–1977	1978–1995	1996–2017
I. Traditional growth accounting								
Output	0.40	..	0.43	0.37	0.40	..	0.43	0.37
Physical capital	−0.23	..	−1.83	0.86	−0.14	..	−1.14	0.53
Human capital	1.69	..	2.37	1.67	0.73	..	0.87	0.63
TFP	..	..	..	..	−0.19	..	0.70	−0.79
II. Growth accounting: private and public capital accumulation								
Output	0.40	..	0.43	0.37	0.40	..	0.43	0.37
Physical capital	..	..	..	..	..	..	..	..
- Public	0.71	..	−0.76	1.72	0.21	..	−0.17	0.40
- Private	−0.67	..	−2.19	0.37	−0.34	..	−0.82	0.14
Human capital	1.69	..	2.37	1.67	0.83	..	0.85	0.63
TFP	..	..	..	..	−0.30	..	0.57	−0.80
III. Growth accounting including the natural capital								
Output	..	..	..	0.37	..	..	..	0.37
Physical capital	..	..	..	0.86	..	..	..	0.14
Natural capital	..	..	..	6.11	..	..	..	1.30
Human capital	..	..	..	1.67	..	..	..	0.39
TFP	..	..	..	..	..	..	..	−1.45

Note: .. = insufficient or no data to perform the calculation.
East Asian Dragons = five East Asian economic "dragons": Indonesia, the Republic of Korea, Malaysia, Singapore, and Thailand; PPP = purchasing power parity; PPP = public-private partnerships; SSA = Sub-Saharan Africa; TFP = total factor productivity.

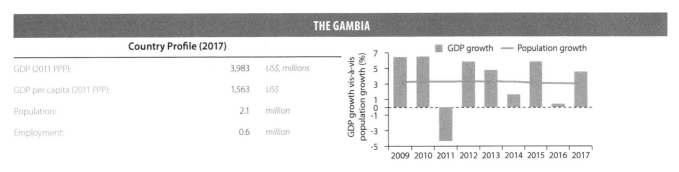

THE GAMBIA

Country Profile (2017)

GDP (2011 PPP):	3,983	US$, millions
GDP per capita (2011 PPP):	1,563	US$
Population:	2.1	million
Employment:	0.6	million

Sectoral shares, 2016 (%)

	Agriculture	Manufacturing	Nonmanufacturing activities	Market services	Nonmarket services
Value added	20.0	4.9	9.2	44.3	21.6
Employment	27.9	9.2	6.2	44.6	12.1

Development accounting

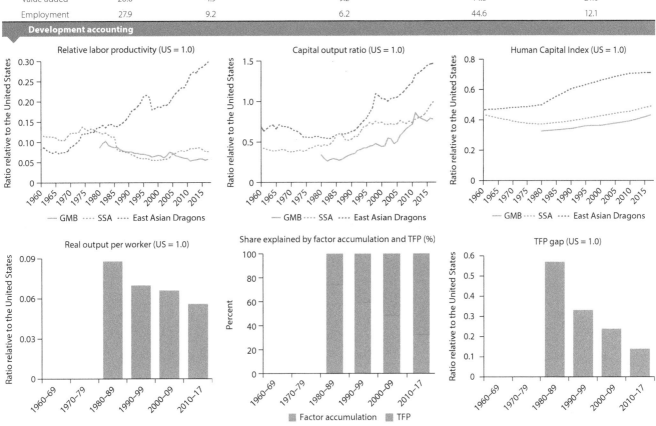

Growth accounting (% per year)

	Observed annual growth rates				Contribution to output growth per worker			
	1961–2017	*1961–1977*	*1978–1995*	*1996–2017*	*1961–2017*	*1961–1977*	*1978–1995*	*1996–2017*
I. Traditional growth accounting								
Output	0.33	..	0.15	0.46	0.33	..	0.15	0.46
Physical capital	1.64	..	1.30	1.88	0.71	..	0.56	0.81
Human capital	0.76	..	0.93	1.10	0.61	..	0.57	0.63
TFP	..	..	..	..	−0.98	..	−0.99	−0.98
II. Growth accounting: private and public capital accumulation								
Output	0.33	..	0.15	0.46	0.33	..	0.15	0.46
Physical capital	..	..	..	..	..	..	..	..
- Public	0.58	..	0.49	0.64	0.27	..	0.16	0.14
- Private	3.87	..	3.85	3.88	1.65	..	1.11	0.80
Human capital	0.76	..	0.93	1.10	0.90	..	0.74	0.63
TFP	..	..	..	..	−2.49	..	−1.85	−1.11
III. Growth accounting including the natural capital								
Output	..	..	..	..	..	..	..	..
Physical capital	..	..	..	..	..	..	..	..
Natural capital	..	..	..	..	..	..	..	..
Human capital	..	..	..	..	..	..	..	..
TFP	..	..	..	..	..	..	..	..

Note: .. = insufficient or no data to perform the calculation.
East Asian Dragons = five East Asian economic "dragons": Indonesia, the Republic of Korea, Malaysia, Singapore, and Thailand; PPP = purchasing power parity; PPP = public-private partnerships; SSA = Sub-Saharan Africa; TFP = total factor productivity.

GHANA

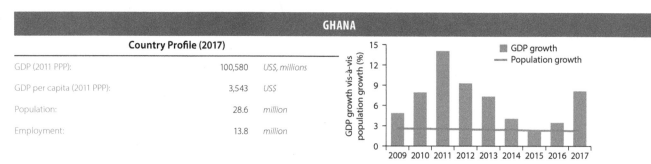

Country Profile (2017)

GDP (2011 PPP):	100,580	US$, millions
GDP per capita (2011 PPP):	3,543	US$
Population:	28.6	million
Employment:	13.8	million

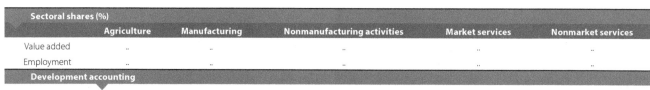

Sectoral shares (%)

	Agriculture	Manufacturing	Nonmanufacturing activities	Market services	Nonmarket services
Value added	..	..	..	..	..
Employment	..	..	..	..	..

Development accounting

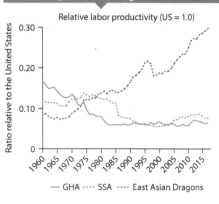
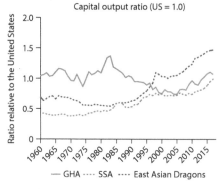
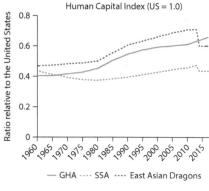

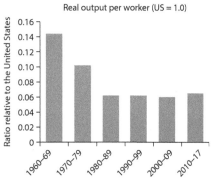
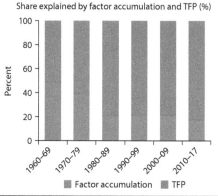

Growth accounting (% per year)

	Observed annual growth rates				Contribution to output growth per worker			
	1961–2017	1961–1977	1978–1995	1996–2017	1961–2017	1961–1977	1978–1995	1996–2017
I. Traditional growth accounting								
Output	0.64	−1.24	0.40	2.29	0.64	−1.24	0.40	2.29
Physical capital	−0.69	−2.14	−1.89	1.41	−0.30	−0.92	−0.82	0.61
Human capital	1.43	1.56	1.94	0.91	0.81	0.89	1.10	0.52
TFP	..	..	..	..	0.13	−1.20	0.11	1.16
II. Growth accounting: private and public capital accumulation								
Output	0.64	−1.24	0.40	2.29	0.64	−1.24	0.40	2.29
Physical capital	..	..	..	..	..	..	..	..
- Public	−0.35	−1.96	−1.26	1.63	−0.08	−0.44	−0.28	0.37
- Private	−0.81	−2.22	−2.20	1.40	−0.17	−0.46	−0.45	0.29
Human capital	1.43	1.56	1.94	0.91	0.81	0.89	1.10	0.52
TFP	..	..	..	..	0.07	−1.23	0.03	1.12
III. Growth accounting including the natural capital								
Output	..	..	..	2.29	..	..	..	2.29
Physical capital	..	..	..	1.41	..	..	..	0.51
Natural capital	..	..	..	22.32	..	..	..	1.68
Human capital	..	..	..	0.91	..	..	..	0.52
TFP	..	..	..	..	..	..	..	−0.42

Note: .. = insufficient or no data to perform the calculation.
East Asian Dragons = five East Asian economic "dragons": Indonesia, the Republic of Korea, Malaysia, Singapore, and Thailand; PPP = purchasing power parity; PPP = public-private partnerships; SSA = Sub-Saharan Africa; TFP = total factor productivity.

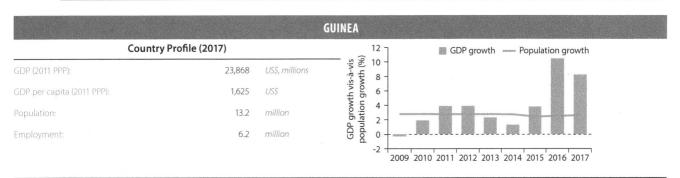

GUINEA

Country Profile (2017)

GDP (2011 PPP):	23,868	*US$, millions*
GDP per capita (2011 PPP):	1,625	*US$*
Population:	13.2	*million*
Employment:	6.2	*million*

Sectoral shares (%)

	Agriculture	Manufacturing	Nonmanufacturing activities	Market services	Nonmarket services
Value added	..	..	..	..	..
Employment	..	..	..	..	..

Development accounting

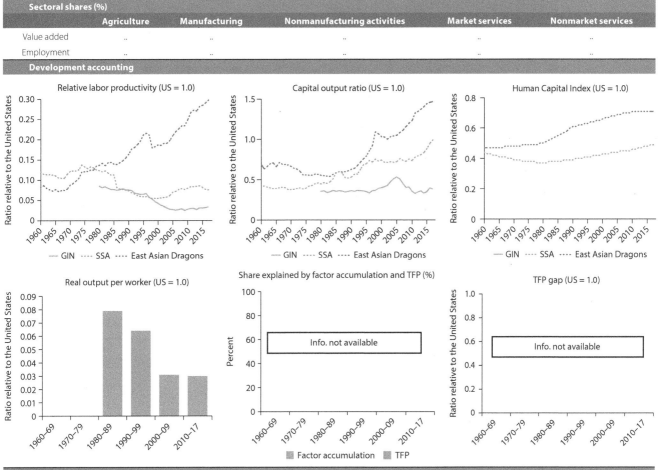

Growth accounting (% per year)

	Observed annual growth rates				Contribution to output growth per worker			
	1961–2017	*1961–1977*	*1978–1995*	*1996–2017*	*1961–2017*	*1961–1977*	*1978–1995*	*1996–2017*
I. Traditional growth accounting								
Output	..	..	..	..	..	..	..	..
Physical capital	..	..	..	..	..	..	..	..
Human capital	..	..	..	..	..	..	..	..
TFP	..	..	..	..	..	..	..	..
II. Growth accounting: private and public capital accumulation								
Output	..	..	..	..	..	..	..	..
Physical capital	..	..	..	..	..	..	..	..
- Public	..	..	..	..	..	..	..	..
- Private	..	..	..	..	..	..	..	..
Human capital	..	..	..	..	..	..	..	..
TFP					..	..	..	..
III. Growth accounting including the natural capital								
Output	..	..	..	..	..	..	..	..
Physical capital	..	..	..	..	..	..	..	..
Natural capital	..	..	..	..	..	..	..	..
Human capital	..	..	..	..	..	..	..	..
TFP	..	..	..	..	..	..	..	..

Note: .. = insufficient or no data to perform the calculation.
East Asian Dragons = five East Asian economic "dragons": Indonesia, the Republic of Korea, Malaysia, Singapore, and Thailand; PPP = purchasing power parity; PPP = public-private partnerships; SSA = Sub-Saharan Africa; TFP = total factor productivity.

GUINEA-BISSAU

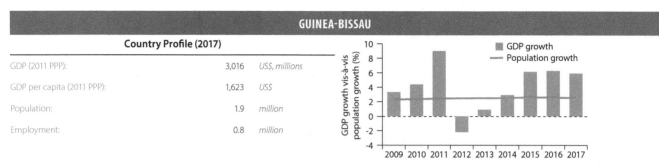

Country Profile (2017)

GDP (2011 PPP):	3,016	US$, millions
GDP per capita (2011 PPP):	1,623	US$
Population:	1.9	million
Employment:	0.8	million

Sectoral shares (%)

	Agriculture	Manufacturing	Nonmanufacturing activities	Market services	Nonmarket services
Value added	..	..	..	..	..
Employment	..	..	..	..	..

Development accounting

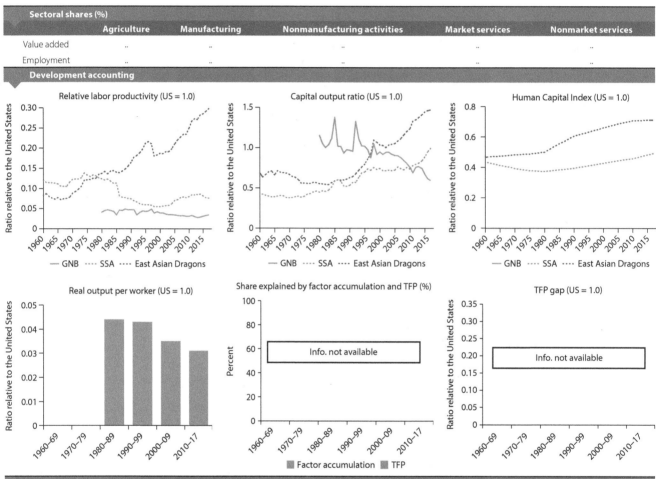

Growth accounting (% per year)

	Observed annual growth rates				Contribution to output growth per worker			
	1961–2017	1961–1977	1978–1995	1996–2017	1961–2017	1961–1977	1978–1995	1996–2017
I. Traditional growth accounting								
Output	..	..	..	..	..	..	..	..
Physical capital	..	.	..	..	..	..	..	..
Human capital	..	..	..	..	..	..	..	..
TFP	..	..	..	..	..	..	..	..
II. Growth accounting: private and public capital accumulation								
Output	..	..	..	..	..	..	..	..
Physical capital	..	..	..	..	..	..	..	..
- Public	..	..	..	..	..	..	..	..
- Private	..	..	..	..	..	..	..	..
Human capital	..	..	..	..	..	..	..	..
TFP	..	..	..	..	..	..	..	..
III. Growth accounting including the natural capital								
Output	..	..	..	..	..	..	..	..
Physical capital	..	..	..	..	..	..	..	..
Natural capital	..	..	..	..	..	..	..	..
Human capital	..	..	..	..	..	..	..	..
TFP	..	..	..	..	..	..	..	..

Note: .. = insufficient or no data to perform the calculation.
East Asian Dragons = five East Asian economic "dragons": Indonesia, the Republic of Korea, Malaysia, Singapore, and Thailand; PPP = purchasing power parity; PPP = public-private partnerships; SSA = Sub-Saharan Africa; TFP = total factor productivity.

KENYA

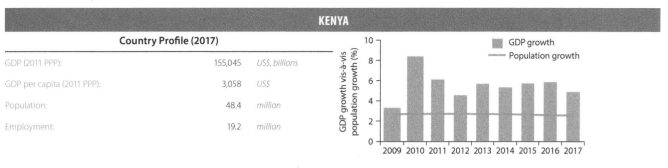

Country Profile (2017)

GDP (2011 PPP):	155,045	US$, billions
GDP per capita (2011 PPP):	3,058	US$
Population:	48.4	million
Employment:	19.2	million

Sectoral shares, 2016 (%)

	Agriculture	Manufacturing	Nonmanufacturing activities	Market services	Nonmarket services
Value added	25.0	11.0	9.9	21.0	33.0
Employment	37.3	11.3	3.4	32.5	15.5

Development accounting

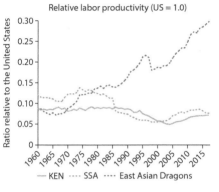
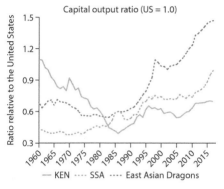
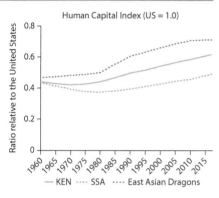

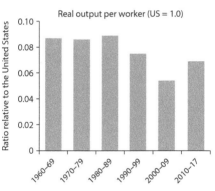
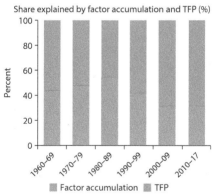
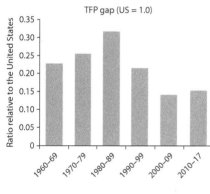

Growth accounting (% per year)

	Observed annual growth rates				Contribution to output growth per worker			
	1961–2017	1961–1977	1978–1995	1996–2017	1961–2017	1961–1977	1978–1995	1996–2017
I. Traditional growth accounting								
Output	0.79	1.26	0.13	0.96	0.79	1.26	0.13	0.96
Physical capital	−0.08	−0.60	−1.19	1.22	−0.03	−0.21	−0.42	0.43
Human capital	1.16	0.98	1.41	1.09	0.75	0.64	0.92	0.71
TFP	..	..	..	..	0.06	0.83	−0.37	−0.17
II. Growth accounting: private and public capital accumulation								
Output	0.79	1.26	0.13	0.96	0.79	1.26	0.13	0.96
Physical capital	..	..	..	..	..	..	..	..
- Public	0.34	−0.47	−0.43	1.60	0.06	−0.09	−0.08	0.29
- Private	−0.19	−0.65	−1.55	1.27	−0.03	−0.11	−0.26	0.21
Human capital	1.16	0.98	1.41	1.09	0.75	0.64	0.92	0.71
TFP	..	..	..	..	0.01	0.81	−0.44	−0.25
III. Growth accounting including the natural capital								
Output	..	..	..	0.96	..	..	..	0.96
Physical capital	..	..	..	1.22	..	..	..	0.46
Natural capital	..	..	..	135.42	..	..	..	0.15
Human capital	..	..	..	1.09	..	..	..	0.77
TFP	..	..	..	..	..	..	..	−0.42

Note: .. = insufficient or no data to perform the calculation.
East Asian Dragons = five East Asian economic "dragons": Indonesia, the Republic of Korea, Malaysia, Singapore, and Thailand; PPP = purchasing power parity; PPP = public-private partnerships; SSA = Sub-Saharan Africa; TFP = total factor productivity.

LESOTHO

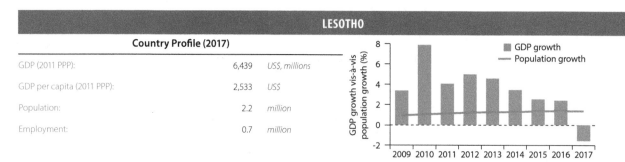

Country Profile (2017)

GDP (2011 PPP):	6,439	US$, millions
GDP per capita (2011 PPP):	2,533	US$
Population:	2.2	million
Employment:	0.7	million

Sectoral shares, 2016 (%)

	Agriculture	Manufacturing	Nonmanufacturing activities	Market services	Nonmarket services
Value added	5.3	10.8	16.9	24.1	42.8
Employment	7.8	12.8	29.6	21.4	28.4

Development accounting

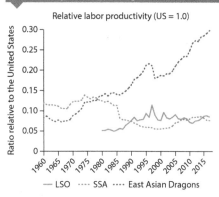

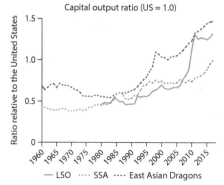

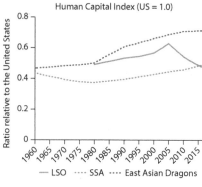

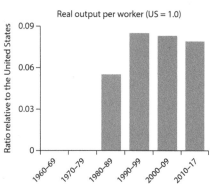

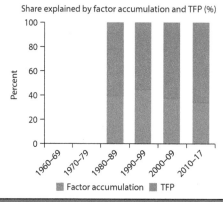

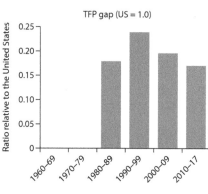

Growth accounting (% per year)

	Observed annual growth rates				Contribution to output growth per worker			
	1961–2017	1961–1977	1978–1995	1996–2017	1961–2017	1961–1977	1978–1995	1996–2017
I. Traditional growth accounting								
Output	3.37	..	3.95	2.98	3.37	..	3.95	2.98
Physical capital	4.71	..	7.08	3.09	1.47	..	2.22	0.97
Human capital	0.38	..	0.99	−0.37	0.14	..	0.71	−0.25
TFP	..	..	..	..	1.76	..	1.02	2.27
II. Growth accounting: private and public capital accumulation								
Output	3.37	..	3.95	2.98	3.37	..	3.95	2.98
Physical capital	..	..	..	..	..	..	..	..
- Public	8.88	..	14.65	4.95	1.40	..	2.42	0.81
- Private	2.83	..	4.78	1.50	0.41	..	0.72	0.22
Human capital	0.38	..	0.99	−0.37	0.25	..	0.69	−0.25
TFP	..	..	..	..	1.31	..	0.13	2.20
III. Growth accounting including the natural capital								
Output	..	..	..	..	..	..	..	..
Physical capital	..	..	..	..	..	..	..	..
Natural capital	..	..	..	..	..	..	..	..
Human capital	..	..	..	..	..	..	..	..
TFP	..	..	..	..	..	..	..	..

Note: .. = insufficient or no data to perform the calculation.
East Asian Dragons = five East Asian economic "dragons": Indonesia, the Republic of Korea, Malaysia, Singapore, and Thailand; PPP = purchasing power parity; PPP = public-private partnerships; SSA = Sub-Saharan Africa; TFP = total factor productivity.

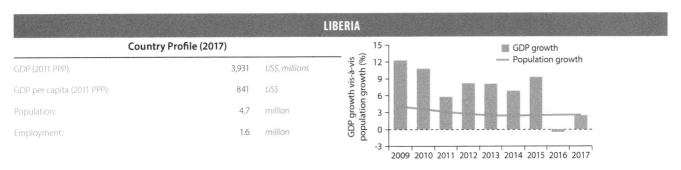

LIBERIA

Country Profile (2017)

GDP (2011 PPP):	3,931	US$, millions
GDP per capita (2011 PPP):	841	US$
Population:	4.7	million
Employment:	1.6	million

Sectoral shares (%)

	Agriculture	Manufacturing	Nonmanufacturing activities	Market services	Nonmarket services
Value added	..	..	..	..	..
Employment	..	..	..	..	..

Development accounting

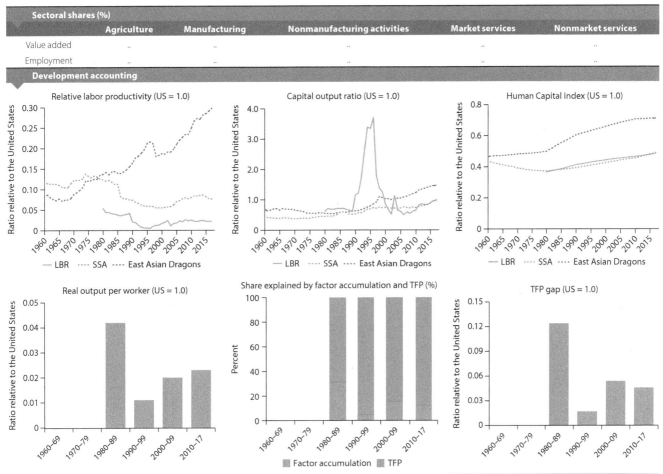

Growth accounting (% per year)

	Observed annual growth rates				Contribution to output growth per worker			
	1961–2017	1961–1977	1978–1995	1996–2017	1961–2017	1961–1977	1978–1995	1996–2017
I. Traditional growth accounting								
Output	1.34	..	−11.46	10.06	1.34	..	−11.46	10.06
Physical capital	−1.55	..	−2.70	−0.77	−0.67	..	−1.16	−0.33
Human capital	0.94	..	1.33	0.82	0.60	..	0.80	0.46
TFP	..	..	..	..	1.41	..	−11.10	9.93
II. Growth accounting: private and public capital accumulation								
Output	1.34	..	−11.46	10.06	1.34	..	−11.46	10.06
Physical capital	..	..	..	..	..	..	..	..
- Public	−1.04	..	−2.24	−0.23	−0.25	..	−0.50	−0.05
- Private	−1.57	..	−3.19	−0.47	−0.34	..	−0.65	−0.10
Human capital	0.94	..	1.33	0.82	0.56	..	0.75	0.46
TFP	..	..	..	..	1.36	..	−11.06	9.75
III. Growth accounting including the natural capital								
Output	..	..	..	..	..	..	..	..
Physical capital	..	..	..	..	..	..	..	..
Natural capital	..	..	..	..	..	..	..	..
Human capital	..	..	..	..	..	..	..	..
TFP	..	..	..	..	..	..	..	..

Note: .. = insufficient or no data to perform the calculation.
East Asian Dragons = five East Asian economic "dragons": Indonesia, the Republic of Korea, Malaysia, Singapore, and Thailand; PPP = purchasing power parity; PPP = public-private partnerships; SSA = Sub-Saharan Africa; TFP = total factor productivity.

MADAGASCAR

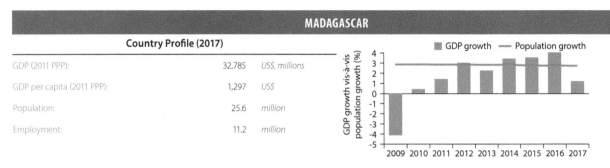

Country Profile (2017)

GDP (2011 PPP):	32,785	US$, millions
GDP per capita (2011 PPP):	1,297	US$
Population:	25.6	million
Employment:	11.2	million

Sectoral shares, 2016 (%)

	Agriculture	Manufacturing	Nonmanufacturing activities	Market services	Nonmarket services
Value added	24.2	11.9	11.9	26.8	25.1
Employment	72.3	6.4	2.8	10.4	8.1

Development accounting

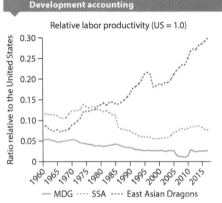

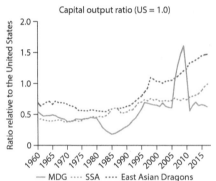

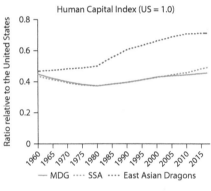

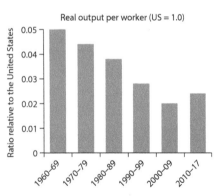

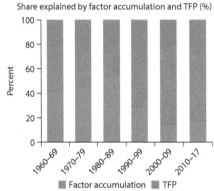

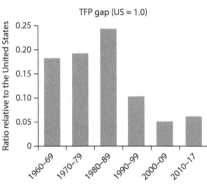

Growth accounting (% per year)

	Observed annual growth rates				Contribution to output growth per worker			
	1961–2017	1961–1977	1978–1995	1996–2017	1961–2017	1961–1977	1978–1995	1996–2017
I. Traditional growth accounting								
Output	−0.68	0.08	−1.86	−0.31	−0.68	0.08	−1.86	−0.31
Physical capital	−0.90	−1.06	−1.94	0.08	−0.39	−0.46	−0.84	0.03
Human capital	0.59	0.08	0.87	0.75	0.33	0.04	0.50	0.43
TFP	..	..	..	..	−0.63	0.49	−1.52	−0.77
II. Growth accounting: private and public capital accumulation								
Output	−0.68	0.08	−1.86	−0.31	−0.68	0.08	−1.86	−0.31
Physical capital	..	..	..	..	..	..	..	..
- Public	−1.95	−1.04	−2.20	−2.45	−0.44	−0.23	−0.50	−0.55
- Private	0.95	−1.12	−1.03	4.16	0.20	−0.23	−0.21	0.86
Human capital	0.59	0.08	0.87	0.75	0.33	0.04	0.50	0.43
TFP	..	..	..	..	−0.77	0.50	−1.65	−1.04
III. Growth accounting including the natural capital								
Output	..	..	..	..	..	..	..	..
Physical capital	..	..	..	..	..	..	..	..
Natural capital	..	..	..	..	..	..	..	..
Human capital	..	..	..	..	..	..	..	..
TFP	..	..	..	..	..	..	..	..

Note: .. = insufficient or no data to perform the calculation.
East Asian Dragons = five East Asian economic "dragons": Indonesia, the Republic of Korea, Malaysia, Singapore, and Thailand; PPP = purchasing power parity; PPP = public-private partnerships; SSA = Sub-Saharan Africa; TFP = total factor productivity.

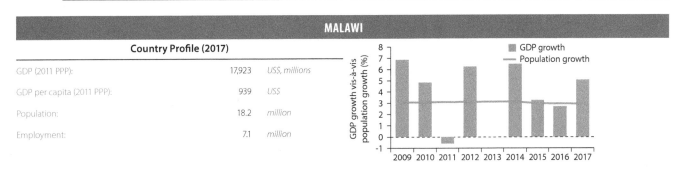

MALAWI

Country Profile (2017)

GDP (2011 PPP):	17,923	US$, millions
GDP per capita (2011 PPP):	939	US$
Population:	18.2	million
Employment:	7.1	million

Sectoral shares, 2016 (%)

	Agriculture	Manufacturing	Nonmanufacturing activities	Market services	Nonmarket services
Value added	29.9	10.2	5.3	26.9	27.7
Employment	84.9	7.4	0.7	3.5	3.5

Development Accounting

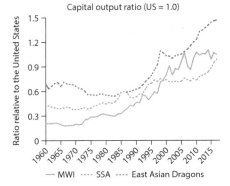

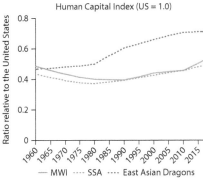

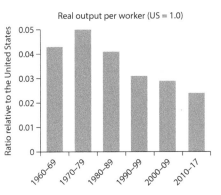

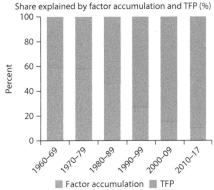

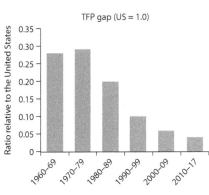

Growth accounting (% per year)

	Observed annual growth rates				Contribution to output growth per worker			
	1961–2017	*1961–1977*	*1978–1995*	*1996–2017*	*1961–2017*	*1961–1977*	*1978–1995*	*1996–2017*
I. Traditional growth accounting								
Output	1.99	5.65	−0.86	1.50	1.99	5.65	−0.86	1.50
Physical capital	1.37	6.78	0.04	−1.72	0.59	2.93	0.02	−0.74
Human capital	0.69	0.05	0.51	1.33	0.39	0.03	0.29	0.76
TFP	..	..	..	..	1.01	2.70	−1.16	1.49
II. Growth accounting: private and public capital accumulation								
Output	1.99	5.65	−0.86	1.50	1.99	5.65	−0.86	1.50
Physical capital	..	..	..	..	..	..	..	..
- Public	2.09	6.84	0.97	−0.66	0.47	1.54	0.22	−0.15
- Private	1.08	6.76	−0.45	−2.07	0.22	1.39	−0.09	−0.43
Human capital	0.69	0.05	0.51	1.33	0.39	0.03	0.29	0.76
TFP	..	..	..	..	0.91	2.69	−1.28	1.32
III. Growth accounting including the natural capital								
Output	..	..	..	..	..	..	..	..
Physical capital	..	..	..	..	..	..	..	..
Natural capital	..	..	..	..	..	..	..	..
Human capital	..	..	..	..	..	..	..	..
TFP	..	..	..	..	..	..	..	..

Note: .. = insufficient or no data to perform the calculation.
East Asian Dragons = five East Asian economic "dragons": Indonesia, the Republic of Korea, Malaysia, Singapore, and Thailand; PPP = purchasing power parity; PPP = public-private partnerships; SSA = Sub-Saharan Africa; TFP = total factor productivity.

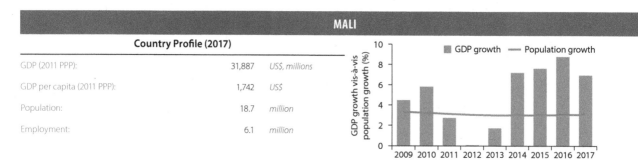

MALI

Country Profile (2017)

GDP (2011 PPP):	31,887	US$, millions
GDP per capita (2011 PPP):	1,742	US$
Population:	18.7	million
Employment:	6.1	million

Sectoral shares, 2016 (%)

	Agriculture	Manufacturing	Nonmanufacturing activities	Market services	Nonmarket services
Value added	45.2	16.2	6.4	20.0	12.2
Employment	66.1	4.2	3.1	18.4	8.2

Development accounting

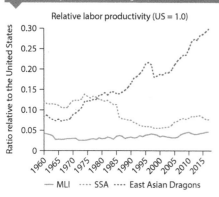

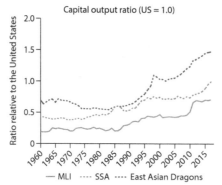

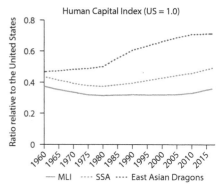

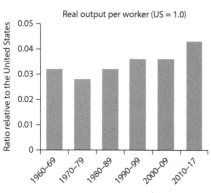

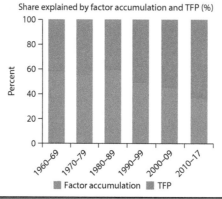

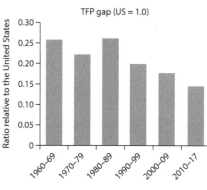

Growth accounting (% per year)

	Observed annual growth rates				Contribution to output growth per worker			
	1961–2017	1961–1977	1978–1995	1996–2017	1961–2017	1961–1977	1978–1995	1996–2017
I. Traditional growth accounting								
Output	1.45	1.19	1.68	1.48	1.45	1.19	1.68	1.48
Physical capital	1.30	0.98	2.45	0.61	0.56	0.42	1.06	0.26
Human capital	0.49	0.13	0.44	0.81	0.28	0.07	0.25	0.46
TFP	..	..	..	..	0.62	0.69	0.37	0.75
II. Growth accounting: private and public capital accumulation								
Output	1.45	1.19	1.68	1.48	1.45	1.19	1.68	1.48
Physical capital	..	..	..	..	..	..	..	..
- Public	0.45	0.97	1.59	−0.89	0.10	0.22	0.36	−0.20
- Private	2.16	0.98	3.70	1.80	0.44	0.20	0.76	0.37
Human capital	0.49	0.13	0.44	0.81	0.28	0.07	0.25	0.46
TFP	..	..	..	..	0.63	0.69	0.31	0.85
III. Growth accounting including the natural capital								
Output	..	..	..	..	..	..	..	..
Physical capital	..	..	..	..	..	..	..	..
Natural capital	..	..	..	..	..	..	..	..
Human capital	..	..	..	..	..	..	..	..
TFP					..	..	..	..

Note: .. = insufficient or no data to perform the calculation.
East Asian Dragons = five East Asian economic "dragons": Indonesia, the Republic of Korea, Malaysia, Singapore, and Thailand; PPP = purchasing power parity; PPP = public-private partnerships; SSA = Sub-Saharan Africa; TFP = total factor productivity.

MAURITANIA

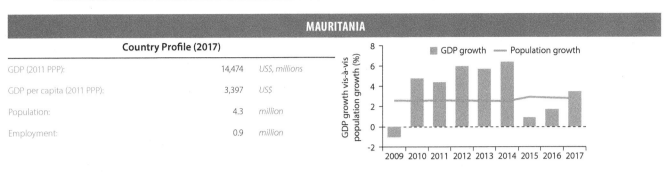

Country Profile (2017)

GDP (2011 PPP):	14,474	US$, millions
GDP per capita (2011 PPP):	3,397	US$
Population:	4.3	million
Employment:	0.9	million

Sectoral shares, 2016 (%)

	Agriculture	Manufacturing	Nonmanufacturing activities	Market services	Nonmarket services
Value added	14.1	5.6	50.6	11.9	17.9
Employment	75.8	6.0	1.7	11.1	5.4

Development Accounting

Relative labor productivity (US = 1.0)

Capital output ratio (US = 1.0)

Human Capital Index (US = 1.0)

— MRT ···· SSA ···· East Asian Dragons

Real output per worker (US = 1.0)

Share explained by factor accumulation and TFP (%)

TFP gap (US = 1.0)

■ Factor accumulation ■ TFP

Growth accounting (% per year)

	Observed annual growth rates				Contribution to output growth per worker			
	1961–2017	*1961–1977*	*1978–1995*	*1996–2017*	*1961–2017*	*1961–1977*	*1978–1995*	*1996–2017*
I. Traditional growth accounting								
Output	0.13	..	−0.86	0.94	0.13	..	−0.86	0.94
Physical capital	1.59	..	−0.79	3.54	0.68	..	−0.34	1.52
Human capital	0.70	..	0.65	1.06	0.50	..	0.37	0.60
TFP	..	..	..	..	−1.05	..	−0.89	−1.18
II. Growth accounting: private and public capital accumulation								
Output	0.13	..	−0.86	0.94	0.13	..	−0.86	0.94
Physical capital	..	..	..	..	..	..	..	..
- Public	2.25	..	0.00	4.10	2.08	..	0.00	0.92
- Private	1.54	..	−1.09	3.69	1.30	..	−0.22	0.75
Human capital	0.70	..	0.65	1.06	1.65	..	0.37	0.60
TFP	..	..	..	..	−4.89	..	−1.01	−1.34
III. Growth accounting including the natural capital								
Output	..	..	..	..	..	..	..	..
Physical capital	..	..	..	..	..	..	..	..
Natural capital	..	..	..	..	..	..	..	..
Human capital	..	..	..	..	..	..	..	..
TFP	..	..	..	..	..	..	..	..

Note: .. = insufficient or no data to perform the calculation.
East Asian Dragons = five East Asian economic "dragons": Indonesia, the Republic of Korea, Malaysia, Singapore, and Thailand; PPP = purchasing power parity; PPP = public-private partnerships; SSA = Sub-Saharan Africa; TFP = total factor productivity.

MAURITIUS

Country Profile (2017)

GDP (2011 PPP):	27,962	*US$, millions*
GDP per capita (2011 PPP):	21,357	*US$*
Population:	1.3	*million*
Employment:	0.6	*million*

Sectoral shares, 2016 (%)

	Agriculture	Manufacturing	Nonmanufacturing activities	Market services	Nonmarket services
Value added	3.7	14.1	6.5	30.3	45.4
Employment	7.1	13.1	11.4	43.4	24.8

Development accounting

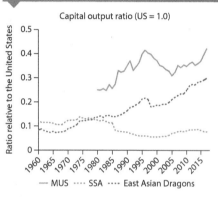

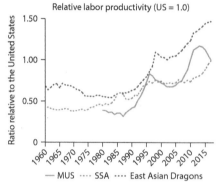

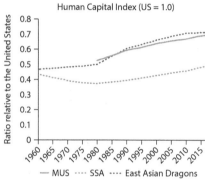

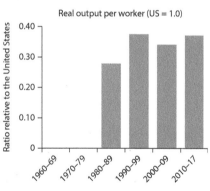

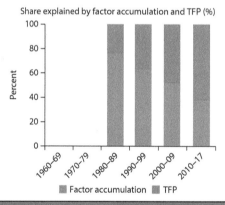

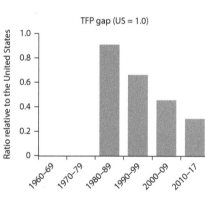

Growth accounting (% per year)

	Observed annual growth rates				Contribution to output growth per worker			
	1961–2017	1961–1977	1978–1995	1996–2017	1961–2017	1961–1977	1978–1995	1996–2017
I. Traditional growth accounting								
Output	3.20	..	3.57	2.95	3.20	..	3.57	2.95
Physical capital	2.65	..	1.91	3.15	1.35	..	0.97	1.60
Human capital	1.12	..	1.38	0.85	0.53	..	0.68	0.42
TFP	..	..	..	..	1.33	..	1.92	0.92
II. Growth accounting: private and public capital accumulation								
Output	3.20	..	3.57	2.95	3.20	..	3.57	2.95
Physical capital	..	..	..	..	..	..	..	..
- Public	2.64	..	2.78	2.55	0.49	..	0.52	0.48
- Private	2.65	..	1.32	3.56	0.84	..	0.42	1.14
Human capital	1.12	..	1.38	0.85	0.55	..	0.68	0.42
TFP	..	..	..	..	1.32	..	1.94	0.91
III. Growth accounting including the natural capital								
Output	..	..	..	..	..	..	..	..
Physical capital	..	..	..	..	..	..	..	..
Natural capital	..	..	..	..	..	..	..	..
Human capital	..	..	..	..	..	..	..	..
TFP	..	..	..	..	..	..	..	..

Note: .. = insufficient or no data to perform the calculation.
East Asian Dragons = five East Asian economic "dragons": Indonesia, the Republic of Korea, Malaysia, Singapore, and Thailand; PPP = purchasing power parity; PPP = public-private partnerships; SSA = Sub-Saharan Africa; TFP = total factor productivity.

MOZAMBIQUE

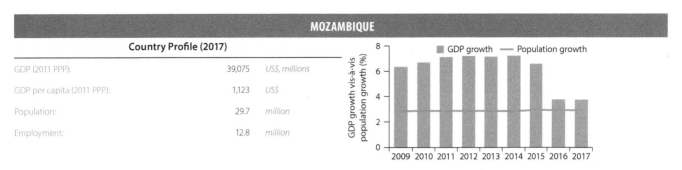

Country Profile (2017)

GDP (2011 PPP):	39,075	US$, millions
GDP per capita (2011 PPP):	1,123	US$
Population:	29.7	million
Employment:	12.8	million

Sectoral shares, 2016 (%)

	Agriculture	Manufacturing	Nonmanufacturing activities	Market services	Nonmarket services
Value added	23.6	9.4	10.1	28.3	28.7
Employment	73.2	0.5	3.8	18.4	4.1

Development accounting

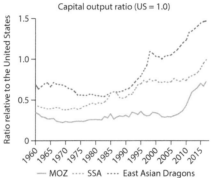
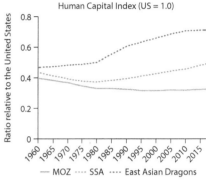

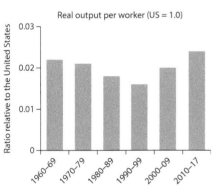
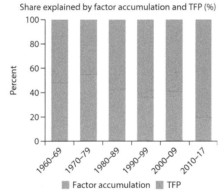
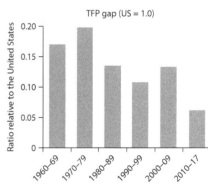

Growth accounting (% per year)

	Observed annual growth rates				Contribution to output growth per worker			
	1961–2017	1961–1977	1978–1995	1996–2017	1961–2017	1961–1977	1978–1995	1996–2017
I. Traditional growth accounting								
Output	2.34	1.97	−0.89	5.27	2.34	1.97	−0.89	5.27
Physical capital	2.87	−0.03	0.97	6.67	1.66	−0.02	0.56	3.86
Human capital	0.21	0.17	0.01	0.41	0.09	0.07	0.00	0.17
TFP	..	..	..	..	0.59	1.92	−1.46	1.25
II. Growth accounting: private and public capital accumulation								
Output	2.34	1.97	−0.89	5.27	2.34	1.97	−0.89	5.27
Physical capital	..	..	..	..	..	..	..	..
- Public	3.65	−0.04	2.32	7.59	1.10	−0.01	0.70	2.29
- Private	3.05	−0.02	−0.05	7.98	0.84	−0.01	−0.01	2.20
Human capital	0.21	0.17	0.01	0.41	0.09	0.07	0.00	0.17
TFP	..	..	..	..	0.31	1.92	−1.59	0.61
III. Growth accounting including the natural capital								
Output	..	..	..	5.27	..	..	..	5.27
Physical capital	..	..	..	6.67	..	..	..	3.34
Natural capital	..	..	..	70.49	..	..	..	1.22
Human capital	..	..	..	0.41	..	..	..	0.15
TFP	..	..	..	..	..	..	..	0.56

Note: .. = insufficient or no data to perform the calculation.
East Asian Dragons = five East Asian economic "dragons": Indonesia, the Republic of Korea, Malaysia, Singapore, and Thailand; PPP = purchasing power parity; PPP = public-private partnerships; SSA = Sub-Saharan Africa; TFP = total factor productivity.

NAMIBIA

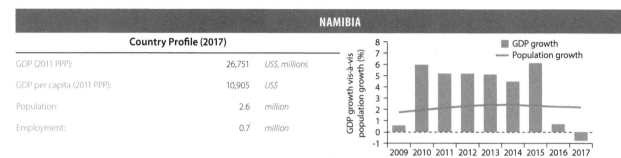

Country Profile (2017)

GDP (2011 PPP):	26,751	US$, millions
GDP per capita (2011 PPP):	10,905	US$
Population:	2.6	million
Employment:	0.7	million

Sectoral shares, 2016 (%)

	Agriculture	Manufacturing	Nonmanufacturing activities	Market services	Nonmarket services
Value added	6.4	10.3	16.1	22.9	44.3
Employment	25.2	5.1	11.9	31.0	26.7

Development accounting

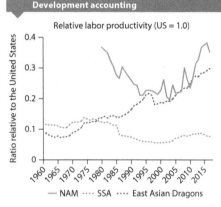

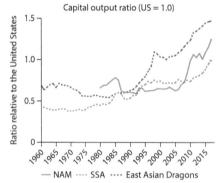

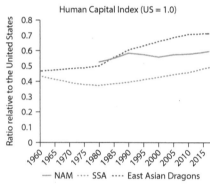

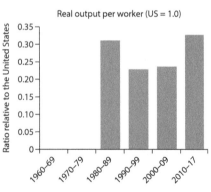

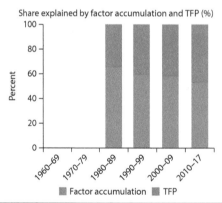

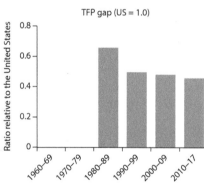

Growth accounting (% per year)

	Observed annual growth rates				Contribution to output growth per worker			
	1961–2017	1961–1977	1978–1995	1996–2017	1961–2017	1961–1977	1978–1995	1996–2017
I. Traditional growth accounting								
Output	0.76	..	−1.71	2.43	0.76	..	−1.71	2.43
Physical capital	1.92	..	−2.50	4.93	0.81	..	−1.06	2.09
Human capital	0.69	..	0.95	0.44	0.37	..	0.55	0.25
TFP	..	..	..	..	−0.43	..	−1.20	0.09
II. Growth accounting: private and public capital accumulation								
Output	0.76	..	−1.71	2.43	0.76	..	−1.71	2.43
Physical capital	..	..	..	..	..	..	..	..
- Public	1.47	..	−2.01	3.84	0.22	..	−0.31	0.60
- Private	2.58	..	−2.98	6.38	0.67	..	−0.80	1.71
Human capital	0.69	..	0.95	0.44	0.38	..	0.55	0.25
TFP	..	..	..	..	−0.52	..	−1.14	−0.12
III. Growth accounting including the natural capital								
Output	..	..	..	2.43	..	..	..	2.43
Physical capital	..	..	..	4.93	..	..	..	1.75
Natural capital	..	..	..	17.68	..	..	..	0.35
Human capital	..	..	..	0.44	..	..	..	0.22
TFP	..	..	..	..	..	..	..	0.11

Note: .. = insufficient or no data to perform the calculation.
East Asian Dragons = five East Asian economic "dragons": Indonesia, the Republic of Korea, Malaysia, Singapore, and Thailand; PPP = purchasing power parity; PPP = public-private partnerships; SSA = Sub-Saharan Africa; TFP = total factor productivity.

NIGER

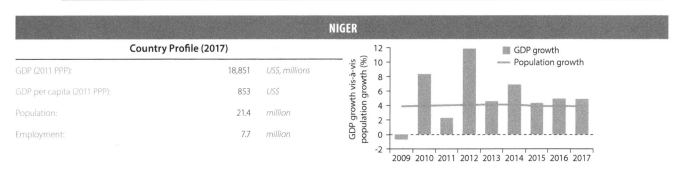

Country Profile (2017)

GDP (2011 PPP):	18,851	US$, millions
GDP per capita (2011 PPP):	853	US$
Population:	21.4	million
Employment:	7.7	million

Sectoral shares, 2016 (%)

	Agriculture	Manufacturing	Nonmanufacturing activities	Market services	Nonmarket services
Value added	40.5	6.6	15.1	19.0	18.8
Employment	76.0	6.9	0.7	11.3	5.1

Development accounting

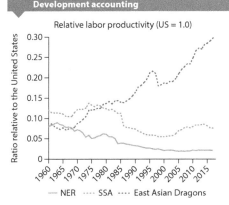

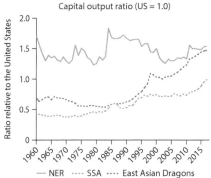

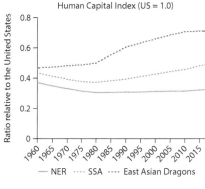

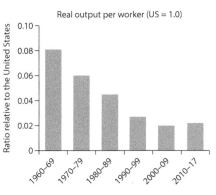

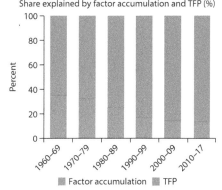

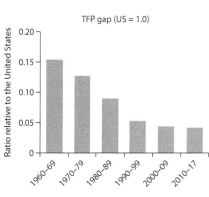

Growth accounting (% per year)

	Observed annual growth rates				Contribution to output growth per worker			
	1961–2017	*1961–1977*	*1978–1995*	*1996–2017*	*1961–2017*	*1961–1977*	*1978–1995*	*1996–2017*
I. Traditional growth accounting								
Output	−0.58	−0.56	−2.15	0.68	−0.58	−0.56	−2.15	0.68
Physical capital	−1.90	−2.19	−2.45	−1.22	−0.82	−0.95	−1.07	−0.53
Human capital	0.32	0.04	0.37	0.50	0.18	0.03	0.21	0.28
TFP	..	..	..	..	0.06	0.37	−1.30	0.93
II. Growth accounting: private and public capital accumulation								
Output	−0.58	−0.56	−2.15	0.68	−0.58	−0.56	−2.15	0.68
Physical capital	..	..	..	..	..	..	..	..
- Public	0.32	−1.98	1.73	0.95	0.07	−0.45	0.39	0.21
- Private	−2.40	−2.21	−3.31	−1.81	−0.50	−0.46	−0.69	−0.38
Human capital	0.32	0.04	0.37	0.50	0.18	0.03	0.21	0.28
TFP	..	..	..	..	−0.34	0.32	−2.07	0.56
III. Growth accounting including the natural capital								
Output	..	..	..	0.68	..	..	..	0.68
Physical capital	..	..	..	−1.22	..	..	..	−0.39
Natural capital	..	..	..	22.42	..	..	..	0.51
Human capital	..	..	..	0.50	..	..	..	0.22
TFP	..	..	..	..	..	..	..	0.34

Note: .. = insufficient or no data to perform the calculation.
East Asian Dragons = five East Asian economic "dragons": Indonesia, the Republic of Korea, Malaysia, Singapore, and Thailand; PPP = purchasing power parity; PPP = public-private partnerships; SSA = Sub-Saharan Africa; TFP = total factor productivity.

NIGERIA

Country Profile (2017)

GDP (2011 PPP):	832,983	*US$, millions*
GDP per capita (2011 PPP):	4,391	*US$*
Population:	192.0	*million*
Employment:	65.4	*million*

Sectoral shares, 2016 (%)

	Agriculture	Manufacturing	Nonmanufacturing activities	Market services	Nonmarket services
Value added	24.5	9.3	12.6	30.9	22.8
Employment	33.6	8.6	4.0	35.0	18.8

Development accounting

Relative labor productivity (US = 1.0)

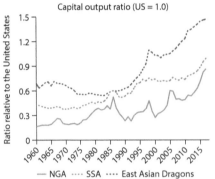

Capital output ratio (US = 1.0)

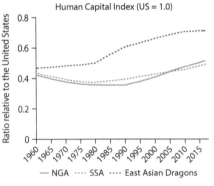

Human Capital Index (US = 1.0)

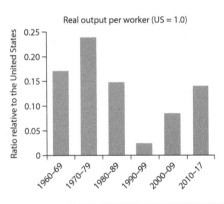

Real output per worker (US = 1.0)

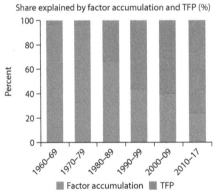

Share explained by factor accumulation and TFP (%)

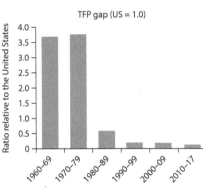

TFP gap (US = 1.0)

Growth accounting (% per year)

	Observed annual growth rates				Contribution to output growth per worker			
	1961–2017	*1961–1977*	*1978–1995*	*1996–2017*	*1961–2017*	*1961–1977*	*1978–1995*	*1996–2017*
I. Traditional growth accounting								
Output	1.65	1.87	0.19	2.68	1.65	1.87	0.19	2.68
Physical capital	3.70	6.09	3.38	2.12	2.57	4.23	2.35	1.47
Human capital	0.91	0.15	0.69	1.67	0.28	0.04	0.21	0.51
TFP	..	..	..	..	−1.19	−2.41	−2.37	0.70
II. Growth accounting: private and public capital accumulation								
Output	1.65	1.87	0.19	2.68	1.65	1.87	0.19	2.68
Physical capital	..	..	..	..	..	..	..	..
- Public	3.39	6.13	4.04	0.74	1.23	2.23	1.47	0.27
- Private	3.93	6.05	2.84	3.19	1.31	2.01	0.94	1.06
Human capital	0.91	0.15	0.69	1.67	0.28	0.04	0.21	0.51
TFP	..	..	..	..	−1.16	−2.41	−2.43	0.85
III. Growth accounting including the natural capital								
Output	..	..	..	2.68	..	..	..	2.68
Physical capital	..	..	..	2.12	..	..	..	0.80
Natural capital	..	..	..	−0.61	..	..	..	−0.09
Human capital	..	..	..	1.67	..	..	..	0.39
TFP	..	..	..	..	..	..	..	1.58

Note: .. = insufficient or no data to perform the calculation.
East Asian Dragons = five East Asian economic "dragons": Indonesia, the Republic of Korea, Malaysia, Singapore, and Thailand; PPP = purchasing power parity; PPP = public-private partnerships; SSA = Sub-Saharan Africa; TFP = total factor productivity.

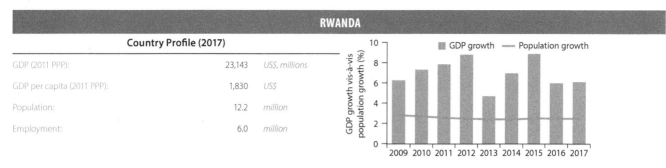

RWANDA

Country Profile (2017)

GDP (2011 PPP):	23,143	US$, millions
GDP per capita (2011 PPP):	1,830	US$
Population:	12.2	million
Employment:	6.0	million

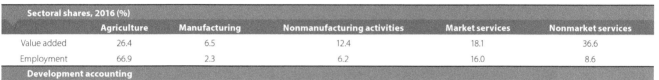

Sectoral shares, 2016 (%)

	Agriculture	Manufacturing	Nonmanufacturing activities	Market services	Nonmarket services
Value added	26.4	6.5	12.4	18.1	36.6
Employment	66.9	2.3	6.2	16.0	8.6

Development accounting

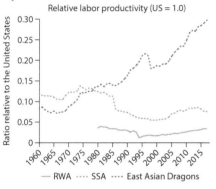

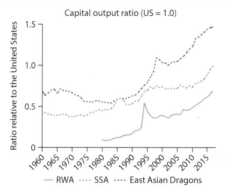

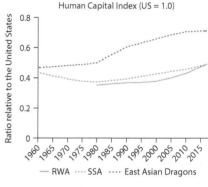

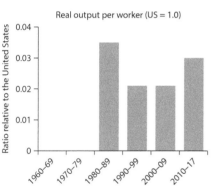

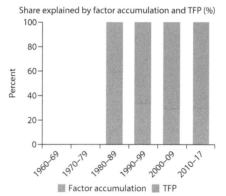

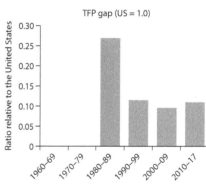

Growth accounting (% per year)

	Observed annual growth rates				Contribution to output growth per worker			
	1961–2017	*1961–1977*	*1978–1995*	*1996–2017*	*1961–2017*	*1961–1977*	*1978–1995*	*1996–2017*
I. Traditional growth accounting								
Output	2.21	..	−1.69	4.87	2.21	..	−1.69	4.87
Physical capital	3.92	..	3.43	4.25	0.94	..	0.82	1.02
Human capital	0.99	..	0.68	1.58	0.92	..	0.52	1.20
TFP	..	..	..	..	0.35	..	−3.03	2.65
II. Growth accounting: private and public capital accumulation								
Output	2.21	..	−1.69	4.87	2.21	..	−1.69	4.87
Physical capital	..	..	..	..	..	..	..	..
- Public	3.66	..	3.89	3.51	0.50	..	0.49	0.44
- Private	4.02	..	2.97	4.74	0.50	..	0.34	0.54
Human capital	0.99	..	0.68	1.58	0.82	..	0.51	1.20
TFP	..	..	..	..	0.40	..	−3.03	2.69
III. Growth accounting including the natural capital								
Output	..	..	..	..	..	..	..	..
Physical capital	..	..	..	..	..	..	..	..
Natural capital	..	..	..	..	..	..	..	..
Human capital	..	..	..	..	..	..	..	..
TFP	..	..	..	..	..	..	..	..

Note: .. = insufficient or no data to perform the calculation.
East Asian Dragons = five East Asian economic "dragons": Indonesia, the Republic of Korea, Malaysia, Singapore, and Thailand; PPP = purchasing power parity; PPP = public-private partnerships; SSA = Sub-Saharan Africa; TFP = total factor productivity.

SÃO TOMÉ AND PRÍNCIPE

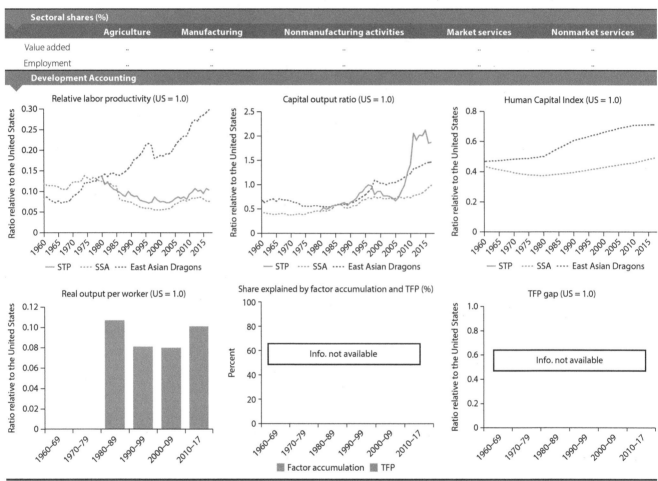

Country Profile (2017)

GDP (2011 PPP):	709	US$, millions
GDP per capita (2011 PPP):	3,456	US$
Population:	0.2	million
Employment:	0.1	million

Sectoral shares (%)

	Agriculture	Manufacturing	Nonmanufacturing activities	Market services	Nonmarket services
Value added	..	..	..	..	..
Employment	..	..	..	..	..

Development Accounting

Growth accounting (% per year)

	Observed annual growth rates				Contribution to output growth per worker			
	1961–2017	*1961–1977*	*1978–1995*	*1996–2017*	*1961–2017*	*1961–1977*	*1978–1995*	*1996–2017*
I. Traditional growth accounting								
Output	..	..	..	..	..	..	..	..
Physical capital	..	..	..	..	..	..	..	..
Human capital	..	..	..	..	..	..	..	..
TFP	..	..	..	..	..	..	..	..
II. Growth accounting: private and public capital accumulation								
Output	..	..	..	..	..	..	..	..
Physical capital	..	..	..	..	..	..	..	..
- Public	..	..	..	..	..	..	..	..
- Private	..	..	..	..	..	..	..	..
Human capital	..	..	..	..	..	..	..	..
TFP	..	..	..	..	..	..	..	..
III. Growth accounting including the natural capital								
Output	..	..	..	..	..	..	..	..
Physical capital	..	..	..	..	..	..	..	..
Natural capital	..	..	..	..	..	..	..	..
Human capital	..	..	..	..	..	..	..	..
TFP	..	..	..	..	..	..	..	..

Note: .. = insufficient or no data to perform the calculation.
East Asian Dragons = five East Asian economic "dragons": Indonesia, the Republic of Korea, Malaysia, Singapore, and Thailand; PPP = purchasing power parity; PPP = public-private partnerships; SSA = Sub-Saharan Africa; TFP = total factor productivity.

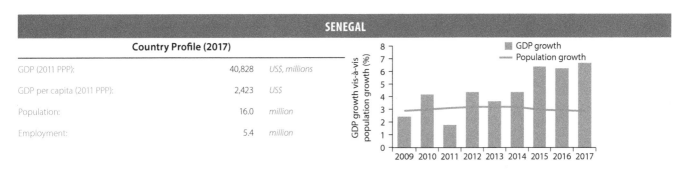

SENEGAL

Country Profile (2017)

GDP (2011 PPP):	40,828	US$, millions
GDP per capita (2011 PPP):	2,423	US$
Population:	16.0	million
Employment:	5.4	million

Sectoral shares (%)

	Agriculture	Manufacturing	Nonmanufacturing activities	Market services	Nonmarket services
Value added	..	..	..	..	..
Employment	..	..	..	..	..

Development accounting

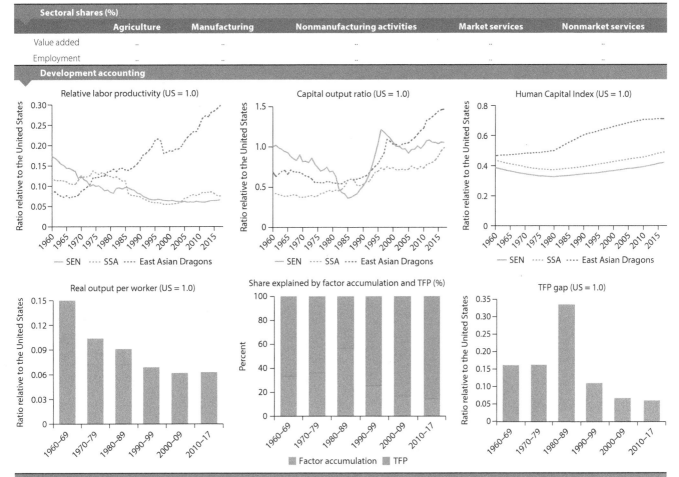

Growth accounting (% per year)

	Observed annual growth rates				Contribution to output growth per worker			
	1961–2017	1961–1977	1978–1995	1996–2017	1961–2017	1961–1977	1978–1995	1996–2017
I. Traditional growth accounting								
Output	−0.45	−1.38	−1.68	1.28	−0.45	−1.38	−1.68	1.28
Physical capital	−1.62	−4.12	−2.65	1.16	−1.03	−2.59	−1.63	0.68
Human capital	0.72	0.15	0.81	1.08	0.29	0.06	0.31	0.45
TFP	..	..	..	..	0.29	1.15	−0.36	0.15
II. Growth accounting: private and public capital accumulation								
Output	−0.45	−1.38	−1.68	1.28	−0.45	−1.38	−1.68	1.28
Physical capital	..	..	..	..	..	..	..	..
- Public	−1.59	−4.09	−2.82	1.36	−0.53	−1.35	−0.91	0.41
- Private	−1.59	−4.13	−2.58	1.18	−0.48	−1.24	−0.76	0.33
Human capital	0.72	0.15	0.81	1.08	0.29	0.06	0.31	0.45
TFP	..	..	..	..	0.27	1.15	−0.33	0.09
III. Growth accounting including the natural capital								
Output	..	..	..	1.28	..	..	..	1.28
Physical capital	..	..	..	1.16	..	..	..	0.71
Natural capital	..	..	..	42.71	..	..	..	0.65
Human capital	..	..	..	1.08	..	..	..	0.48
TFP	..	..	..	..	..	..	..	−0.55

Note: .. = insufficient or no data to perform the calculation.
East Asian Dragons = five East Asian economic "dragons": Indonesia, the Republic of Korea, Malaysia, Singapore, and Thailand; PPP = purchasing power parity; PPP = public-private partnerships; SSA = Sub-Saharan Africa; TFP = total factor productivity.

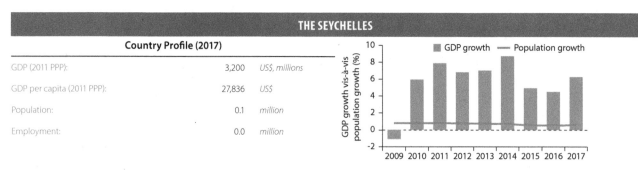

THE SEYCHELLES

Country Profile (2017)

GDP (2011 PPP):	3,200	US$, millions
GDP per capita (2011 PPP):	27,836	US$
Population:	0.1	million
Employment:	0.0	million

Sectoral shares (%)

	Agriculture	Manufacturing	Nonmanufacturing activities	Market services	Nonmarket services
Value added	..	..	..	..	..
Employment	..	..	..	..	..

Development Accounting

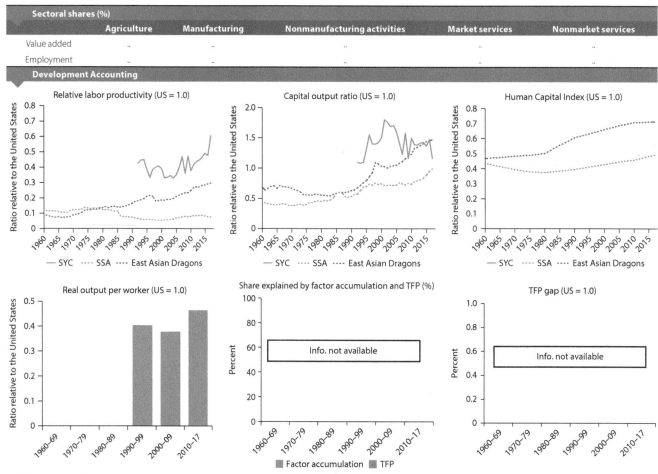

Growth accounting (% per year)

	Observed annual growth rates				Contribution to output growth per worker			
	1961–2017	1961–1977	1978–1995	1996–2017	1961–2017	1961–1977	1978–1995	1996–2017
I. Traditional growth accounting								
Output	..	..	..	..	..	..	..	..
Physical capital	..	..	..	..	..	..	..	..
Human capital	..	..	..	..	..	..	..	..
TFP					..	..	..	..
II. Growth accounting: private and public capital accumulation								
Output	..	..	..	..	..	..	..	..
Physical capital	..	..	..	..	..	..	..	..
- Public	..	..	..	..				
- Private	..	..	..	..				
Human capital	..	..	..	..				
TFP					..	..	..	..
III. Growth accounting including the natural capital								
Output	..	..	..	..				
Physical capital	..	..	..	..				
Natural capital	..	..	..	..				
Human capital	..	..	..	..				
TFP					..	..	..	..

Note: .. = insufficient or no data to perform the calculation.
East Asian Dragons = five East Asian economic "dragons": Indonesia, the Republic of Korea, Malaysia, Singapore, and Thailand; PPP = purchasing power parity; PPP = public-private partnerships; SSA = Sub-Saharan Africa; TFP = total factor productivity.

SIERRA LEONE

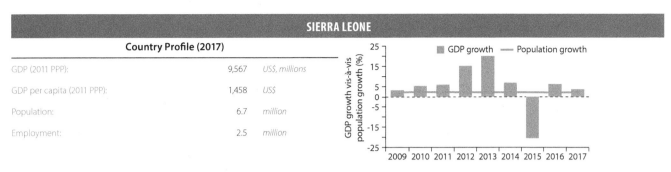

Country Profile (2017)

GDP (2011 PPP):	9,567	US$, millions
GDP per capita (2011 PPP):	1,458	US$
Population:	6.7	million
Employment:	2.5	million

Sectoral shares, 2016 (%)

	Agriculture	Manufacturing	Nonmanufacturing activities	Market services	Nonmarket services
Value added	53.0	2.1	9.5	14.6	20.8
Employment	59.1	3.1	3.2	29.4	5.3

Development accounting

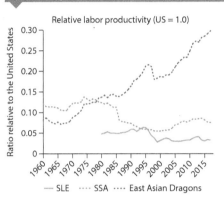

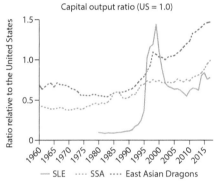

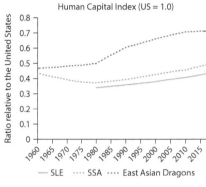

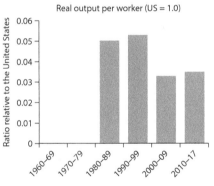

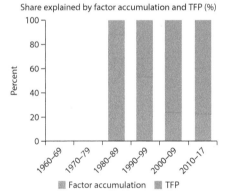

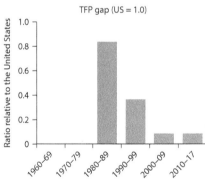

Growth accounting (% per year)

	Observed annual growth rates				Contribution to output growth per worker			
	1961–2017	*1961–1977*	*1978–1995*	*1996–2017*	*1961–2017*	*1961–1977*	*1978–1995*	*1996–2017*
I. Traditional growth accounting								
Output	0.00	..	−0.99	0.67	0.00	..	−0.99	0.67
Physical capital	−0.28	..	−0.17	−0.35	−0.13	..	−0.08	−0.16
Human capital	0.74	..	0.85	0.99	0.51	..	0.48	0.53
TFP	..	..	..	..	−0.38	..	−1.39	0.31
II. Growth accounting: private and public capital accumulation								
Output	0.00	..	−0.99	0.67	0.00	..	−0.99	0.67
Physical capital	..	..	..	..	..	..	..	..
- Public	0.23	..	0.81	−0.16	0.00	..	0.19	−0.04
- Private	−0.16	..	−0.97	0.40	0.00	..	−0.21	0.09
Human capital	0.74	..	0.85	0.99	0.02	..	0.44	0.53
TFP	..	..	..	..	−0.02	..	−1.42	0.10
III. Growth accounting including the natural capital								
Output	..	..	..	..	..	..	..	..
Physical capital	..	..	..	..	..	..	..	..
Natural capital	..	..	..	..	..	..	..	..
Human capital	..	..	..	..	..	..	..	..
TFP	..	..	..	..	..	..	..	..

Note: .. = insufficient or no data to perform the calculation.
East Asian Dragons = five East Asian economic "dragons": Indonesia, the Republic of Korea, Malaysia, Singapore, and Thailand; PPP = purchasing power parity; PPP = public-private partnerships; SSA = Sub-Saharan Africa; TFP = total factor productivity.

SOUTH AFRICA

Country Profile (2017)

GDP (2011 PPP):	666,245	US$, millions
GDP per capita (2011 PPP):	12,105	US$
Population:	56.1	million
Employment:	19.6	million

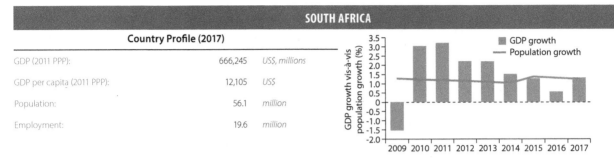

Sectoral shares, 2016 (%)

	Agriculture	Manufacturing	Nonmanufacturing activities	Market services	Nonmarket services
Value added	2.4	13.7	14.3	24.6	45.0
Employment	4.5	11.1	12.1	40.9	31.3

Development Accounting

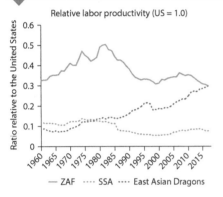

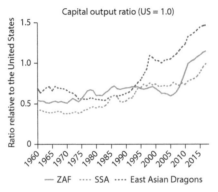

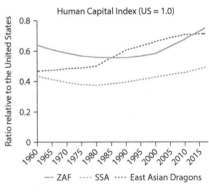

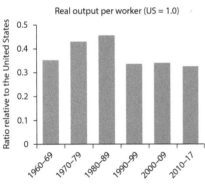

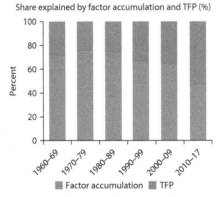

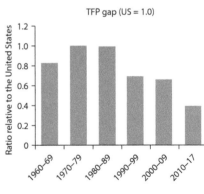

Growth accounting (% per year)

	Observed annual growth rates				Contribution to output growth per worker			
	1961–2017	1961–1977	1978–1995	1996–2017	1961–2017	1961–1977	1978–1995	1996–2017
I. Traditional growth accounting								
Output	1.16	3.62	−0.48	0.60	1.16	3.62	−0.48	0.60
Physical capital	1.70	4.66	0.08	0.75	0.71	1.94	0.03	0.31
Human capital	0.85	0.35	0.44	1.57	0.49	0.20	0.26	0.91
TFP	..	..	..	..	−0.05	1.47	−0.76	−0.63
II. Growth accounting: private and public capital accumulation								
Output	1.16	3.62	−0.48	0.60	1.16	3.62	−0.48	0.60
Physical capital	..	..	..	..	..	..	..	..
- Public	2.07	5.34	1.87	−0.29	0.32	0.82	0.29	−0.04
- Private	1.65	4.46	−0.66	1.36	0.43	1.17	−0.17	0.36
Human capital	0.85	0.35	0.44	1.57	0.49	0.20	0.26	0.91
TFP	..	..	..	..	−0.09	1.42	−0.85	−0.63
III. Growth accounting including the natural capital								
Output	..	..	..	0.60	..	..	..	0.60
Physical capital	..	..	..	0.75	..	..	..	0.18
Natural capital	..	..	..	5.28	..	..	..	0.24
Human capital	..	..	..	1.57	..	..	..	0.64
TFP	..	..	..	..	..	..	..	−0.46

Note: .. = insufficient or no data to perform the calculation.
East Asian Dragons = five East Asian economic "dragons": Indonesia, the Republic of Korea, Malaysia, Singapore, and Thailand; PPP = purchasing power parity; PPP = public-private partnerships; SSA = Sub-Saharan Africa; TFP = total factor productivity.

SUDAN

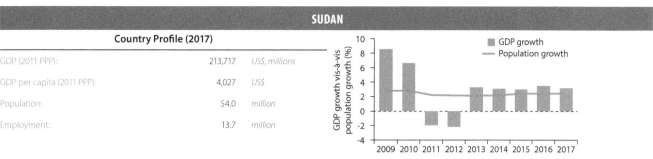

Country Profile (2017)

GDP (2011 PPP):	213,717	US$, millions
GDP per capita (2011 PPP):	4,027	US$
Population:	54.0	million
Employment:	13.7	million

Sectoral shares (%)

	Agriculture	Manufacturing	Nonmanufacturing activities	Market services	Nonmarket services
Value added	..	..	..	..	..
Employment	..	..	..	..	..

Development Accounting

Relative labor productivity (US = 1.0)

Capital output ratio (US = 1.0)

Human Capital Index (US = 1.0)

— SDN ···· SSA ···· East Asian Dragons

Real output per worker (US = 1.0)

Share explained by factor accumulation and TFP (%)

TFP gap (US = 1.0)

▮ Factor accumulation ▮ TFP

Growth accounting (% per year)

	Observed annual growth rates				Contribution to output growth per worker			
	1961–2017	1961–1977	1978–1995	1996–2017	1961–2017	1961–1977	1978–1995	1996–2017
I. Traditional growth accounting								
Output	1.16	3.59	−0.65	1.87	1.16	3.59	−0.65	1.87
Physical capital	3.28	−1.92	−1.55	8.89	0.69	−0.40	−0.32	1.86
Human capital	0.82	0.37	0.89	0.91	0.65	0.29	0.71	0.72
TFP	..	..	..	..	−0.17	3.70	−1.03	−0.71
II. Growth accounting: private and public capital accumulation								
Output	1.16	3.59	−0.65	1.87	1.16	3.59	−0.65	1.87
Physical capital	..	..	..	..	..	..	..	..
- Public	5.79	−1.91	−0.96	13.77	0.63	−0.21	−0.10	1.50
- Private	2.79	−1.92	−1.61	7.89	0.28	−0.19	−0.16	0.79
Human capital	0.82	0.37	0.89	0.91	0.65	0.29	0.71	0.72
TFP	..	..	..	..	−0.40	3.70	−1.09	−1.14
III. Growth accounting including the natural capital								
Output	..	..	..	1.87	..	..	..	1.87
Physical capital	..	..	..	8.89	..	..	..	0.57
Natural capital	..	..	..	80.20	..	..	..	9.82
Human capital	..	..	..	0.91	..	..	..	0.65
TFP	..	..	..	..	..	..	..	−9.16

Note: .. = insufficient or no data to perform the calculation.
East Asian Dragons = five East Asian economic "dragons": Indonesia, the Republic of Korea, Malaysia, Singapore, and Thailand; PPP = purchasing power parity; PPP = public-private partnerships; SSA = Sub-Saharan Africa; TFP = total factor productivity.

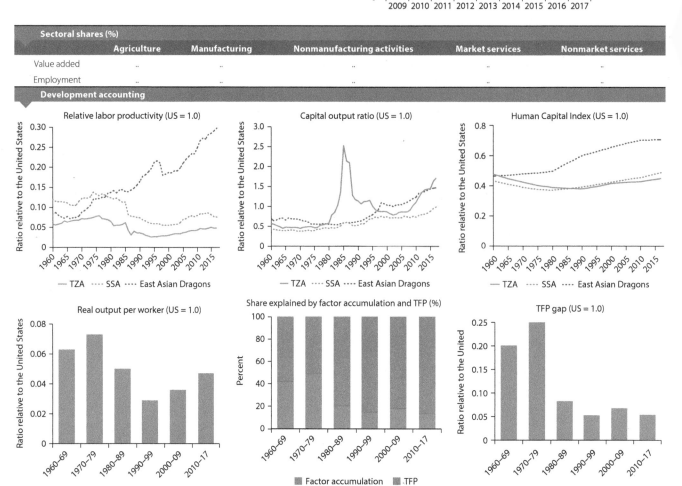

TANZANIA

Country Profile (2017)

GDP (2011 PPP):	134,398	US$, millions
GDP per capita (2011 PPP):	2,368	US$
Population:	55.3	million
Employment:	24.5	million

Sectoral shares (%)

	Agriculture	Manufacturing	Nonmanufacturing activities	Market services	Nonmarket services
Value added	..	..	..	..	..
Employment	..	..	..	..	..

Development accounting

Growth accounting (% per year)

	Observed annual growth rates				Contribution to output growth per worker			
	1961–2017	1961–1977	1978–1995	1996–2017	1961–2017	1961–1977	1978–1995	1996–2017
I. Traditional growth accounting								
Output	1.69	1.97	0.12	2.74	1.69	1.97	0.12	2.74
Physical capital	1.38	2.69	−1.11	2.41	0.67	1.30	−0.54	1.16
Human capital	0.46	0.01	0.39	0.85	0.24	0.01	0.20	0.44
TFP	..	..	..	..	0.79	0.67	0.46	1.14
II. Growth accounting: private and public capital accumulation								
Output	1.69	1.97	0.12	2.74	1.69	1.97	0.12	2.74
Physical capital	..	..	..	..	..	..	..	..
- Public	0.58	2.70	−0.62	−0.08	0.15	0.68	−0.16	−0.02
- Private	1.61	2.69	−1.41	3.26	0.37	0.62	−0.32	0.75
Human capital	0.46	0.01	0.39	0.85	0.24	0.01	0.20	0.44
TFP	..	..	..	..	0.93	0.67	0.40	1.57
III. Growth accounting including the natural capital								
Output	..	..	..	..	..	..	..	..
Physical capital	..	..	..	..	..	..	..	..
Natural capital	..	..	..	..	..	..	..	..
Human capital	..	..	..	..	..	..	..	..
TFP	..	..	..	..	..	..	..	..

Note: .. = insufficient or no data to perform the calculation.
East Asian Dragons = five East Asian economic "dragons": Indonesia, the Republic of Korea, Malaysia, Singapore, and Thailand; PPP = purchasing power parity; PPP = public-private partnerships; SSA = Sub-Saharan Africa; TFP = total factor productivity.

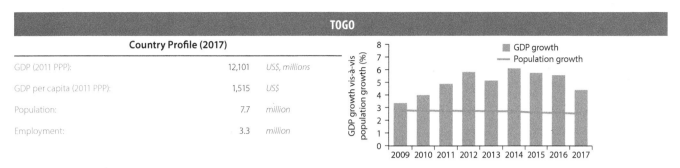

TOGO

Country Profile (2017)

GDP (2011 PPP):	12,101	US$, millions
GDP per capita (2011 PPP):	1,515	US$
Population:	7.7	million
Employment:	3.3	million

Sectoral shares, 2016 (%)

	Agriculture	Manufacturing	Nonmanufacturing activities	Market services	Nonmarket services
Value added	27.7	10.1	6.9	22.6	32.7
Employment	39.1	13.3	4.2	31.6	11.8

Development accounting

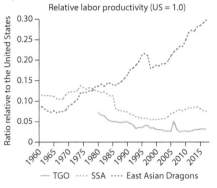
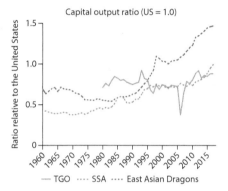
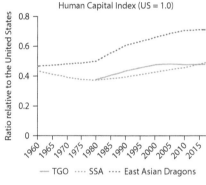

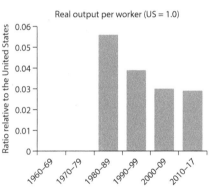
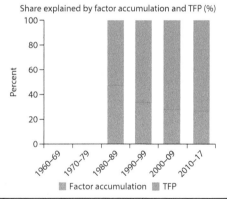
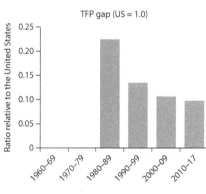

Growth accounting (% per year)

	Observed annual growth rates				Contribution to output growth per worker			
	1961–2017	*1961–1977*	*1978–1995*	*1996–2017*	*1961–2017*	*1961–1977*	*1978–1995*	*1996–2017*
I. Traditional growth accounting								
Output	−0.92	..	−2.24	−0.01	−0.92	..	−2.24	−0.01
Physical capital	−1.25	..	−2.90	−0.12	−0.24	..	−0.56	−0.02
Human capital	0.95	..	1.67	0.50	0.77	..	1.31	0.40
TFP	..	..	..	..	−1.45	..	−2.99	−0.39
II. Growth accounting: private and public capital accumulation								
Output	−0.92	..	−2.24	−0.01	−0.92	..	−2.24	−0.01
Physical capital	..	..	..	..	..	..	..	..
- Public	−2.31	..	−2.77	−1.99	−0.23	..	−0.29	−0.20
- Private	0.02	..	−3.07	2.14	0.00	..	−0.29	0.20
Human capital	0.95	..	1.67	0.50	0.76	..	1.37	0.40
TFP	..	..	..	..	−1.44	..	−3.04	−0.41
III. Growth accounting including the natural capital								
Output	..	..	..	−0.01	..	..	..	−0.01
Physical capital	..	..	..	−0.12	..	..	..	0.00
Natural capital	..	..	..	114.33	..	..	..	0.38
Human capital	..	..	..	0.50	..	..	..	0.01
TFP	..	..	..	..	..	..	..	−0.41

Note: .. = insufficient or no data to perform the calculation.
East Asian Dragons = five East Asian economic "dragons": Indonesia, the Republic of Korea, Malaysia, Singapore, and Thailand; PPP = purchasing power parity; PPP = public-private partnerships; SSA = Sub-Saharan Africa; TFP = total factor productivity.

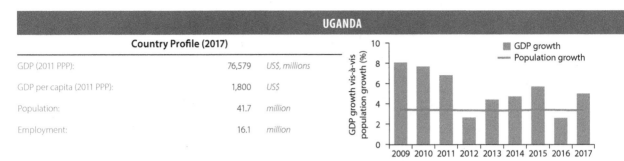

UGANDA

Country Profile (2017)

GDP (2011 PPP):	76,579	US$, millions
GDP per capita (2011 PPP):	1,800	US$
Population:	41.7	million
Employment:	16.1	million

Sectoral shares, 2016 (%)

	Agriculture	Manufacturing	Nonmanufacturing activities	Market services	Nonmarket services
Value added	23.0	9.6	12.2	27.4	27.8
Employment	70.3	4.2	2.8	15.1	7.6

Development accounting

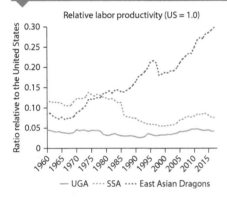

Relative labor productivity (US = 1.0)

— UGA ···· SSA ---- East Asian Dragons

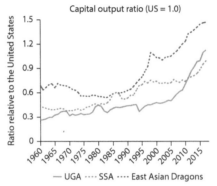

Capital output ratio (US = 1.0)

— UGA ···· SSA ---- East Asian Dragons

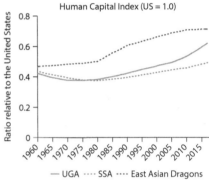

Human Capital Index (US = 1.0)

— UGA ···· SSA ---- East Asian Dragons

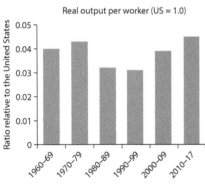

Real output per worker (US = 1.0)

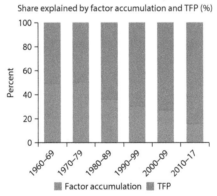

Share explained by factor accumulation and TFP (%)

■ Factor accumulation ■ TFP

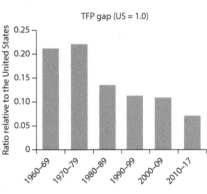

TFP gap (US = 1.0)

Growth accounting (% per year)

	Observed annual growth rates				Contribution to output growth per worker			
	1961–2017	1961–1977	1978–1995	1996–2017	1961–2017	1961–1977	1978–1995	1996–2017
I. Traditional growth accounting								
Output	1.32	0.69	0.03	2.86	1.32	0.69	0.03	2.86
Physical capital	3.34	3.63	0.70	5.27	1.44	1.57	0.30	2.27
Human capital	1.25	0.44	1.35	1.79	0.71	0.25	0.77	1.02
TFP	..	..	..	..	−0.83	−1.13	−1.04	−0.43
II. Growth accounting: private and public capital accumulation								
Output	1.32	0.69	0.03	2.86	1.32	0.69	0.03	2.86
Physical capital	..	..	..	..	..	..	..	..
- Public	4.96	3.68	6.07	5.03	1.12	0.83	1.37	1.13
- Private	2.98	3.62	−0.59	5.40	0.61	0.75	−0.12	1.11
Human capital	1.25	0.44	1.35	1.79	0.71	0.25	0.77	1.02
TFP	..	..	..	..	−1.12	−1.14	−1.98	−0.40
III. Growth accounting including the natural capital								
Output	..	..	..	..	..	..	..	..
Physical capital	..	..	..	..	..	..	..	..
Natural capital	..	..	..	..	..	..	..	..
Human capital	..	..	..	..	..	..	..	..
TFP	..	..	..	..	..	..	..	..

Note: .. = insufficient or no data to perform the calculation.
East Asian Dragons = five East Asian economic "dragons": Indonesia, the Republic of Korea, Malaysia, Singapore, and Thailand; PPP = purchasing power parity; PPP = public-private partnerships; SSA = Sub-Saharan Africa; TFP = total factor productivity.

ZAMBIA

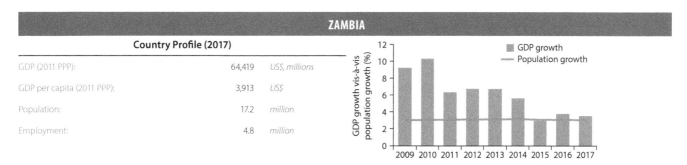

Country Profile (2017)

GDP (2011 PPP):	64,419	US$, millions
GDP per capita (2011 PPP):	3,913	US$
Population:	17.2	million
Employment:	4.8	million

Sectoral shares, 2016 (%)

	Agriculture	Manufacturing	Nonmanufacturing activities	Market services	Nonmarket services
Value added	7.8	8.5	24.1	33.0	26.6
Employment	51.7	4.6	7.2	20.5	16.0

Development accounting

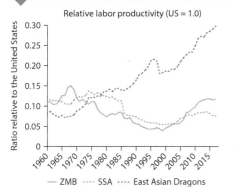

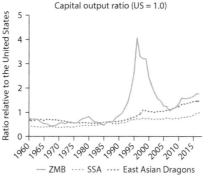

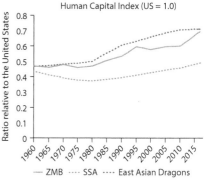

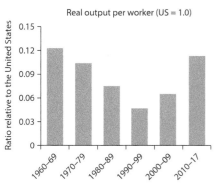

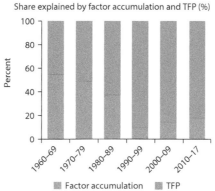

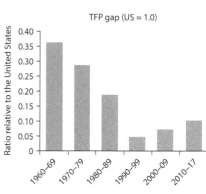

Growth accounting (% per year)

	Observed annual growth rates				Contribution to output growth per worker			
	1961–2017	1961–1977	1978–1995	1996–2017	1961–2017	1961–1977	1978–1995	1996–2017
I. Traditional growth accounting								
Output	0.81	1.09	−1.92	2.82	0.81	1.09	−1.92	2.82
Physical capital	−1.48	−0.27	−4.33	−0.08	−0.64	−0.12	−1.87	−0.03
Human capital	1.26	1.02	1.82	0.98	0.72	0.58	1.04	0.56
TFP	..	..	..	..	0.73	0.63	−1.09	2.29
II. Growth accounting: private and public capital accumulation								
Output	0.81	1.09	−1.92	2.82	0.81	1.09	−1.92	2.82
Physical capital	..	..	..	..	..	..	..	..
- Public	−1.59	−0.14	−3.25	−1.34	−0.36	−0.03	−0.73	−0.30
- Private	−1.04	−0.42	−5.93	2.48	−0.21	−0.09	−1.22	0.51
Human capital	1.26	1.02	1.82	0.98	0.72	0.58	1.04	0.56
TFP	..	..	..	..	0.67	0.64	−1.00	2.05
III. Growth accounting including the natural capital								
Output	..	..	..	2.82	..	..	..	2.82
Physical capital	..	..	..	−0.08	..	..	..	−0.02
Natural capital	..	..	..	26.46	..	..	..	3.30
Human capital	..	..	..	0.98	..	..	..	0.44
TFP	..	..	..	..	..	..	..	−0.91

Note: .. = insufficient or no data to perform the calculation.
East Asian Dragons = five East Asian economic "dragons": Indonesia, the Republic of Korea, Malaysia, Singapore, and Thailand; PPP = purchasing power parity; PPP = public-private partnerships; SSA = Sub-Saharan Africa; TFP = total factor productivity.

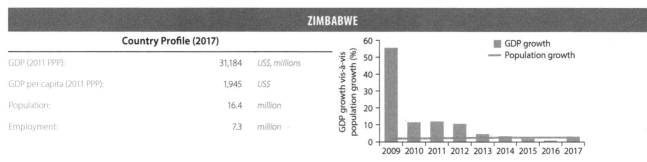

ZIMBABWE			
Country Profile (2017)			
GDP (2011 PPP):	31,184	*US$, millions*	
GDP per capita (2011 PPP):	1,945	*US$*	
Population:	16.4	*million*	
Employment:	7.3	*million*	

Sectoral shares (%)

	Agriculture	Manufacturing	Nonmanufacturing activities	Market services	Nonmarket services
Value added	..	..	..	..	..
Employment	..	..	..	..	..

Development accounting

Relative labor productivity (US = 1.0)

Capital output ratio (US = 1.0)

Human Capital Index (US = 1.0)

— ZWE ····· SSA ···· East Asian Dragons

Real output per worker (US = 1.0)

Share explained by factor accumulation and TFP (%)

TFP gap (US = 1.0)

■ Factor accumulation ■ TFP

Growth accounting (% per year)

	Observed annual growth rates				Contribution to output growth per worker			
	1961–2017	1961–1977	1978–1995	1996–2017	1961–2017	1961–1977	1978–1995	1996–2017
I. Traditional growth accounting								
Output	0.33	..	−0.82	1.11	0.33	..	−0.82	1.11
Physical capital	−1.89	..	−3.17	−1.02	−0.72	..	−1.21	−0.39
Human capital	1.34	..	1.60	1.29	0.91	..	1.07	0.80
TFP	..	..	..	..	0.15	..	−0.67	0.71
II. Growth accounting: private and public capital accumulation								
Output	0.33	..	−0.82	1.11	0.33	..	−0.82	1.11
Physical capital	..	..	..	..	..	..	..	..
- Public	−1.53	..	−3.02	−0.51	−0.41	..	−0.55	−0.10
- Private	−2.02	..	−3.21	−1.21	−0.49	..	−0.53	−0.22
Human capital	1.34	..	1.60	1.29	1.10	..	0.90	0.80
TFP	..	..	..	..	0.13	..	−0.63	0.64
III. Growth accounting including the natural capital								
Output	..	..	..	1.11	..	..	..	1.11
Physical capital	..	..	..	−1.02	..	..	..	−0.23
Natural capital	..	..	..	−0.81	..	..	..	−0.04
Human capital	..	..	..	1.29	..	..	..	0.57
TFP	..	..	..	..	..	..	..	0.82

Note: .. = insufficient or no data to perform the calculation.
East Asian Dragons = five East Asian economic "dragons": Indonesia, the Republic of Korea, Malaysia, Singapore, and Thailand; PPP = purchasing power parity; PPP = public-private partnerships; SSA = Sub-Saharan Africa; TFP = total factor productivity.